Chicken Soup
for the Soul.

angels
all
around

Chicken Soup for the Soul: Angels All Around
101 Inspirational Stories of Miracles, Divine Intervention, and Answered Prayers
Amy Newmark

Published by Chicken Soup for the Soul, LLC www.chickensoup.com
Copyright ©2019 by Chicken Soup for the Soul, LLC. All Rights Reserved.

Front cover photo of man on path courtesy of iStockphoto.com/ppart (©ppart)
Front cover, back cover, and interior images of feathers courtesy of iStockphoto.com/Gluiki (©Gluik)
Photo of Amy Newmark courtesy of Susan Morrow at SwickPix

Cover and Interior by Daniel Zaccari

Distributed to the booktrade by Simon & Schuster. SAN: 200-2442

Publisher's Cataloging-In-Publication Data
(Prepared by The Donohue Group, Inc.)

Names: Newmark, Amy, compiler.
Title: Chicken soup for the soul : angels all around : 101 inspirational stories of miracles, divine intervention, and answered prayers / [compiled by] Amy Newmark.
Other Titles: Angels all around : 101 inspirational stories of miracles, divine intervention, and answered prayers
Description: [Cos Cob, Connecticut] : Chicken Soup for the Soul, LLC, [2019]
Identifiers: ISBN 9781611599930 | ISBN 9781611592924 (ebook)
Subjects: LCSH: Angels--Literary collections. | Angels--Anecdotes. | Miracles--Literary collections. | Miracles--Anecdotes. | Providence and government of God--Literary collections. | Providence and government of God--Anecdotes. | LCGFT: Anecdotes.
Classification: LCC BL477 .C45 2019 (print) | LCC BL477 (ebook) | DDC 202/.15/02--dc23

Library of Congress Control Number: 2019940300

PRINTED IN THE UNITED STATES OF AMERICA
on acid∞free paper

25 24 23 22 21 20 19   03 04 05 06 07 08 09 10 11

angels all around

101 Inspirational Stories of Miracles, Divine Intervention, and Answered Prayers

Amy Newmark

Chicken Soup for the Soul, LLC
Cos Cob, CT

Changing your life one story at a time®
www.chickensoup.com

Table of Contents

❶

~Miraculous Intervention~

1. Daddy, Why Did You Push Me? *Jackie Carman Blankenship* 3
2. Airport Angel, *S.L. Blake* 6
3. Lucy's Angel, *Ginny Huff Conahan* 9
4. The Farewell Party, *Glenice Wilson* 12
5. Butterflies, *Julia Gousseva* 15
6. Divine Doorman, *Lisa McCaskill* 19
7. Hot Springs Magic, *S.R. Karfelt* 22
8. The Voice, *Tory Wegner Hendrix* 26
9. An Angel's Tools, *Randi O'Keefe* 29
10. A Beautiful Day in the Neighborhood, *Lisa Romeo* 32

❷

~Touched by an Angel~

11. Bill, *Jeff Hill* 37
12. Pennsylvania Turnpike, *Anita Stone* 41
13. The Repairman, *Suzanne Miley* 45
14. Still There for Me, *Kathryn Radeff* 48
15. An Angel from Arizona, *Billie Holladay Skelley* 51
16. Unexplained, *Dorothy Dale* 55
17. An Angel in Black, *Gwyn Schneck* 57
18. Angels' Food, *Delores E. Topliff* 60
19. Help in a Time of Trouble, *Christine Brown* 63

❸
~Comfort from Beyond~

20. Snow Angels, *Wendy Portfors*.................................67
21. Angels at the Window, *Evangeline Neve*.....................70
22. I'm Okay Now, *Steve Schultz*................................72
23. As Promised, *Jayne M. Adams* 75
24. Sparks of Light, *Carrie K. Linde*...........................79
25. Dimes from Heaven, *C. R. Chan*............................83
26. The Sign, *Gail Gabrielle* 86
27. A Time to Sparkle, *Laurie Batzel*...........................89
28. See You in Heaven, *Kristi Allen*............................93
29. Always a Father, *D'ette Corona*.............................95

❹
~Angels in Disguise~

30. Cardinal Red, *Karen Ross Samford*...........................99
31. The Lady Who Lived Over the Hill, *Kathleen Ruth*...........103
32. The Writing Coach, *Maureen Boyd Biro* 106
33. The Angels on the Train, *Ryan Freeman* 110
34. Just What I Needed, *Elizabeth C. Crognale* 113
35. The Flat Tire, *Renée Vajko-Srch* 117
36. The Perfect Companion, *Theresa Brandt*.....................121
37. A Gentle Voice, *Jeri McBryde* 124
38. Do Angels Carry Cash? *Kathleen Kohler* 126
39. Angel Soup, *Marya Morin*..................................129

❺
~Guardians and Protectors~

40. Someone to Watch Over Me, *David-Matthew Barnes*...........134
41. Grounded, *G. E. Mimms* 136
42. Heavenly Escorts, *Elizabeth Rose Reardon Farella*...........139
43. How Did She Know? *Melody R. Ringo* 142

44. Jadyn's Guardian Angel, *Yvonne Hall* 144
45. Airborne, *Soneakqua J. White* 147
46. The Angel Who Saved My Daughters, *Dorann Weber* 149
47. Doctor's Orders, *Lynn Darmon* 152
48. A Brief Encounter, *Karleen Forwell* 155
49. The Day I Got My Own Angel, *Lisa Leshaw* 157
50. Prayer Card, *Hayley Pisciotti* 160

❻

~Answered Prayers~

51. On Angel Wings, *M.J. Shea* 164
52. How God Took My Burden, *Darlene Grace Peterson* 167
53. The Parking Lot Angel, *Tree Langdon* 171
54. Never Give Up, *Lori Phillips* 174
55. Prayers and Positive Thoughts, *Joanne Guidoccio* 178
56. The Day the Wind Stood Still, *Mary Edwards* 182
57. The Handkerchief, *Deborah J. Konrad* 184
58. Divinity on Seventh Street, *Gail Walkowich* 187
59. The Day I Met an Angel, *Jackie Eller* 189

❼

~Divine Messengers~

60. I Met My Angel at Dog Point, *David Davis* 192
61. Divine Comfort, *Barbara Bennett* 195
62. No! Don't Take It! *Sara Schafer* 197
63. The Unexpected Messenger, *Dayle Allen Shockley* 200
64. Go and Get It, *Francine L. Billingslea* 203
65. A Dream Come True, *Ruth Douglas* 206
66. An Angel's Whisper, *Sergio Jauregui* 209
67. Someday, *Lenore Petruso* 213
68. Heeding the Angel, *Dana D. Sterner* 215
69. And the Angels Sang, *Sheryl Hutchinson* 218

8

~Miracles Happen~

70. Faithful Fingers, *Caroline S. McKinney* 222
71. The Invisible Life Saver, *Carolyn Jaynes*..............................224
72. The Angels Are a Little Deaf, *Jeffrey Guard*.......................226
73. A New Start, *Renee C. Houghton* 230
74. A Divine Bug, *Tammy Parker* 233
75. Midnight Stranger, *Kathleen Kohler* 236
76. My Icy Miracle, *Donna Keenan*...239
77. Your Daughter Is Alive, *Sandra Hesler*................................242
78. Mavis's Ladybug, *Sid Korpi*..245
79. A Miraculous Recovery, *Mary Jo Marcellus Wyse*.................248

9

~Divine Coincidences~

80. Perfect Timing, *Janet Rich*..253
81. Hidden Messages, *Sergio Del Bianco* 256
82. A Tap on the Shoulder, *Judith Burnett Schneider*.................259
83. Synchronicity on the Ski Trail, *Stephanie Kovala*.................263
84. Humpback's Song, *M. Elizabeth Gage*...................................267
85. A Second Chance, *M. Jean Pike* 270
86. Looking for the Sale Sign, *Tyann Sheldon Rouw*.................274
87. A Warm Night in Vermont, *Jean S. Anker* 278
88. A Watchful Eye, *Gwen Cooper*...282
89. The Dragon-Wagon, *Mandi Raybuck* 285
90. Secret Garden Angel, *Marlene Bryenton* 289
91. More than a Souvenir, *Jennie Ivey*..291

❿

~Messages from Heaven~

92. Photographs from Mom, *Amy Rovtar Payne*.........................295
93. Hummingbird Angel, *Donna Adams Stare* 298
94. The Weathervane, *Debra Zemke*.......................................300
95. Marco, *Carrie Roope*...303
96. A Fragrant Reminder, *Kathy Whirity*.................................307
97. Get Up! *Steve Schultz* 309
98. Time for Mass, *Fran Signorino*...312
99. The Pull of the Magnet, *Teresa Otto*..................................314
100. The Mansion of Many Rooms, *Joshua J. Mark*.....................316
101. Buggy Ride, *Melinda Pritzel*..320

Meet Our Contributors..323
Meet Amy Newmark 339
Thank You..341

Chapter
1

Miraculous
Intervention

Daddy, Why Did You Push Me?

Don't believe in miracles — depend on them.
~Laurence J. Peter

When our girls, Autumn and Emerald, were little, my husband Sam and I loved taking them to Drakes Creek Park in Hendersonville, Tennessee. We usually stopped en route to pick up a loaf of bread so the girls could feed the ducks by the side of the lake.

One afternoon, while feeding the squawking mallards, five-year-old Autumn kept getting too close to the water. I would make her move back, but before we knew it, she would be right back at the edge. Sensing that I was getting overly anxious, Sam suggested that I go check on my mom, who was sitting at a picnic table up the slope from the water. He was watching the girls.

I'd gone about halfway up the slope toward my mom when I heard the unmistakable splash of a body entering the water. By the time I turned around, I saw my husband pulling our daughter from the water by one arm. Fearing the worst because of the jagged rocks that were just under the water at the edge of the lake, I ran back to them in a panic. As I reached them, I heard my unscathed daughter ask, "Daddy, why did you push me when I started falling?"

Sam, who was now kneeling in front of her, responded, "Honey,

I didn't push you. I was standing next to Emerald. When I looked over, you just kind of lurched out into the water. That man helped me pull you out."

Autumn replied, "Daddy, I felt a push on my back after I started falling."

Gently, Sam placed his hands on her shoulders, looked straight into her eyes, and said, "I promise you, Autumn, I did not push you." Then he pulled her into a tender embrace. Looking around for a moment and then turning to me, he said, "Hey, Jack (he always called me that unless we were arguing), where's the guy who helped me pull Autumn out of the water?"

I looked at him quizzically and replied, "Honey, what are you talking about? There was no one but you who lifted her out."

"Jack, there was a man who grabbed her other arm and helped me pull her out. I couldn't have gotten her out by myself."

Just as I was about to respond, a lady approached us holding a baby blanket exactly like the one that had been Autumn's favorite as a toddler. She said, "I saw your little girl fall in, and I thought y'all could use this to dry her off." I reached for it and offered thanks at the same time that Sam asked her if she'd seen where the man went who had helped get our daughter out of the lake. The woman responded, "Sir, I didn't see nobody but you get her out." Sam asked her if she was sure, and she assured him she was positive that she'd seen only him.

A few minutes later, when we reached my mother — who'd seen everything from her vantage point at the picnic table — she told us the same thing as the woman with the blanket. She hadn't seen anyone help Sam pull Autumn out.

We knew we'd had an angelic intervention. The jagged rocks under the water went in six or eight feet so it was a miracle that Autumn somehow fell right past them into the safer area. The push she felt propelled her right over those rocks, so she didn't get even a scratch. No one but Sam saw the man who helped, except Autumn felt his push.

I've never forgotten that miraculous encounter. And when Autumn gave birth to her daughter two and a half years ago at the age of twenty,

I gave her the little receiving blanket that the woman at the park gave us the day the angel saved her from serious injury or even death.

—Jackie Carman Blankenship—

Airport Angel

A guardian angel walks with us, sent from up above,
their loving wings surround us and enfold us with love.
~Author Unknown

I t was the morning after my twenty-fourth birthday. Instead of catching up on lost sleep from a late night out, I was sitting in the back seat of a car heading to the airport so my boyfriend could complete his yearlong deployment to Afghanistan.

There were five people in the car, but hardly any words were spoken during the forty-minute drive. We sat in silent understanding, each building up the courage to say goodbye to a person we all loved, unsure if there were any words that could make the goodbye easier. I replayed the first half of the month in my head, astonished that two weeks—his allotted mid-deployment leave time—had passed so quickly. Our relationship was fairly new, so my stomach was a knot of nerves.

When we arrived at the airport, we each obtained a security pass so we could walk our hero to the gate. As fate would have it, he had missed his original flight and was rebooked on a later one, giving us a little more time together. We gladly stole every extra second we could.

Sitting in the stiff airport seat, reality hit. I sat on his right side, our hands still clasped together, while his mom sat on his other side, her head gently resting on his left shoulder. None of us spoke, and I tried my best to push down the lump in my throat when I saw a tear slide down his mother's cheek.

That unleashed my own tears, but I tried not to let him see me cry. I didn't want him to feel guilty for leaving when I knew it wasn't a choice but a duty. He had made a promise to his country and the Army long before making any promises to me.

Before we were ready, the time had come for him to board the plane. We rose from our chairs and stood in a line, each of us taking a turn to say our form of "See you later." I stayed to the far right, wanting my soldier to be able to give his family a proper farewell. Too soon, it was my turn, and my boyfriend and I embraced, shedding tears for the uncertainty that lay ahead.

I had never dated someone in the service before, so the experience was entirely new. I knew with all my heart I was falling in love with him, but I was scared the risk wouldn't be worth the heartbreak should the worst thing happen. I wanted to hold on tight to him and never let go, but I reluctantly pried my arms from around his neck and blinked the tears from my eyes so I could see him clearly.

"Focus," I said, as much to him as to myself.

I saw a flash of movement to my right. By the time I turned my attention to the source, a man was standing next to us.

"Here," he said to my soldier. "Take this. It will keep you safe."

The man held out his hand to my boyfriend, who was hesitant to take what the man was offering.

"I know this is difficult, but you'll be alright. You'll come home," the man said with a smile. Opening his hand, he revealed a silver chain necklace with a small pendant hanging from it. My boyfriend opened his hand and accepted the gift from the stranger.

He turned to me as he patted my boyfriend on the back. "He's going to come home to you. Everything is going to be okay, all right? Don't worry," he said. He glanced at all of us with reassurance.

The five of us smiled and gave a collective thank you. My boyfriend hugged the complete stranger. Full of gratitude, we turned our attention to the necklace in my boyfriend's hand. He held it up, revealing that the pendant was that of Saint Michael.

We all looked at each other in wonder and appreciation to have experienced such a kind gesture from a total stranger. Then we realized he was no longer standing next to us and was nowhere to be seen.

The gate attendant made the final boarding announcement. With one more hug and kiss, my boyfriend placed the necklace around his neck and vowed not to take it off through the remainder of his deployment.

After he walked out of sight, his family and I tried our best to find the kind stranger but he was nowhere to be found.

My then boyfriend, now my husband, wore that necklace throughout his entire deployment. Saint Michael, known throughout many religions as the Angel of War, the leader of all angels and of the army of God, rested around his neck for eight months. Only after he returned safely did he take it off, and we still have that necklace to this day.

None of us has an explanation for what happened at the airport all those years ago. We try to picture the man, but none of us can remember what he looked like. We simply remember the way he made us feel, and we refer to him as our angel because there doesn't seem to be any other explanation.

—S.L. Blake—

Lucy's Angel

A good man's prayers will from the deepest dungeon
climb heavens' height, and bring a blessing down.
~Joanna Baillie

Five-year-old Lucy would not come out from under the table in reading class again. My teenage daughter, Molly, was trying to coax her out to sit at the table and practice learning her ABCs. As the remedial reading teacher, I worked with Lucy every day to give her extra help in reading. Molly volunteered every week to come and encourage Lucy.

It was not going well because Lucy's eyes were terribly cross-eyed and she could not see the page, the alphabet, or many of the toys and books in my classroom.

After class, Molly complained to me. She said that Lucy would never learn to read until she could see! Of course, I knew that, but I explained to her that I had tried to get help for Lucy's vision problem, but to no avail. My job was to help each child learn, whatever the situation might be. So we needed to encourage Lucy to sit at the table and practice reading and writing her ABCs.

Since my husband and I had three children of our own and very little extra money at that time, I needed to do the best I could as a teacher in that situation. I told my daughter that I would be sure to get Lucy an eye operation if I ever had the money—if I were ever visited by an angel who would help me win the lottery, I would get Lucy's eyes fixed.

Every Friday night, my husband and I went out on an inexpensive date. We went to a country-western saloon where we were trying to learn to do the two-step. On Fridays the saloon had a drawing to attract more customers. The place was always packed with 500 people because everyone wanted to win the cash.

Each week, $100 was added to the pot. One night the pot was up to $2,500. As we entered the saloon, we were handed a raffle ticket. Later that evening, the DJ selected four numbers and mine was one of them — out of 500 people! I felt like a beautiful, little angel was on my shoulder!

I brought my ticket to the stage with a trembling hand. I had to pick a key from among ninety-nine keys in a basket to try to open the treasure chest. The other three people went first but could not open the chest. If I had the right key, I could open the treasure chest and get $2,500. I looked very closely at the keys. They appeared to look exactly the same at first glance. However, I swear one appeared a little shinier than the rest and beckoned to me to choose it.

It was as if an angel were guiding my hand to select that particular key. In my heart, I knew I had been helped to choose that key by divine intervention.

My exquisite key slipped right in and opened the chest with the money inside! I already knew exactly how the money would be spent.

The next morning, I called Lucy's dad, Johnny, a young, single father with four children under the age of eight. He was overworked and trying his best to provide his kids with a stable life. I explained about the money I had won. I told him I felt the money was given to me to help Lucy with her eyes. I really felt an angel had been on my shoulder the evening before, helping me choose the correct key.

Johnny gave me permission to take Lucy to the doctor. The ophthalmologist said her eyes could be fixed, but there was a short window of time. After children reach a certain age, the problem is permanent. He said we only had a few months.

A problem arose during the last appointment before the surgery. The doctor said Lucy would need to stay in bed and rest for three days after the surgery so her eyes could heal. Johnny said he could not take off from work, and it would not be a calm environment at his home anyway. So I agreed to have Lucy stay at my house for a few days until she could go home.

My teaching friends were afraid that I would get in trouble for having a student stay with me. They warned that it could result in serious problems down the road, especially since I did not know the family very well. I told them that this miracle occurred because God had used me to get Lucy's eyes fixed. The angel on my shoulder that evening would not let me down now.

After the operation, Lucy did stay with me for a few days. When the bandages were taken off, we knew the operation was a success! She could now see well enough to see the world around her better.

At school, Lucy no longer hid under the table. She was happy to join our small reading group to work on learning to read. She enjoyed looking at books, and learning the alphabet and how to write. She was happier and had more self-confidence.

Years later, I am still in touch with Lucy. She is now a mother with two daughters of her own. Every time I see Lucy and her beautiful blue eyes, I know that God works in mysterious ways.

—Ginny Huff Conahan—

The Farewell Party

Angels are the bridge between heaven and earth.
~Megan McKenna

My friend Linda was in the hospital. That day, I planned to see her family: her two sisters and ninety-year-old mom from Nova Scotia, her son in Toronto, and her other son and his wife who lived here in Alberta. This loving family had come together to cheer Linda, who was in the Intensive Care Unit after a setback. Their weeklong visit would end the next day.

I already knew the family from their prior visits to support Linda during her bone-marrow transplant. It had been a long struggle for Linda, but she had been doing better until this recent setback. My plan was to meet them for lunch at the hospital and then drive back home in the afternoon. But right after I closed my front door, I heard a little voice say, "Go back and book a hotel. Take the wine."

There was a hotel across the street from the hospital, and I had just bought a couple of bottles of wine, but why did I have to do this? It seemed like the most unlikely thing to do, but somehow I knew I had to do it. I unlocked my door, put down my purse, and phoned the hotel across the street from the hospital. They had only one room for one night. I booked it.

Nothing made sense, but I didn't have time to argue. I rationalized that Linda's mom or her two sisters might appreciate a glass of wine and a good sleep in a real bed instead of camping out in Linda's room or the waiting room. If that were the case, so be it. I stood a minute pondering whether I should take the red or the white wine I had purchased the previous day. Then I chuckled to myself, thinking I could always bring one bottle back home, so I packed both.

I went straight to the hotel, parked and registered. After I put my bag inside the hotel-room door, I ran to meet Linda's family. Her son Matt and her sister Debbie met me and shared their concerns. Linda was still struggling and would not be released from ICU by nightfall. They felt uneasy about leaving her.

We went up to the waiting room to join the rest of the family. Right then, the nurse came and called both sons to see the doctor. Matt and John returned and asked all of us to join them in the little room. Matt said, "Mom has talked to the doctor. There is no more to be done, she says. Mom has thanked the doctor and all the staff."

Matt paused. "The doctor thanked Mom for being an incredible patient and asked if he could do anything more for her." Matt's voice broke, and then he continued, "And Mom said she would like to have a glass of wine with her family." All was quiet for a moment.

"I don't know where we will get that, but…"

"I can get that," I said, and I ran out of the room and across the street to the hotel.

As I hurried, I thought, *Linda hates wine from a paper or Styrofoam cup. Maybe the hotel room will have two glasses in the bathroom.* To my surprise, there was a nice kitchen, with four wine glasses and four water goblets in the cupboard. I wrapped them in my clothes with the wine and tore back across the street.

Linda's sons invited me into her room, and they poured the wine. There were eight of us and eight glasses. Two bottles of wine seemed to be just right.

When a nurse appeared with a stack of cups, she was surprised. "Oh, you already have real glasses. I guess you won't need these."

Linda was lucid, and her son John helped her with a straw to sip her wine. Linda smiled, and we all stood around the bed and enjoyed the party. As she looked at each of us intently like never before, she said, "What a handsome crew. This room is brimming with love."

Stroking Linda's bald head, her mom told her how beautiful she was, inside and out. She said that now Linda would go to join her dad. Then Linda, her mom and sisters began to sing an Irish song the dad had taught them: "Put Me in Your Pocket (So I'll Be Close to You)."

Linda spoke to all of us, and we said our final goodbyes.

Then Linda told one of her sons, "I don't have any fresh produce, but I have some frozen pizzas in the freezer if you want."

He smiled. "No, Mom, we are happy with a glass of wine. Are you?"

"Yes. I haven't felt this good in months." She closed her eyes, and we all stayed until she passed.

Exhausted but awed, sad but content, we bid each other farewell.

We never used the $200 hotel room — only the elegant glasses. But how fortunate that little voice had urged me to bring the wine and get the room. It was worth paying for the room just to have those glasses for Linda! My guardian angel knew exactly what she was doing.

— Glenice Wilson —

Butterflies

*Love is like a butterfly: It goes where it pleases
and it pleases wherever it goes.*
~Author Unknown

I t was a bright September morning, the first day of my senior year in high school. The school was located on a small, tree-lined street, and the branches of tall poplars and birches were inches away from our classroom window. Some leaves were still green, but many were already turning yellow, red, and orange.

The school building was old, and everything about it seemed worn and in need of repair. The desks creaked, the blackboard had scratches, and the large picture in a heavy frame that hung above the teacher's desk was so dusty that it was hard to discern the landscape it portrayed.

"We're getting a new biology teacher," my friend Gail told me. "I hope she's nice."

"I hope so, too."

I sat down next to Gail, and we chatted and watched other students walk in and take their seats. We had been at the same school for many years, and we knew everyone. Then a new girl walked in. She was petite, with dark hair and pale skin. She wore a checkered skirt, a white top, and a plain jacket. I didn't see any jewelry or make-up, not even a hint of mascara. But that's not what surprised me most. I expected her to find a seat with the other students. Instead, she walked to the teacher's desk.

"My name is Ms. Keto," she said. "I'm your new biology teacher."

"She's so young," Gail whispered.

Ms. Keto, apparently having heard the comment, smiled and said, "Everyone tells me I look too young to be a teacher, but I have my degree and teaching credentials. As for my youth, I'll tell you what my grandmother always tells me. 'Don't worry. Youth is a drawback that goes away with time.'" Her eyes sparkled as she said it.

We chuckled and settled down for the lesson. Ms. Keto kept our attention for the entire period, telling us about her studies in marine biology, the expeditions she took, and the interesting projects she planned for our class. She was knowledgeable and spoke with a sense of authority, yet she was friendly and approachable. Her positive attitude infused our old school with energy, and everything seemed newer somehow. Even the old, dusty picture up on the wall looked brighter.

In a few weeks, the whole class fell in love with Ms. Keto. Besides teaching biology, she started a science club and a hiking club. Gail and I joined both.

One day, Ms. Keto brought her guitar to school, and a bunch of us often stayed after classes singing and enjoying tea with delicious, home-baked cookies. Ms. Keto told us that her grandmother baked the cookies for us.

"But she doesn't know us," Gail said.

"True," Ms. Keto said. "But she knows a lot about you. She loves listening to stories about my classes and students. We sit in the kitchen and talk every night."

"You live with your grandmother?" Gail asked.

I blushed. Why did she always ask these embarrassing questions? I was worried that Ms. Keto would be upset.

Instead, Ms. Keto simply smiled. "Yes, Gail. I moved in with her at the beginning of the school year because she needs a little help once in a while. And I enjoy living with her very much."

Weeks turned into months, and the school year fell into a routine, with classes, homework assignments, and club projects. The weather got colder and wetter, the days grew shorter and darker, and I spent more time after school with Ms. Keto and other students.

Then, in November, our principal told us that Ms. Keto would be gone for a week.

"Why?" Gail asked. "Is she sick?"

"She isn't sick," the principal responded. "And she'll tell you the rest herself if she chooses to."

After a week, Ms. Keto came back. She told us that her grandmother had died unexpectedly. Ms. Keto looked small and sad, and the sparkle was gone from her eyes. She was dressed the same but now wore a butterfly pin on her jacket.

"Is the butterfly pin new?" Gail asked, making me cringe.

"No," Ms. Keto said. "It's quite old. It was a gift from my grandmother. She always said that butterflies are like angels. They can protect us from harm."

"Do you believe it?" Gail asked.

Ms. Keto sighed. "I'm a biologist, a scientist, and I know what butterflies are." She walked to the teacher's desk and started organizing her papers.

The day was dark and cold, and the first snow had already covered the ground with a thin layer of white. The poplars and birches outside had dropped their leaves and covered the roof of the storage shed below with a layer of yellow, red, and orange.

"Ms. Keto," Gail spoke up. "Do you believe that butterflies are angels?"

"It's November," Ms. Keto said. "There are no butterflies now. And we have a week's worth of lessons to catch up on."

As she said it, I looked out the window. A flock of red, yellow, and orange wings fluttered up into the sky. I couldn't believe my eyes.

"Butterflies!" I exclaimed. "Look!"

Ms. Keto came to the window. Everyone else ran up and crowded around her. The butterflies were soaring and twirling in the air, their colorful wings bright against the gray autumn sky. Mesmerized, we stood in silence and watched them.

The moment was interrupted by a loud crash next to Ms. Keto's desk.

Stunned, I watched the dusty picture hit the desk, leaving a deep indentation, its heavy frame bouncing off the chair and breaking it. Glass shattered and scattered all over the floor.

"Ms. Keto could have been killed," Gail whispered. "The butterflies saved her."

I looked out the window again but didn't see any butterflies. Red, yellow, and orange leaves were slowly falling from the sky onto the roof of the storage shed below. What we saw a few moments earlier must have been those same leaves picked up and spun by a whirlwind.

Ms. Keto touched her pin. "I'm going to finish class early today," she said. "Let's clean up this mess, and then I'd love for us to stay and talk, just like we used to. My grandmother would have wanted me to spend time with you." She smiled. The sparkle was back in her eyes.

— Julia Gousseva —

6

Divine Doorman

One thing you can say for guardian angels: they guard.
They give warning when danger approaches.
~Emily Hahn

Many years ago, before the advent of cell phones, I volunteered to direct the church Christmas play. Overwhelmed by the enormity of my task, I rushed to make costumes and props as the date of the performance drew nearer.

Early Saturday morning, I headed to the church with sewing machine in tow, parked in front of the basement entrance, and lugged the first batch of materials through the double glass doors. The pastor, who knew I was on the way, helped me unload items and then said, "Could you lock that door? I might forget that it's open later if you don't." One quick clockwise motion slid the lock in place.

Two hours later, the wise men were finished. Mary — check. Joseph — check. But there were still seven sheep, five shepherds, and a host of angels who needed costumes. As the pastor left for lunch, he let me know that all the upstairs doors had been locked since I would be alone in the church building. I began assembling the simple white tunics that would clothe the angels.

I was deeply engrossed in the preparation of a set of cardboard wings when a series of frantic, rapid knocks startled me. Had the pastor forgotten his keys? I looked to the door. It wasn't the pastor. A young woman cupped her hands around her face to peer in, and then she resumed her desperate knocking.

I approached the door. I could clearly hear her asking for help through the glass. Old clothes, messy hair — was she someone whose life could change with a kind word or deed from me? I was still pondering the thought when she spoke again.

"Something is wrong with the car. Could I come in and use the phone? We're trying to get my baby to the doctor. I need help." The words were punctuated by a mournful cry from the back seat of a sputtering blue car.

I paused only a moment before I nodded. The phone was just inside. She could make her call, and help would be on the way.

I put my hand on the lock and turned. It wouldn't budge. Did I break it when I locked it earlier? I attempted to turn the lock again. This time, I tried jiggling it. That deadbolt wasn't moving. It felt like it had been welded in place. I'd have to get the pastor to check it out when he returned.

"Please let me in," she whined.

"The door is jammed. Give me the number, and I'll call."

"I need to look it up."

The telephone began to ring, but I ignored the call and attempted once more to open the jammed lock. Then I stopped as a feeling of foreboding engulfed me. I looked back to the car and then at the woman. There were two men in the back seat.

"This isn't going to budge. Let me tell you how to get to the gas station up the street," I said. The car was running, after all, and the gas station was very close.

But she lingered. "Please let me use this phone. It won't take a minute."

The phone began ringing once more.

"Excuse me, I have to get that. Go to the gas station." I left the woman and answered the phone.

"Hello?"

"Hey." It was the pastor. "I'll be back as soon as I can. I just got a call from Pastor Williams over at Greater Vision. There are some people — a woman, two men, and they have a baby — who are going around to churches and stealing things. They've already robbed one church this morning. If they stop by, don't let them in."

I swallowed hard. "I think they were just here."

The pastor was silent for a moment. "I'll be right there."

Pastor Jack was there in a flash and approached the glass doors. I walked over and pointed to the lock.

"Pastor, that lock is jammed. You'll have to go around."

"Hmmmm," he said. He took out his key and opened the door—no jiggle, no effort. He entered the basement and turned the lock.

"Wait," I said. I had to try. I unlocked the door with no effort at all. I locked it and repeated the process. "It wouldn't open."

"So, tell me what happened..." he said.

And I did. He smiled and tested the lock once more.

"Well, you know, sometimes we entertain angels unaware. And if God can shut a lion's mouth to protect Daniel, He can shut a door for you. I think you had a guardian this morning."

I smiled and nodded as goose bumps dotted my arms.

—Lisa McCaskill—

7

Hot Springs Magic

Sometimes our grandmas and grandpas
are like grand-angels.
~Lexie Saige

Just a few days after the birth of our second child, my husband Scott suggested we pack up and head for Hot Springs on vacation. We'd never been there, and after months of bed rest during my second difficult pregnancy, I was dying to get out and go somewhere.

We'd driven past Hot Springs many times without being able to stop, but a group of cabins in the woods near a small lake had caught our eye. They even had a lodge and would cook us dinner at six o'clock every evening.

We loaded up our little car with diapers and a Snoopy fishing pole. In addition to two tired parents, a baby, and a toddler, we took Gunner Boom, our high-strung bird dog. By the time we crammed in some luggage, the baby in her car seat probably had the most room.

Every moment of the drive, Belle sobbed, wanting only what any newborn wants and can't have in a moving vehicle — to be held. Two-year-old Oliver politely requested she pipe down and wondered why he couldn't hold his fishing pole in the car. He kept up this refrain for hours. Poor Gunner — crammed into the tightest space possible — whined louder than both kids, a deep-throated complaint of abject canine misery.

It seemed a hundred years with all the starts and stops, but we finally got to Hot Springs and spilled out of the car. Scott unpacked and I nursed Belle while sitting on a picnic table. Oliver ran in and out of the cabin with his fishing pole still safely in its shrink-wrap packaging. Gunner fetched a box turtle from the creek and refused to give it up until we all gave chase and demanded it.

We missed the six o'clock dinner by hours and ate pancakes, trying to convince Oliver that the turtle hadn't been harmed. We promised he could see for himself tomorrow because now it was bedtime. But the little ones weren't as interested in sleep as their parents.

It took hours for Oliver to fall asleep in the little bed next to Scott. The fishing pole helped. Belle wanted me-time with Mom and to be held, sobbing every time I tried to put her into the crib.

Her crying started Gunner whining again, so I left the room before Scott and Oliver woke up. The small second bedroom was little more than a screened porch, but it had a daybed. Burrowing under blankets to keep warm, I held my fussy girl close and rested my head on my arm.

It probably didn't take me long to drift off. I lost track of time. With Belle content at last beside me, the only sound was wind in the trees and water trickling in the nearby creek. I dreamed we were floating in those treetops, warm and comfortable deep in the woods.

A familiar voice poked at me, like a finger jabbing my chest, whispering deep in my ear.

"Saffi."

I ignored it, wanting to drift forever.

"Saffi. Saffi. Saaaaaaffi!"

Snuggling deeper into my dream, I continued to ignore it.

"Saff-a-no-ski! SAFF-A-NO-SKI!" The voice and old nickname penetrated. My eyes filled with tears, and my breath caught. How was this possible?

"Granny?"

"There you are, Saff-a-no-ski! I thought you were going to ignore me!"

"Granny!" She'd died less than a year before, and I couldn't believe she was here. "It's so good to hear your voice!" Tears spilled down my cheeks, and I began to sob.

"Aw! It's okay, Saffi! But I need you to do something for me. Right now."

"Okay," I said, unable to stop crying. How could Granny be here if she was dead?

"Pay attention to me! I'm talking to you! I want you to wake up."

"Okay, but I miss you so much! I can't believe you're here!"

"Wake up, Saffi. Wake up! NOW!"

Nobody ever ignored Granny when she raised her voice. I opened my eyes, still sobbing with the joy of hearing her again. It took me a moment to realize where I was, lying on my stomach on an unfamiliar bed.

We're at that place in Arkansas. Where's the baby?

At that moment, I realized with absolute horror that she was under me. I'd rolled over on top of her as I slept, shoving her deep into the soft mattress beneath me.

Yanking Belle into my arms, I shouted for Scott. She wasn't moving. She hung in my arms, limp and quiet.

Scott shoved open the door and flipped on the light. At that exact moment, Belle opened her eyes. They were dark as night. She opened her mouth wide and roared. It was the most beautiful sound I'd ever heard, and I added my own terrified sobs to them.

"What's going on?" Scott said.

"Granny woke me up!" I said. "Granny told me to get up, and I was lying on top of the baby!"

"She's okay." He cupped her face, examining her. "Any baby who can cry like this is just fine."

As a woman with a scientific mind, I've thought of that night many times over the years. I know I heard Granny's distinctive gravelly voice as plainly as I'd ever heard it when she was alive. Sometimes, I tell myself that my subconscious knew I'd rolled on top of Belle. That bone-numbing exhaustion kept me from being able to wake up. That my brain used the memory of Granny to force me awake.

I try to make myself believe that rational explanation.

But what I know for sure is that a year after Granny left this world, she spoke to me clearly in a voice I'd know anywhere. Granny kept my world intact that night just like she did when she was alive.

—S.R. Karfelt—

The Voice

The guardian angels of life fly so high as to be beyond
our sight, but they are always looking down upon us.
~Jean Paul Richter

I was tired of being a watched pot that wouldn't boil, so I welcomed the labor pains when they began. I was almost two weeks overdue with our second daughter. The household was sleeping, and I whispered to the baby, enjoying the final moments of her being all mine.

Once at the hospital, I submitted to the rhythms of labor. Time had a funny way of ceasing to exist even though I was surrounded by a husband, doula, and nurse. I had retreated into the focus I needed. At the tenth hour, I was told all was progressing nicely.

I remember it vividly like a light switch went off. One minute I was fine; the next I felt like I couldn't breathe. I knew something was wrong. Pulling myself out of "the zone," I told the nurse what I was experiencing. She replied, "If you're talking, you're breathing." She proceeded to put an oxygen mask on me. "You may be having a panic attack."

I knew that wasn't true and was about to reply when the obstetrician walked into the room. I explained my symptoms. She checked all the vital-sign information for both my baby and me. Everything was still textbook according to the machinery. The doctor knew how committed I was to a vaginal delivery. She stayed with me for a few minutes, and our eyes met. She said, "Are you ready for a C-section?"

Without hesitation, I said, "Yes!" I saw the dismay on the faces of my husband and my doula; they knew of my wishes for a natural experience. I could not explain to them that something was very wrong, as a flurry of activity had begun in preparation for an emergency C-section.

I was wheeled to the OR without my husband. Surrounded by medical staff, I'd never felt more scared or alone. I prayed that the baby would be okay, and it dawned on me that maybe I should pray for myself, too.

The suffocating feeling continued. Anesthesia had to be administered faster than normal. At first, I felt my legs go numb and then my waist, but it didn't stop there. The eerie numb feeling continued slowly up my body, one vertebra at a time, until I couldn't move any part of my body from the neck down.

I felt a deep primal scream well up inside me as blinding fear took over. My worst nightmare was coming true. I was being buried alive and couldn't do anything to stop it. I felt tears sliding out of my eyes, but I couldn't move my hand to wipe them away. I had a fleeting thought that I hoped they could get the baby out before I died. I needed to see her just once, and I wondered how my husband would cope being a single dad of two girls.

I was on the precipice of pure panic when I heard a voice. Floating above me, a gentle but firm voice said, "Breathe!" I took a breath, and then another. Fear was still clawing at the back of my throat. The voice repeated, "Breathe!" I obeyed. When the prep for the C-section was complete, my husband was let into the OR. I have a vague recollection of him standing by my head, but I was so focused on not screaming that I couldn't talk. I felt the doctor make the first incision, and my right leg moved. The obstetrician asked the anesthesiologist why my leg was moving. Before he could answer, I said, "Because I can feel what you're doing." The doctor looked up at me in surprise and said, "You must hold still. I have to get this baby out immediately!" There was no mistaking her sense of urgency. My needs came second.

The voice above me said, "It's going to be okay. You're both going to be okay."

I held onto those words. I felt a loving presence envelop me as

I floated to the ceiling to join the voice. Sheltering me from pain and fear, the voice was keeping me in a dreamy fog.

Once the C-section was over, I snapped back to the present. There was a flurry of activity on the other side of the surgical drape.

I screamed, "Why isn't my baby crying?"

No one answered.

I yelled my question again.

The doctor said, "Your baby has been taken to the NICU. The cord was wrapped around her entire body, including her neck." She paused from her suturing and looked at me. "If you had tried to deliver vaginally, she wouldn't have made it."

Letting this information sink in, I understood that my baby and I were so connected that I could sense her slow strangulation. I felt like I couldn't breathe because that was happening to her.

Eventually, the nurse brought my daughter into the OR. Still under the effects of anesthesia, I couldn't move, but my husband held our baby up near my head so I could hear her beautiful cries. I could sense the comforting presence of the voice slowly fading from the room. Was it an angel, spirit guide, God, divine intervention, or my subconscious? Honestly, I've stopped trying to give it a label. It doesn't matter, because the voice saved my life and that of my daughter, Davina Grace.

—Tory Wegner Hendrix—

9

An Angel's Tools

*Not everything we experience can be
explained by logic or science.*
~Linda Westphal

I drove around a corner through the old stockyards district to take a shortcut home. As soon as I pulled into the far right lane, my hopes of getting home sooner than expected were crushed. A slow-moving train blocked my path.

Having spent all my life in the same city, I was all too familiar with the train tracks that bisected neighborhoods. I knew that even though no train was supposed to block traffic at any given intersection for more than ten minutes at a time, it was rarely a reality. Sometimes, they would stop for minutes at a time, slowly back up, and then pull forward again. I had no choice but to take my place behind the long line of cars that were idling behind the flashing red crossbars. Most likely, I would be waiting for fifteen to twenty minutes.

There were four lanes of traffic: two on my side of the train and heading east, and two lanes heading west toward me on the unseen opposite side of the tracks. Unwritten railroad etiquette dictated that each new vehicle entering the line would pull up as close as possible to the car ahead. We all knew that the closer we got to the vehicle in front of us, the faster we could be on our way once the train had passed and the bars were raised. Plus, squeezing in tightly meant that the cars entering the lane behind us would be less likely to be blocking traffic.

As I pulled in to take my place behind the car in front of me, I clearly heard a voice in my head. "Leave one car length between you and the car ahead of you."

I was stunned. Leaving one car length between cars was not only unheard of, but it was rude. Sure that I was imagining things, I took my foot off the brake to creep forward.

"Leave one car length between you and the car ahead."

I put my foot on the brake again and left an entire space between vehicles, but not without worry. Would the driver behind me honk for me to pull forward? What happens if a car in the left lane pulls all the way forward, leaving me standing out as an anomaly?

As soon as I thought about the cars in the left lane, a new driver pulled up and stopped his vehicle directly to the left of mine, also leaving a full car length between himself and the car ahead of him. I felt relief that at least I was not the only one breaking protocol. I was curious as to why the car next to me also stayed behind. Did he hear the same voice in his head? Or was he simply following my example?

My musings were interrupted by the loud blare of a siren. My first thought was panic, wondering how in the world an emergency vehicle was going to navigate around this train. It simply would not be possible.

As I whipped my head around to locate the origin of the siren, an ambulance — lights flashing and horn blasting — emerged from between two buildings and entered the space conveniently left by the adjacent driver and me. I was stunned when I saw the paramedic maneuver the vehicle past our windshields and then swing left into the car-free westbound lane.

Immediately, my mind was full of what-ifs. What if I hadn't listened to the voice? What if the driver of the car next to me had pulled forward instead of staying behind with me? What if the egress of the ambulance was totally blocked until the train moved — five, ten, or fifteen minutes later?

The train was still rumbling and clanging past when the truth of the situation hit me.

Someone was supposed to live that night.

Someone's angel was in a battle to save his or her life.

The driver next to me and I were simply tools used by that loving entity to ensure that someone would rise to see another day.

— Randi O'Keefe —

10

A Beautiful Day in the Neighborhood

Miracles do not, in fact, break the laws of nature.
~C.S. Lewis

After weeks of rain, on a glorious April afternoon in New Jersey, I took my three-week-old son on his first outing to the park. His four-year-old brother chattered along the mile-long path around the sparkling duck pond.

"Look, little Paul, there's a goose. Honk!" Sean said, pointing. "And a dog. Hi, puppy!"

We lasted only one lap, with a twenty-minute stop on a bench, because I was still winded from the pneumonia I'd contracted while eight months pregnant. Sean fed the ducks and watched a swooping bird, talking to his brother as if the infant might miraculously answer.

I was grateful to be out with my newborn somewhere other than the pediatrician's office, where we'd been several times already. Paul had been whisked to neonatal intensive care moments after his birth with fluid clogging his lungs, and we'd had to come home without him.

Friends and relatives assured me they were praying, sending "good vibes" and positive thoughts. One gave me a crystal. Another said Paul's guardian angel was watching. I thanked them but secretly dismissed much of it. He'd get better with proper medicine and care, and he did.

Now, after March's gloom, the skies had cleared, literally and in our hearts. So I took my children to our safe and lovely park, something

I had yearned to do throughout my pregnancy, which was plagued by illness.

When we were stowing the stroller back in the minivan, Sean asked when we could come back. Very soon, I assured him. It was spring. Paul was healthy. Why not?

At home, Paul napped while I rested on the couch. Sean ate lunch with my mother, who was visiting from her home in Las Vegas, and then they headed to the back yard. I glanced out the kitchen window, noticing the sun lighting up the faces of people I loved. Mom pushed Sean on his swing while he pumped his skinny, little legs.

Paul woke and nursed, and then I paced the house, patting his warm back. Suddenly, I had an overwhelming urge to be out there, too.

"How about it, little guy? Want to go outside?" I cooed just as Paul burped.

Our kitchen empties into a kind of crooked breakfast nook/mud room that the previous owners must have slapped on as an afterthought. In stocking feet, it's easy to notice the tilt to the thin wood floor, and in winter, the heat can't compete with three walls of fifty-year-old jalousie windows.

But on a day like this, the "porch" was perfect, which was why I had rolled the bassinet from its usual spot in the living room to a warm patch beneath a porch window. What a convenience it was to have that bassinet! It let me move my infant from room to room, keeping Sean, a nervous child, calm about whether his baby brother was "doing okay." And because Paul fell asleep on his own, I liked being able to lay him down at the first blush of fatigue, allowing him to nap on his own schedule.

"Okay, buddy, just let me get on my shoes," I told Paul. I slipped my feet into my old "yard sneakers," which were all stretched out and with backs so rundown that they remained flat under my heel. "Let's go see your brother and Noni. See, Sean's on the swing!"

Paul tried to push up his head and follow my finger. His little body jerked in one of those non-verbal movements of baby excitement, like jumping in place against my chest.

Before reaching the back door, I took a quick look around, wondering if I should grab the cordless phone, the baby's blanket, or a juice box for Sean. I decided against all three. I pulled open the interior wood door and let my left hand fall on the screen-door handle.

Then I heard something. Or maybe I felt something. Or perhaps both.

Put down the baby. Put the baby in the bassinet. Don't take the baby outside.

Strangely, I did what I was told. Without hesitation.

Without knowing why, I laid Paul gently in the bassinet and cranked open a window so I could hear him from outside.

Then I stepped through the open screen door and fell down the two steps that lead to our slate patio, breaking my left foot in five places and severely spraining my right ankle.

I cried out in pain. Sean and Mom came running, and in seconds they were both crying, too. Only Paul was quiet inside, safe in his bassinet.

Mom called a neighbor to help get me into a patio chair, and we summoned my husband home from work. I sobbed and sobbed, so grateful that I'd placed my tiny son in a safe place. Surely, if he'd been in my arms when I fell — well, I didn't even want to think about that.

In the hospital, a nurse remarked that in falls like mine, one usually scrapes hands and forearms, or maybe an elbow, trying to break the fall, but it looked like I never put out my arms. I tried to reason why, but all I could remember, in the millisecond before I hit the ground, was clutching my arms to my chest. What was I trying to protect?

The next day, people assured me that I had much to be thankful for. It hadn't happened in the park. My mother was there, and I wasn't alone with Sean in the yard. And thank goodness it hadn't happened weeks earlier when I was nine months pregnant.

Hardly anyone said it was a good thing that I wasn't holding Paul when I fell. When Mom came back outside after getting the phone, she reported that Paul was sleeping, and I never mentioned why he came to be in the bassinet in the first place. I didn't tell anyone for a long time. Only I knew that my baby was in my arms until five seconds before I fell. I couldn't explain how or why someone like me, who typically dismissed talk of angels or guardians or the whisperings of the universe as so much hooey, had listened to whatever, or whomever, spoke to me that day.

Since that afternoon, I listen closely to my gut. I pay heed to urgent cautions in my head, what comes to me in dreams, or warnings that seem to come from nowhere. Paul is twenty-one now, and he's a little tired of the bassinet story. That's okay. I do hope, though, that he'll listen to his own inner voices or guidance, too.

— Lisa Romeo —

Chapter 2

Touched by an Angel

11

Bill

I am convinced that these heavenly beings exist and
that they provide unseen aid on our behalf.
~Billy Graham

W[hen the application came in the mail, I wasn't sure
I should bother filling it out. It was from the largest school district in the state, with more than 400
applicants for every opening. My letters of recommendation were solid, but my GPA was less than stellar.

An acquaintance "in the know" informed me that in order for the
district to get the applications down to a manageable number, the first
cut was always by GPA. I had no one who could put in a good word for
me, and rumor had it they liked to hire from within. The application
form itself was daunting — five pages ending with an essay section on
why the applicant should be considered for employment. I was about
to toss it out when my wife reminded me that I had nothing to lose.

I filled it out. Reluctantly.

Two weeks later, I was invited for an interview. My appointment
was for 1:00 p.m. I arrived ten minutes early. When I walked through
the main door, most of the hallway lights were off and the office was
empty. My first thought was that I had gone to the wrong building. I
wasn't sure where I should wait or even if I should.

1:05 came and went. Fifteen more minutes passed. Then twenty.
Should I go somewhere to make sure I have the right place? Maybe I

got the time wrong. Maybe I've blown it. Maybe I should go back to building houses.

At the peak of my confusion, I decided to leave and headed for the door.

"Don't go," a voice called out.

A man walked toward me at a brisk pace. He was slender, almost gaunt, a couple of inches shorter than me, and his hair was pepper gray.

He was wearing dark pants and a light blue shirt with the school-district logo on the pocket. Above the pocket, "Bill" was embroidered in heavy red thread. The handle of a crescent wrench leaned out of one back pocket, and a dust rag crept out the other.

"Everyone's out to lunch. That's why it's empty. You must be the new guy they're hiring."

His manner was friendly, and he held out his hand. It was a hand that had worked in oil, grease, dirt and dust for years. An honest hand.

I shook it gladly.

"I haven't been hired yet," I replied. "I haven't even had an interview."

"I know the job is yours if you want it. John—he's the boss—isn't planning on interviewing anyone else unless you turn it down."

This was really weird. How would a custodian know the employment decisions of the principal of the school?

"The thing is," he continued, "sometimes John doesn't have anyone to talk to, so he talks to me. I know a great deal about what goes on around here."

"Sounds encouraging," I said.

However, I was extremely suspicious of the quality of this information.

"You can wait for him in this outer office." Bill pointed to two chairs along a paneled wall. "They'll be back soon."

"Thanks."

"Well, I better get back to work," Bill said. "Good luck."

I took a chair and waited.

When John did arrive, he was most amiable. He apologized for being late, shook my hand firmly, and told me he was glad to finally meet me. The interview was nothing like what I was expecting. It consisted of him leading me around the building, telling me what went on at different areas, showing me where my room would be, and explaining how he saw me fitting into their plans. He even showed me where the private coffee stash was... the good stuff.

"Just for you, me, the nurse, and my secretary," he said.

At the end of the tour, we sat in his office and had an informal chat. We talked about educational philosophy, our backgrounds, where I saw myself in ten years, family, even hobbies. He then told me something that made me chuckle.

"I noticed you filled out your application in pencil."

"Yes. I didn't want to use whiteout."

"You know, NASA spent thousands of dollars trying to develop a pen that would work in zero gravity. The Russians just used pencils."

He grinned, and I thought, *good point, literally*.

He offered me a fair contract, and I signed it.

As I was pulling out of the parking lot, I caught sight of Bill working on an outside water faucet. He turned when he saw me, flashed a big grin, and waved.

School started a month later. My second day there, I wandered about trying to find Bill. I wanted to say hello and thank him for the encouragement he'd given me on the day of my interview. I also wanted to get the real story on how he was so confident I would be offered the job. He was nowhere to be found. *Must be on vacation,* I surmised. When another week went by and I still hadn't seen him, I went in to talk to John.

"I've been trying to find Bill," I said.

"Bill who?"

"You know, Bill the custodian. I never caught his last name. He is an older guy, slender, gray hair, wears frameless glasses. He told me you talk over decisions with him occasionally."

John adjusted his seat and sat up a bit straighter. There were question marks all over his face.

"The only custodians we have here are Tony, Ray, and Lisa. They're all younger folks. I never talk business with them. And we've never had a custodian working here named Bill."

"But I met him on the day of my interview," I assured him. "He was working here. He had the uniform, district logo and everything. He told me the building was dark because everyone was at lunch. He even told me the job was mine for the taking and that you weren't planning on interviewing anyone else unless I turned it down."

John's eyes widened like eyes do when a person is experiencing a mixture of mystery and fear. I could tell he was thinking, and that his mind was searching, reaching, racing.

"I did think those exact thoughts," he whispered finally. "But I never spoke them to anybody… except in prayer."

We let that statement hang out there for a few seconds.

We kept looking at each other, waiting for the other person to say something.

Neither one of us did. Ever.

I stayed for thirty-one years.

—Jeff Hill—

Pennsylvania Turnpike

I think that someone is watching out for me,
God, my guardian angel, I'm not sure who that is,
but they really work hard.
~Mattie Stepanek

Two eighteen-wheelers lay jackknifed across the road. Dozens of snow-covered cars were turned over in ditches. Others were still sliding out of control, colliding with each other. Drivers of every form of transportation were fighting for survival in a swirl of falling snow.

My husband Joe, our new baby, and I had just approached the Pennsylvania Turnpike after one of the state's worst snowstorms blanketed the road. Terrified and shaking, we could go no farther, but it was too late to turn back.

We were on the way to Buffalo, New York. My in-laws were hosting a luncheon to welcome our new infant into the family circle, and we had not anticipated this storm.

Joe got out of the car and began directing what little traffic there was in order to keep cars from sliding and crashing into us. I sat in the front passenger seat, trembling, holding my baby girl tightly in my arms. Snow continued to fall. As dusk set in, we began to feel the temperatures fall. It was so cold.

"We can't just sit here," said Joe. "I'm going to try to find an exit ramp and see if I can get us out of this mess."

Although I pleaded with him not to leave us, I knew we were in a dangerous situation and would soon freeze without any help. We kissed and hugged as though it were our last moment on Earth together.

"I love you," I called out as I saw his distant form faintly disappearing from view. I prayed silently for the next thirty minutes. "I don't want to die. Please, please, can't someone — anyone — hear me?" I guess the rest of the people in their cars did the same because no one could be seen outside.

After what seemed like forever, I saw a figure heading toward the car. It was Joe, a white outline of a man. Ice particles stuck to his hair and eyebrows. Without a word, he yanked open the driver's door, sat down and started the engine.

"What are you doing?" I asked.

He put the car in reverse. "I am going to try to inch up a snow mound that I saw. I think it's an off ramp."

Joe was right: It was a ramp. Barely visible, we found out later it had sheer twenty-foot drops on both sides. But we were lucky. At the top of the ramp, we slid slowly down and spotted a pub on the side of the road. Joe went inside and asked if we could sleep there.

"No room here," said the bartender. "We're already overloaded."

As Joe began to move toward the outside door, a young man who had been seated at the bar approached him. "I live a mile up the road," he said. "You are welcome to stay with my wife and me."

I was not in favor of the plan, but it was either follow the stranger or sit outside and freeze to death. Besides, who knew when or if we would be rescued.

We followed the stranger, who drove a red pickup. The man told us his name was David. Soon, we came to a small cabin set back in a wooded area. A young woman stood in the doorway waving us inside.

It was a small home with a fireplace, kitchen and one bedroom. The warmth felt good, and I knew my child was going to be safe. David's wife smiled at my child. "We have hot chocolate if you like," she offered. She also heated up one of the three baby bottles that I had filled with formula for our trip. David held the baby while I took off my wet coat.

The couple offered us dinner and gave us their bed to sleep in while they slept on the floor with roll-up foam pads. There was a small crib in the bedroom, but it was empty, with no mattress or blanket. No toys spun overhead. I decided not to ask any questions that might have opened wounds.

It was a restless night, but I did get some sleep. The next thing I knew, it was morning. I opened my eyes and saw Joe sitting in a rocker next to the window holding our baby.

"There is breakfast in the kitchen," he announced. "Bacon, eggs and grits are on the small hotplate."

"Where are David and his wife?" I asked.

"Beats me," said Joe. "I'm sure they will be home soon." He paused. "In the meantime, eat up."

For the next twenty-four hours, we stayed in the cabin, listening to snow plows clearing the road outside.

Strangely, no one returned to the cabin. I thought maybe David and his wife were at work, but why wouldn't they have come home at night?

We packed the car and headed toward the pub to ask the bartender where the owners of the cabin were.

"No one lives in that cabin," the bartender told us. "It has been vacant for three years, ever since the Baker family lost their lives on a holiday trip."

The bartender told us that David Baker and his family had been on the Pennsylvania Turnpike when a tanker truck struck their sedan from behind. "The driver lost control, and the tanker veered, rolled over and skidded into the Bakers' car. Fire broke out, and flames instantly surrounded the car." His lips quivered. "Several locals tried to save them, but the family was killed immediately."

"Dear God!" I blurted out. "We must be dead."

"No, ma'am," the bartender said. "The Bakers are dead."

"But… I saw them. I talked to them," I cried, now sobbing. "They fed us and gave us their bed."

"Sorry, ma'am," the bartender said.

We got to our destination that afternoon. I cannot explain what happened that day on the Pennsylvania Turnpike. Years later, I read that angels are all around us. I decided that my angel is named David. Since that experience, I have had a deep feeling of protection around me. Sometimes, I whisper to David, thanking him for his grace.

— Anita Stone —

13

The Repairman

True healing involves body, mind and Spirit.
~Alison Stormwolf

I t was a confusing time in my life. I had been unceremoniously ousted from my high-paying marketing position and was still struggling with a lot of "Who am I, and why am I here?" type of questions. Of course, life marches on even when we're in the throes of a personal identity crisis, and in my case that meant a broken dishwasher.

Our family's finances at the time were abysmal. Finally, after several months of dealing with mountains of dirty dishes strewn around the kitchen, I bought a dishwasher with the last bit of credit on our credit card.

I was ecstatic when two young men showed up to install my new best friend. It was stainless steel and amazingly quiet — too quiet, as it turned out.

I used my sleek new companion several days in a row. Every time I ran the dishwasher and took out the dishes, they were still dirty. I called the store to ask for help, and they promised to send someone out the next morning to check into the problem.

Marty, the repairman, showed up right on time. He was around fifty, slender, and had a cowboy sort of air about him. I was comfortable with him immediately. He seemed open and friendly, competent and wise. We walked to the kitchen, and within five minutes Marty had determined that the installers hadn't opened a water valve completely, so there wasn't adequate water reaching the dishwasher.

I was relieved the problem was so simple and easily fixed. I thanked him and offered him some coffee. He accepted a mug and leaned back against the kitchen counter. After taking a sip, he asked me if I believed in angels. His question caught me off guard; it didn't fit with our conversation up to that point. I asked what prompted him to ask me that. He said he'd noticed I had several angel and cherub paintings and figurines around my home and garden. Feeling slightly disconcerted, I avoided his original question and agreed that I did collect them.

Then he took a postcard from his toolbox and handed it to me. It was from a store in Independence, Missouri, about forty-five minutes from my home. He said I should go there sometime because the owner had many angel objects for sale. I asked Marty how he found out about the store. He proceeded to tell me an amazing story.

About six months before I met Marty, his only daughter had been killed in a car accident on a nearby highway. She was a passenger in the front seat, riding with a couple of friends. The driver's cell phone rang, and he dropped it while trying to answer it. When he bent over to pick it up, he lost control of the car and slammed into a concrete barrier. Marty's daughter was the only person killed.

She was in her early twenties at the time of her death. She and Marty were very close. He said he loved to grow roses in his back yard, and he called them his babies. After he got home from work during the warmer months, he would go out to tend his roses. His daughter would often join him in the garden.

Marty would cut one perfect rose and hand it to her wordlessly. It was his way of telling her how much he valued her and how beautiful she was to him.

Just a few days after her death, Marty had a dream. His daughter told him that she was fine, he needn't worry about her, and he should move forward with his life. When he woke, he felt a sense of calm and peace.

Unfortunately, his wife felt no such peace. She was despondent and could see no point to anything in life. Marty tried to help his wife by telling her about his dream, but she seemed to be out of his reach.

A few months later, Marty and his wife were driving around in downtown Independence. He kept asking her where she wanted to go for lunch, but she was unresponsive. Marty's anger, which had built up over the last few months while his wife shut him out, threatened to explode. He took a deep breath and said he was going to drive around the square until she made a decision about where they were going.

He drove around and around, receiving no response from his wife. When he had tired of driving, he stopped the car and turned toward her to try to reason with her one more time. When he looked behind her, he saw they were in front of a store called the Angel Lady. He had never heard of this store and could not explain why, but he told his wife they must go inside.

As they entered the store, Marty immediately felt a sense of peace and love wash over him. The store was in an old house and consisted of several small rooms filled with angel paintings, figurines, books, and music — anything one could imagine with an angel theme. As they entered the second room, Marty looked up and saw a painting of an angel holding a rose. The angel's face looked just like his daughter's. He showed it to his wife and said they must buy it. For the first time since their daughter's death, Marty's wife seemed to be present. She agreed that they must have the painting for their home.

This experience was the turning point for Marty's wife in accepting and moving beyond their daughter's death. He said that was the reason he carried cards from the Angel Lady with him wherever he went. He felt there were always people who needed to experience the healing that he and his wife had.

It was time for Marty to go to his next service call. He had more appliances to repair, and more souls to touch — or repair. I was reminded yet again that life always goes on, and we never know when and where we will meet angels on our path.

— Suzanne Miley —

14

Still There for Me

Brothers and sisters are as close as hands and feet.
~Vietnamese Proverb

After graduating from high school, I was hired as a flight attendant for Eastern Airlines. A few months later, when I was about to start the training program, the airline began experiencing financial difficulties. Heavy debt loads and labor disputes forced the company to begin shutting down. Soon after, the airline stopped flying. So I took different jobs for a few years and then pursued my second career goal: becoming a professional writer. For twenty-plus years, I worked as a travel and health writer for magazines and newspapers. But as an adventurer, I never gave up on my dream to work in the airline industry.

My brother George was always very supportive. Often, I went to him for advice and inspiration. He called me early every morning and helped me focus on the positive, encouraging me to pursue new experiences. He was a successful businessman and happy to share his wealth with family and friends. He was also intelligent, funny, and a gifted musician. I admired and adored him. He encouraged me to look for a job opening in the airline industry and apply again.

"It's never too late," he said. "Don't give up on your dream."

I decided to apply for a customer-service position with JetBlue, and the interview went well. A few months later, I received a call telling me I was hired and would begin training soon. After I hung up the phone, I sat at my desk, amazed.

"I told you," my brother said, smiling. "That's great! I knew you could do it! Now you'll get great benefits and be able to travel all over. And as your family member, I can travel, too!"

Not long after our conversation, my brother suddenly started feeling ill. Shockingly, he was diagnosed with Amyotrophic Lateral Sclerosis, also known as Lou Gehrig's disease. ALS is a progressive neurodegenerative condition that affects nerve cells in the brain and spinal cord.

"There is no cure," the doctor said.

"How long do I have?" my brother asked as tears welled in our eyes.

"No more than six months," the doctor replied.

As we left the doctor's office, my brother told me, "Don't let this ruin your new job. Go get your training. It's only for two weeks."

"I can't leave you now," I said. "I'll postpone it."

The disease progressed so rapidly that my brother soon needed twenty-four-hour care. Hospice was called, and he was gone a few months later.

Time went by, and I felt in my heart that my brother was still insisting that I take the airline job. All that winter, my heart ached for him. I prayed, "If I'm supposed to have this job, then please let it work out. But if not, I'll put this dream out of my heart."

The next day, I got the call that arrangements had been made for me to fly to Florida to finish paperwork and get airport clearance before going to the academy in Orlando for training. I returned home on the late flight. It was my first time flying at night by myself, and I was a little nervous. Finally, we landed. I got off the plane and collected my luggage.

It was late, so the airport was deserted. I sat on a bench waiting for a friend to pick me up when a tall, handsome man with dark hair and dark eyes suddenly stood next to my seat. He was dressed in a long overcoat with tan khaki pants and a white dress shirt. He was talking on his cell phone and carrying a briefcase. I was surprised because I hadn't seen him enter the lobby.

When I looked up at him, he smiled. I didn't expect to experience such emotion when I looked into this man's eyes. He smiled again, nodded, and started talking on his cell phone as he walked away slowly. He not only looked identical to my brother but also dressed and walked like him. My brother was always on his cell phone with clients and always carried his briefcase. I stood up.

"Wait," I said. I wanted to hug this man. He stopped, turned and looked back at me. The tears fell down my cheeks as our eyes met, and he nodded again, smiling. I put my head down briefly and then looked up. He was gone. I stood alone in the airport. I didn't move a muscle, but a feeling of peace came over me.

Just then, I felt a tap on my shoulder. "Are you okay?" my friend said. "I've been outside trying to get your attention. You're in a daze."

"Did you see that man?" I asked.

"What man? It's midnight. There's no one in the airport now. You were sitting on the bench alone."

"No," I said. "He was standing next to the bench. He looked just like George! His hairstyle… the way he was dressed. It was my brother!"

"I didn't see anybody," he replied.

The next morning, I didn't feel the same sadness I had felt every morning since my brother died. And the ache in my heart seemed less painful. Since that night, I often hear a soothing voice that seems to speak from deep within, reminding me that we are always connected to those we love and will see them again when we travel into the next life.

—Kathryn Radeff—

15

An Angel from Arizona

All God's angels come to us disguised.
~James Russell Lowell

On May 22, 2011, a devastating EF5 tornado struck Joplin, Missouri. This twisting monster demolished 8,000 structures, injured more than 1,100 people, and took 161 lives. Initially, the scope of the destruction was difficult to comprehend, and many residents, including me, felt overwhelmed. The world as we knew it seemed over. Faced with confusion, uncertainty, loss, and despair, we looked for any light to lead us out of the darkness.

Our house suffered major damage, but the home of my parents, who were in their eighties, was decimated. Their roof blew away, and the roof from a nearby school crashed into the front of their house. In seconds, the home they had known for years became uninhabitable.

As soon as my parents were safely relocated, I tried to determine if any of their remaining possessions could be saved. Regrettably, I discovered their roof, before departing for parts unknown, had dropped massive amounts of fiberglass insulation. This pink material made everything appear to be coated in cotton candy, but the glass fibers within it had ruined most of their furniture and clothing.

My parents had hoped, however, that I might be able to save some of their books and pictures. Unfortunately, every time I tried to remove a photo album from a drawer or a book from a shelf, the nonstop rain drenched what I was trying to protect. Between the rain and the glass fibers, it all seemed hopeless.

Trying to fight off despair, I took a minute to stand in what was left of my parents' bedroom. When I looked up through their nonexistent roof, I saw gray clouds floating above me, and suddenly everything seemed so surreal. Rain coated my upturned face, flooded my eyes, and flowed into my mouth. Overwhelmed, I felt like I was drowning. I needed fresh air, so I ran outside.

Standing on my parents' front lawn in the rain, I could breathe better, but I still had an overwhelming sense of hopelessness. Suddenly, from out of nowhere, a short, thin, elderly man appeared at my side. One second, I was alone, and a second later, he was next to me. It seemed like he rose up through the ground or fell out of the sky. He was just there... right beside me.

Startled, I took a step back, but he put my mind at ease by saying, in a very comforting voice, "Everything is going to be alright."

Confused, I asked him, "Where did you come from?"

"I'm from Arizona," he answered. "I heard about the disaster and came to help."

"I used to live in Arizona," I informed him.

He smiled and nodded like he was already aware of this information.

"You need to get a tarp over that roof," he told me. "Everything inside is going to be ruined if you don't get a cover over the house."

"I can't get up there in this rain," I explained. "There's no ladder, and I don't have a tarp."

"Would you like me to fix it?"

"Oh, that would be great, but ... how can you fix it?"

"I can. No problem."

With that response, he glided through the rain toward the house. Climbing on the debris that covered the front of the house, he clambered up to the roof—or to what pieces were left of it. For his age, he seemed exceptionally agile. I remember thinking he must be some kind of acrobat to move so nimbly and quickly. As I stared through the rain, he pulled out some type of shiny cutting tool and proceeded to cut off pieces of white, rubbery-looking material from the school's displaced roof. Working swiftly, he fastened these pieces to the remaining rafters and beams.

I watched him until I remembered I was supposed to be saving my parents' prized possessions. I went back inside and found some towels and plastic bags in a cupboard. Using the towels to dry off several photo albums and books, I placed these treasured items into the plastic bags for protection from the rain.

Suddenly, I realized it was no longer raining in the house. Looking up, I saw white, rubbery fabric covering the roof. He'd done it. That acrobatic man from Arizona had succeeded in putting a tarp over the whole house.

I ran outside to thank him, but my elderly gymnast was nowhere to be seen. I walked around the house, looking up as I went, but there was no sign of him. I wanted to tell him how grateful I was for his help because now I could save more of my parents' cherished possessions.

Thinking this man might have moved on to help others in the neighborhood, I walked up and down the street asking if anyone had seen him. No one, however, had seen or heard of my helper.

One neighbor, in particular, seemed skeptical about my description of this man's appearance and actions.

"You'd have to be crazy to climb up on such an unsound structure in this rain," he said. "You could easily slip, fall, or have the rest of the roof collapse beneath you. Plus, you'd have to have a big tool to cut that thick tarp."

Another neighbor remarked that it would take several men to pull the heavy, wet tarp across the roof, and still another questioned why a man from Arizona would drive all the way to Missouri to help and how he could have gotten here so fast. I had no explanations for any of their concerns, but the tarp was proof the man had been there. It was in place and blocking the rain.

Walking back toward my parents' house, I encountered a woman who said she'd heard me talking to the neighbors.

"I think you saw an angel," she said. "There are a lot of them around right now."

"I saw a nice man," I told her, "and he was real."

"Yes, angels are real," she answered.

The rain continued for days, but because of the tarp, I was able to save many of my parents' favorite books, important papers, and family pictures. They were so grateful to have those mementos and keepsakes.

I never saw the elderly, acrobatic man again. I never got to thank him, but I have concluded the woman I met on the street was right. This man was an angel sent to help me in my hour of need — and I was not alone. In fact, many people reported seeing angels in Joplin after the tornado, and several children described "butterfly people" who wrapped their wings around them to keep them safe.

I didn't see any wings on my helper, but with the heavy rain and in my anxious state, I might have missed them. All I know is that he was a light in the darkness. He gave me assistance, comfort, and hope. Like so many others after the tornado, I believe I saw an angel. Mine just said he came from Arizona.

— Billie Holladay Skelley —

16

Unexplained

A God wise enough to create me and the world
I live in is wise enough to watch out for me.
~Philip Yancey

The summer after I turned fifteen, I worked as a waitress at Sunnybrook Farm, a resort near where I lived, a few miles from South Haven, Michigan. One of my duties was to help clean up the dining room and kitchen after the guests were done.

One afternoon, after we had finished our cleaning detail, the waitresses and busboys were standing around in the spacious kitchen chatting with the cooks. We had developed some close friendships that summer and often talked for a while before leaving for the day.

As I stood there, I felt a sharp jolt from behind, as if someone had fallen against me. To regain my balance, I took a step forward and a little to my left.

A split second later, a large object hit the floor right where I had been standing. The kitchen vent fan had somehow torn apart. The electric motor, which weighed at least forty pounds, had crashed into the floor, doing extensive damage. Had I still been in that spot, I would surely have been badly injured — if not killed.

Everyone gathered around me, making sure that I was not hurt, and commenting on how lucky I was that I had moved at that precise time.

When I told them that someone had shoved me, they were puzzled.

There had been no one else in the kitchen—and no one behind me—so no one who could have pushed me out of harm's way.

But "someone" did.

—Dorothy Dale—

17

An Angel in Black

*An angel can illuminate the thought and mind of man
by strengthening the power of vision.*
~Saint Thomas Aquinas

It was a warm October morning in Arizona. Typical of the desert, the morning began on the cooler side, but quickly warmed up to a beautiful day of sunshine — perfect for a walk in shorts and tennis shoes. Lots of people were at the park this morning — men were fishing, women were jogging, children were playing.

As we walked, we talked about Ann's marital struggles. We had met in an abuse-recovery program. She was currently feeling trapped in an emotionally destructive marriage. However, she also had two young daughters to think about. Ann's husband and the children had dual citizenship in a foreign country. Ann was terrified he would take the children abroad and she would never see them again. Although she loved her husband, she was almost at a breaking point. The verbal and emotional abuse was killing her and had all but broken her spirit. Throughout our morning walk, she was brought to tears repeatedly.

As we rounded the last turn of the path, Ann looked directly in my eyes. "What should I do? Do I leave him? Could he take my children?"

"I don't know. I just don't know," I said.

We sat down on a bench so Ann could have a good cry. I prayed aloud for her. We sat in silence; there were no more words to speak. Ann's problem was huge, and there was no easy answer. She had hard decisions to make. We sat still, allowing God and nature to calm our worries. The beautiful sun warmed our faces, and the birds sang.

Then we saw a young woman approaching us. She wore a black, hooded running suit. The long sleeves and long pants were oddly out of place on this warm day. The hood tied under her chin made it seem like she was ready for cold weather. She did not look like she belonged in Arizona. All we could see was a beautiful, round face shining from the dark hood. Her eyes were glued on Ann as she walked directly to her.

"Can I give you a hug?" the stranger asked. This question jolted both of us from our thoughts. Quickly, I eyed the woman to make sure she did not have a weapon or bad intent. Her face calmed me, though, and her smile was full of kindness and concern. I will never forget how her face seemed to shine, round and bright like the sun. Her eyes were full of love. Ann looked at me as if asking what she should do. In that split second, I nodded my head.

Ann stood, and the woman embraced her with a firm, strong hug. She held Ann tightly while she whispered in her ear, "Keep hope. The Lord will make a way."

Ann stammered back, "Thank you; is there anything I can do for you? Are you okay?" However, without a word, the woman in black turned to leave. As quickly as she had appeared in front of us, she turned and started on her way. Ann sat down, stunned at what had just taken place.

"What's your name?" I called out after her as she began to disappear over a hill.

"Lauren," she replied, looking back over her shoulder. With that, she was out of our sight.

Ann and I sat in silence again, but this time we were stunned and flabbergasted. The entire encounter had taken only a few seconds.

"What just happened?" I questioned.

"Do you think that was an angel?" Ann voiced.

"Yes, I do." I knew a miracle had unfolded right in front of us. "She came for you. I was just the witness."

"I know she came for me. She came to give me a message: God is going to make a way." My dear friend's eyes welled up with tears, but a slight smile began to form on her face.

We got up and began to walk briskly around the lake again, in the same direction as Lauren. Although there were only minutes separating us, we never saw her again. The woman in the black running suit was nowhere to be found.

For months to come, we processed this day and Lauren's message. We were glad we had both been present so we could verify the facts with each other. We visited the same bench at the same time on the same day of the week, but we never saw Lauren again. The two of us continued to believe that we had been visited by an angel and witnessed a miracle.

Ann's situation didn't change that day, but her heart did. She had a renewed hope and strength. Lauren's spirit ministered to Ann. She brought God's love to one of his children who was discouraged and broken. We came to the park that unforgettable day with heavy hearts, but we left amazed and full of hope.

— Gwyn Schneck —

18

Angels' Food

Angels live among us. Sometimes they hide their wings,
but there is no disguising the peace
and hope they bring.
~Author Unknown

One rainy spring day, Mom became a single mother. My little brother was two, my sister was eight, and I was fourteen. Those first weeks were especially hard before our small monthly support payments began. Mom found work in a potato-chip factory, but didn't get paid right away.

That first Saturday morning as she left for work, Mom said, "I don't know what you'll cook for supper. My boss put a rush on my beginning paycheck so I'll have it Monday, but I'm out of money, and our shelves are as bare as Mrs. Hubbard's cupboards." She laughed, but tears filled her eyes. "I forget. Does that nursery rhyme have a happy ending?"

"No, but we'll do better," I said. "I'll ask Jesus to get us food today." My words sounded bold even to me. She shook her head and went to work.

I had planted a garden out back. The lettuce and peas were up, but nothing was ready to eat. I poked through the kitchen and discovered Mom was right. We had enough cereal for our breakfast but that would be the end of the milk. We had half a package of dry macaroni, one medium-sized can of tomatoes, and a quart of home-canned green beans. That didn't sound appetizing, but I could do something with it.

While my sister and brother played, I prayed and tidied the house. I was washing our front-room window when a cheery man in a blue denim shirt and narrow-brimmed hat wobbled past our house on a bicycle and turned into our driveway. He climbed our porch steps and rang the doorbell. Although I'd never seen him before, his big smile made me trust him.

When I opened the door, he asked, "Have you heard about the new grocery store a mile from here? Today's their grand opening."

I nodded. I'd seen their signs as I rode past on the school bus.

"They're giving away gift coupons to celebrate." He pulled three white cards from his shirt pocket and handed them to me. "The first is for a jumbo-size loaf of bread, the second is for a gallon of milk, and the third lets you choose a half-gallon of your favorite flavor of ice cream."

I stared. "Really? There's no purchase required?"

"None at all. These are free. Go and see."

I thanked him and watched as he got back on his bike and rode down the street without stopping at any other house.

Could it be true? We had to find out. I took my battered blue bicycle and put my sister on the seat behind me and my brother in the basket. We pedaled to the store, where colorful balloons still announced the grand opening. After I parked the bike, we walked inside and showed our cards to the nearest clerk. "It says these are gift cards. Is a purchase necessary?"

She peered down. "No. You have gift certificates. These items are absolutely free."

My sister, brother, and I could hardly believe it. We grabbed a jumbo-size loaf of Wonder Bread and a gallon of pasteurized milk. We went to the ice-cream section and agreed on Cherry Delight. We left the store with blinding smiles. I tucked the groceries in the basket around my brother and raced home before the ice cream could melt.

When Mom returned, we had nice plates, silverware, and food on the table. Our glasses held fresh milk.

"Where did you get this?" Mom asked.

"I prayed," I said. And then I opened our freezer to show her the ice cream.

"Really," she repeated. "Where did all this come from?"

I told her about the man on the bicycle while we ate one of the happiest meals of our lives. Even our vegetable macaroni tasted okay with a little extra seasoning.

She shook her head again, this time with a sense of wonder.

Monday morning at the school bus stop, I asked other kids up and down our street if a man representing the new grocery store had stopped by their houses.

"What man?" they asked.

I told them about the man on the bicycle and the cards he gave me.

"Free food? You're kidding. We would remember if we'd seen him."

But he had brought food for our table — maybe angels' food, including the Cherry Delight ice cream that is still my favorite. That day taught me to expect good things, even in hard times, and to keep my eyes wide open so I won't ever miss seeing the unexpected.

— Delores E. Topliff —

19

Help in a Time of Trouble

Believe in guardian angels. They believe in you
and are forever by your side.
~Author Unknown

They say when it rains it pours, and I never believed it more than I did at that point. It had been a year of pain and struggles, and I'd just been hit with the biggest blow of all. I sat there cradling my warm cup of coffee, hoping it could warm the chill inside.

It started in July when a car ran my car off the highway into one of the concrete dividers. I nearly died. The impact forced my left eye from its socket and damaged the optic nerve. My face was crushed, I had a concussion, and my neck was fractured. To top it off, the doctors couldn't get the bleeding to stop, so they said I wouldn't make it. If I did make it, they said, I would likely be blind or paralyzed, possibly both.

I don't remember much about the accident. But I do remember the stranger in white who helped me at the scene. My right eye was blurry and damaged, so I never really got a good look at him, but I could make out the figure of a body in a white or cream-colored outfit. He held my hand and told me that it would be okay. My head wasn't clear enough to understand then, but I knew I appreciated the comfort of having someone with me and holding my hand.

When I asked the paramedics about the stranger, they said there was no one there when they arrived. But I felt sure of what I had heard and seen, even if I had been half-conscious. Of course, there were times when I wondered if it had just been my imagination, and maybe the paramedics had been right. I didn't realize then that it was my first encounter with an angel who had been sent to help me through a difficult time.

Two months later, my mother lost everything in a hurricane. Her home was totally destroyed, and everything she owned was damaged. When she tried to keep the doors closed to lessen the damage, the force of the winds injured her. The entire area around her had been destroyed, and there were no contractors available for months. It felt like more than we could take.

Two months after that disaster, my dad was diagnosed with lung cancer. The doctors said his lungs were totally covered in spots, and there was nothing they could do for him.

At this point, it was November, and I just wanted the year to be over because I didn't think it was possible to survive anything more. Surely, the next year would be better. How could it not?

On the morning of December 5th, I got a call that proved things could still get worse. My twenty-four-year-old sister had been killed by a drunk driver. The words still ring in my ears.

Sitting at the dining-room table, it seemed all hope was lost. The smell of my coffee was the only thing tying me to this world. My mind and heart seemed to be falling deeper and deeper into despair.

As I stared off into the distance, one eye covered with a patch and the other still adjusting to doing all the work, I saw a figure pass by my left side. She walked behind me and laid a hand on my shoulder. She was wearing a white or cream-colored gown. I thought it might have been my grandmother, who always wore her cream-colored housecoat around the house. Then I heard a slightly familiar voice say, "It's going to be okay."

I turned to look, not sure if I was still expecting my grandma or not, but no one was there. I could still feel the print of the hand on my shoulder and hear the words spoken softly in my ear. I felt tears streaming down my face again, but this time it was with renewed hope and comfort. The chill was gone, and I could feel the warmth of everlasting love and care flood my soul. It would not bring my sister back to me, of course, but it would help me go on.

After that, though the year had been hard and long, I knew I hadn't gone through it alone. God had sent an angel to give me strength and remind me He was always there. No matter how hard things get, He will give me strength to make it through. It showed me that I was never alone, especially in the hardest times.

— Christine Brown —

Chapter
3

Comfort from Beyond

20

Snow Angels

Snowflakes are snow angels
blowing kisses from heaven.
~Author Unknown

I grew up in a family of six children. Regardless of the temperature, we learned to make our own fun outdoors. We enjoyed making impressions on the freshly fallen snow. We would lie on our backs and move our arms and legs in a sweeping motion. When we stood up, we were careful not to disturb our creations — our snow angels.

Years after I married and moved away from my childhood city, I still made snow angels. My husband Brian and I would search out fresh snow, unmarked by our dogs, and lie down side by side, just far enough apart to move our arms and legs. Afterward, we would stand and look down with pride at what we had created.

After thirty-nine years together, Brian lost his battle with cancer less than nine months after the diagnosis. I lost my sparkle and the desire to go outside and make snow angels.

Months later, I purchased a cedar bench and had it erected on the walking path through the wetlands park near my home. The bench was inscribed in memory of Brian. Two weeks after the bench was finished, winter arrived unexpectedly. I was surprised when I looked out the kitchen window and saw the tree branches drooping under the weight of wet snow. The sun was just peeking out from behind the clouds, and the trees looked beautiful, glistening with ice crystals.

I love photography and was anxious to go outdoors and capture some photos before the sun had fully risen. It would melt the overnight snow, and the glory of what I was looking at would be gone. With a fresh cup of coffee in my hand and my camera tucked under my winter jacket, I stepped outdoors. The crisp winter air bit at my exposed skin. I quickened my step. Snowflakes were still drifting down slowly. A peaceful calm enveloped me.

During the summer, the wetland pond was alive with waterfowl but now the pond was silent. All I could see were the deer tracks across the ice.

It was absolutely silent as I walked, and it was easy to get lost in my thoughts. The only sound was the crush of snow beneath my feet. As I approached Brian's bench, mine were the only footprints. No one had walked before me. And yet, I saw two perfectly created snow angels, side by side, just a couple of feet from the bench. I wondered who could have created them. Snow was falling steadily now, yet the impressions were clear.

I turned and looked toward the pond. The bulrushes still stood tall, covered in a crisp ice frosting. The snow leading to the pond was pristine. I looked backwards from where I stood on the path. The only blemishes were the marks my own boots had left. There were no other footprints. I glanced around and realized the snow was totally undisturbed everywhere around me.

My attention turned back to the angel impressions. There was no reason for someone to lie down so close to the bench to create the angels with so much open area just a few feet away. As I stared at the angels, a realization slowly dawned on me. I smiled inwardly, knowing this was a sign from heaven. The angels were my husband's way of letting me know that he was here with me in this moment. I felt a swell of emotion building, but instead of letting the emotion push me to sadness, I embraced the blessing that our life together had been.

I captured the images with my camera. Then I brushed the snow from the bench and sat down. I leaned back and closed my eyes, thinking about the hundreds of times that Brian and I had made snow angels. It seemed a silly thing to do at our age, but whenever we stood up, we were proud of the angels we had created.

I can't explain how the snow angels appeared or why the angels were so close to Brian's bench, but it doesn't matter. All that matters is that it brought me comfort.

Years have passed since that day, and never again have I found snow angels. I believe that Brian knows I have learned to live without him, and time has healed my loneliness.

I plan to resume making snow angels in the winter–for both of us.

— Wendy Portfors —

21

Angels at the Window

Is death the last sleep? No—it is the last
and final awakening.
~Sir Walter Scott

I remember running from the room as my mother shuddered in my dad's arms. Within a few seconds, I was back in there, trying to help. Of course, there was nothing I could do.

The hospice nurse was on the way; we could do nothing but hold her and pray. I could tell by the way Dad was looking at her and praying that he thought it was the end.

None of this was unexpected—we knew that my mother's cancer was terminal. What shocked us was the speed and timing. Within just a few hours, Mom's health had deteriorated drastically, and it seemed the weeks we thought we had left together had come down to only these few minutes.

As the convulsions stopped, Mom went still and limp in my dad's arms, no longer breathing. He looked at the window at the foot of her bed in our tiny apartment. There was nothing to say.

Between ten and twenty long seconds later, Mom suddenly drew a deep breath and announced cheerily, "I'm back!" Then, more dreamily, "It's very beautiful there."

Shocked, we helped her back under her covers, and she was asleep within seconds.

Dad and I just looked at each other. Finally, he spoke. "When I looked at the window, I saw two angels there. I was sure she was gone, that they had come to take her."

When Mom woke later, she was still weak but felt refreshed. She had no memory of either the convulsions or what she'd said. She asked us to tell her again and again what she'd said about it being beautiful there, and about the angels Dad had seen. Every time we repeated it to her, she seemed a little happier and more at peace. This little glimpse of what we believe to be her guardian angels watching over and waiting for her gave her — and all of us — strength for what we knew was ahead.

The hospice nurse arrived and confirmed what we suspected: Mom's time was short. We called my sister, who had planned to fly up the coming weekend, and told her to get on a plane as fast as she could. She arrived the following day, and we were all around Mom when she slipped into unconsciousness — still smiling and gripping our hands — and finally left with the angels.

— Evangeline Neve —

22

I'm Okay Now

When you open your mind to the impossible,
sometimes you find the truth.
~From the television show, Fringe

he asked if she could speak with me after school. It was my
first year as a high-school English teacher, and the first time
this student had ever spoken to me. Sure enough, at the end
of the school day she walked into the classroom.

"Mr. Schultz, you have to promise me that you won't make fun
of me for what I'm about to tell you."

"Of course I won't. What did you want to talk to me about?"

She said, "I'm going to tell you something I've never told anyone
before. I come from a family of mediums."

Foolishly, I blurted out, "Oh, like little people?"

Unnerved, she said, "No, mediums can see dead people. You
know how you were reading that letter in class today about your
friend Brandon who died? He was standing next to you while you
were reading it."

Now she had my attention! I looked around the room for hidden
cameras as I thought this might be some kind of new teacher initiation
prank, but she looked very sincere and serious.

In class, we were doing an assignment called "The Letter You
Wish You Sent" about reaching out to someone who is in trouble
and letting them know how we feel. I told them the story of my best
friend from middle school, Brandon, who got into drinking and drugs

in high school and ended up dying from them a few years later. My letter to him shared how much he had meant to me and how sorry I was he got into such a dark place. I wish I could have saved him. I never showed them a photo of Brandon, but this student started describing him exactly.

She described his bowl haircut and corduroy shorts. Then she asked if she could use my board to write on. She explained that she would receive random sayings and numbers, but she wasn't always sure what they meant. Maybe I could figure them out.

She wrote: 1996, 2, 6th, Tish, Masuda, Bulldog, and some other stuff. She asked if they made any sense to me. I couldn't believe it! I said, "I met Brandon in 1996 in second period. We sat next to each other in Mrs. Tischer's 6th grade English class at Masuda Middle School. My nickname for him was Bulldog."

I had never experienced anything like it. How could this be real?

She said, "Angels are with us more than we ever realize."

She said Brandon wanted me to have this message: "I'm okay now. You don't have to worry about me anymore. There's nothing you could have done. I feel your love still. I'm okay now."

I had chills! She said, "I wasn't going to say anything, but he really wanted me to give you that message. Your letter meant a lot to him and how you keep him alive by telling his story to us." I thanked her, and she left like it was no big deal.

Immediately, I went and asked several of my fellow teachers to come into my classroom and look at the board while I explained what had happened. I kept asking if this had been a prank. Were they in on this, or had they ever heard of this before? But they denied being involved and shared my disbelief.

The student never said another word the rest of the semester, but I guess she didn't need to. I've been teaching for ten years now, and no student's words have ever affected me like the words that girl spoke to me.

I love how, as an angel, Brandon took the form of how he looked when I knew him best — that innocent, fun-loving child who helped me not to be so scared and shy because he was boisterous and brave.

Every year, I still do that assignment. I continue to read my letter to Brandon and tell his story. I show pictures of him now, too. And every time I read the letter, I wonder if the little bulldog with the bowl-cut hair and corduroy shorts — with whom I used to play basketball and have sleepovers — is still standing next to me listening.

But thanks to the brave girl who dared to speak her truth to her teacher a decade ago, I don't have to wonder anymore about how my friend is faring. I know he is okay now.

— Steve Schultz —

As Promised

Flowers grow out of dark moments.
~Corita Kent

I watched as my lovely mother gazed out her bedroom windows at the sunset. The awful word "terminal" was still fresh in our minds. "Three months to live," we were told. "Make her comfortable."

We had just moved to a new state and created a beautiful bedroom suite for her in our home. There were windows all around, as sunny and cheery as we could make it. She'd come with only a few suitcases—everything she owned in the world after she sold her house up north. She also clung to two scraggly Christmas cacti she wouldn't give up because a favored niece had given them to her. They didn't even bloom at Christmas. They were dying in my care too and I hated them for the constant reminder.

After we settled her in her new quarters, we began to deal with the reality we faced together. We denied the truth of the hideous diagnosis, got angry at the impotence of the medical world, tried to bargain with God, and then got depressed—trying to hide our sadness from one another through all of those stages.

One day my mother turned to me and said, "I'm not through yet. I still have things to do."

"What things, Mama?"

"There's a reason I ended up here." I turned away, rolling my eyes. She meant she had more work to do on me. I said nothing and fiddled with her oxygen.

"Mama, I'll see about finding a priest. Would you like that?" I had no idea where any church was in this town, nor was I in the mood for finding one. But I would do it if it would make her happy. I asked the only other person I knew there, our real estate agent, who said she'd make some calls. She was going to try to get a church volunteer to come and read some prayers or bring communion.

The next morning, our doorbell rang. When I opened the door, a tall priest introduced himself. He was an imposing older man, dressed in full black garb and a white Roman collar. I had always felt uncomfortable around priests for some reason, and I usually averted my eyes. But Father John's eyes held mine fast; I could not look away. I invited him in, and we walked together to Mama's room. He stopped me at her door and said he'd see her alone.

"I'll anoint her and hear her confession if she wants. I'll come for you when our private time is over." Before the door closed behind him, I saw a beautiful smile spread across Mama's face. She took his hand and said, "I've been waiting for you."

He began to visit regularly. I'd leave them alone and hear them laughing and talking.

The real estate agent stopped by to see if anyone had showed up to tend to Mama's spiritual needs. I said, "Yes, a very nice Father John." Her mouth dropped.

"He's the pastor of the biggest church in the state. He doesn't make house calls. She's not even a registered member of his church!"

"Well, he's been coming every week," I said, a little offended. "He says she's an angel—not literally, of course. But yesterday, before he left on his trip to Rome, he came especially to ask her to pray for him."

***

Two more weeks passed. Family members flew in and out. Mama loved their visits, talking animatedly and with the sense that her earthly time was drawing to a close. She had so many things she wanted to say.

Finally, we were alone once again. She was tired but happy. She confessed she had yet to pray for Father John. He'd confided he was terrified of flying, and she needed a little time to keep that promise so he'd get home safely. I kissed her and said goodnight, but she reached for my hand.

"Wait!" she said. "What would you like from me?"

"I don't know, Mama. What do you mean?" I was embarrassed and confused. "A keepsake? Maybe a ring or something?" I had avoided having this conversation for three months and hated the idea of talking about her "stuff."

"No. That's not what I mean, honey. I mean… what kind of sign?"

I stared at her, knowing I had been so pre-occupied with keeping her alive, so manic about making her comfortable, that she had reached the acceptance stage way ahead of me. I wasn't ready.

"A sign," she insisted, forcing my thoughts back to her question.

"Aw, please don't, Mama." Avoiding her eyes, my gaze fell on the neglected Christmas cacti. "Okay, Mama. Flowers then. Send me a sign with flowers. I'll know it's you."

She shrugged at the simplicity of the request and smiled. She knew I had no expectations. "Flowers it is. Now off you go. I've got some praying to do." I closed her door.

She slipped into a coma that night. Two nights later, she drew her last breath while her beloved Father John was winging his way home.

We flew her back to New England for a September burial, laying her to rest by our father's side. We stayed on for a few days with family, telling a life's worth of stories about Mama to each other. Too soon, it was time to return and face her empty rooms.

***

The stillness was heartbreaking. The oxygen concentrator sat silent in the corner, no longer whoosh-pumping air into Mama's poor, damaged lungs. I passed her bed, running my hand along the mattress, but the warmth she once radiated was gone.

I moved to her dark sitting room to open the plantation shutters. The light began to reveal a sight my mind could not grasp. Going from window to window, I opened more until the room was bright with daylight, and then I blinked and looked again. The two near-dead Christmas cacti lay at my feet. Tumbling from every brown, scaly limb of those sad plants were hundreds of blossoms—red ones, white ones, pink ones—covering the floor of the room. I sat down among them and cried joyful tears.

I went to that room often to commune with my mother, surrounded by her gift of flowers. The riotous bloom, which started out of season — months before Christmas — continued for nine months. I loved the significance of that because my mother had always talked about how she carried me for nine months. Now these blossoms comforted me for another nine months, and when they died, I felt my mother whispering, "Time to heal, sweetheart. Time to make your own beauty now." I swept up the dead stems and flowers, threw out the plants, and created a studio there. I know my mother watched and smiled as I unpacked my easel, oils, and brushes. I have tried to paint her, but there's no way on earth to capture my mother's beauty. It lives on in my memories, however, and in the story of the Christmas cacti that came back to life months early, the sign that my mother promised.

—Jayne M. Adams—

24

Sparks of Light

Unable are the loved to die. For love is immortality.
~Emily Dickinson

Anxiously, I described for my fiancé a recurring dream that had plagued me for more than ten years. "I see myself only from behind, walking, holding hands with what I think is a little boy. The back of the child's short, golden-blond hair sparkles in the sunshine. We cross amber-colored grass and kneel. We're visiting a cemetery."

I exhaled deeply and averted my eyes. "I know it's my child, and the father is gone. Not that he left us or wasn't part of our lives." I hesitated a moment. "He's passed away. We're at his grave."

I waited nervously for his reaction.

"People can dream their worst fears," he suggested with what felt like "old soul" wisdom. This confidence calmed me... for a time.

We married. Then amid years of painful and seemingly hopeless infertility treatments, I came to a bittersweet realization: The dream wouldn't come true if I couldn't conceive a child.

Finally, we had the miracle of a positive test. We announced the news to his mother right away. Covering her mouth, she inhaled sharply. "Oh, no! Just a few nights ago, I dreamed you gave birth to a beautiful baby girl. I held and rocked her. Angels appeared before me, and one took the baby from my arms. I was about to demand he give her back, but he calmed me. He said she wasn't ready and promised she would be back in three months. They disappeared with her." She wiped tears from under her glasses, but quickly pulled her posture upright and smiled. "Let's forget all that and just be happy!"

***

In my third month I had a miscarriage. The angel was right. She obviously wasn't ready. And, also as predicted, exactly three months later, I was pregnant again.

Talk of my dream resurfaced. Would it be a boy or a girl? My husband reminded me that his mother's dream came true, and in her dream the baby was a girl. Maybe we had nothing to worry about.

It was a girl… a sweet, little girl with dark brown hair.

Five months later, wondering why I wasn't taking off baby weight, I unexpectedly found myself two months along. Blessed indeed. But again we held our breath. It looked like another girl on the ultrasound. My husband noted happily, "See! It's a girl. Your dream isn't true." Born happy, healthy and right on time in late February, she had fine, golden-blond peach fuzz for hair.

Early August was incredibly hot… too hot to be pouring concrete for a large driveway. My husband's face was gray as he came inside, sweaty and overheated. He admitted he hurt as if a horse had kicked him square in the chest. He tried a cold shower. It didn't help.

At the emergency room, I was ushered into a small waiting room. When the attendant finally let me see him, he was sporting dozens of tubes and cords. The doctor noted calmly that he was having a heart attack. I stood dumbfounded.

"I don't want to die. Please don't let me die," he pleaded with the doctor.

The machines started blaring and I was whisked away. I told myself he was lucky to be in the hospital while having a heart attack. Surely this would be a routine matter for the doctors.

I anxiously awaited the doctor who finally came in and asked if I wanted them to keep trying.

"What?" I could hardly fathom what he meant. "Do everything possible!"

He said that Rob needed an immediate heart transplant, which wasn't possible. He had also inhaled fluid into his lungs, and his color was a "bit bluish."

These unbelievable statements ricocheted in my head, but I was still in denial.

"Maybe you should come see for yourself," he said, leading the way.

I rushed to my husband's bedside. A staff member was straddling him and doing chest compressions. It felt so foreign to see no life in his still face.

"Well?" the doctor asked. I watched for a moment, with tears welling in my eyes, and then I made the call. The man stopped and climbed down.

***

I don't remember how I got home that night. I stood alone in the quiet darkness, my throat tight, with my forehead pressed against the cool wall. How could they not have saved a thirty-three-year-old man? How could I have left him there? He was going to have an autopsy, and the image of his lifeless face rattled me. I replayed the scenes over and over again like an unrelenting nightmare.

The envelope containing the papers to purchase our first life-insurance policy sat in the mail holder by the door, ironically planned to go out that day. I marveled at how that morning two people got up with a full to-do list and two sweet babies to care for. Then, just like that, one person ended the day alone.

My depression deepened over the next month leading to my thirtieth birthday. The Twin Towers fell four days later, making it even worse. I was numb. Life with two babies seemed too big a journey to face alone.

One afternoon, in deep contemplation, I gazed into the sweet face of my one-and-a-half-year-old and wondered how she processed her dad's absence. Suddenly, she jumped up and ran to the front door where he always scooped her up when he entered. It was their routine. I followed. She stood at the silent door looking up with her arms stretched high above her head.

"Dada, up! Dada, up!" she said with a little giggle of delight.

I froze and warily scanned the ceiling for what she was seeing. There was a brilliant pinpoint of light there. A slight halo around it reminded me of mist. Mist with hints of rainbow colors. I stood awestruck, mostly in disbelief, as she walked back to the kitchen with a look of complete contentment.

The visits to my older daughter and the sparks of light occurred again and again over the first few months after my husband's sudden death. They pierced the dark veil that was smothering me. Whether they were signs from my late husband or something else equally miraculous, I can't say. But I could no longer deny what I was seeing and feeling.

In prayer, I finally let go of my burdens. My soul vibrated with a feeling of love and support. I believe I had permission to say goodbye, to begin the healing process. Now I knew I wasn't alone. For this reassurance and for my two now teenage daughters, I am forever grateful.

— Carrie K. Linde —

25

Dimes from Heaven

In thee my soul shall own combined
the sister and the friend.
~Catherine Killigrew

"There's been an accident." With those four words, my life changed. My youngest sister, Macala, only seven years old, had been run over by a tractor she was sitting on after it hit a large rock and she was thrown to the ground.

The next few months were the hardest of my life. Every little thing reminded me of her. Being sixteen years her senior, I had taken care of her for all of her life. We looked so much alike that we were often mistaken for mother and daughter. She brightened my world with her smiles, hilarious stories, and hugs. She never left me without saying, "I love you, Con."

While we planned the funeral, journalists showed up at the door at all hours searching for a human-interest story. As numerous people (with heartfelt intentions) informed me that it "would be okay," I struggled to make it through my everyday life, feeling like things would never be okay again.

I was living with my wonderful grandparents, having gone through a very rough time prior to Macala's passing. While watching TV in bed one evening, a cowboy hat hanging on my closet door started to swing back and forth. I got up to see what was causing the hat to swing. To my surprise, there was nothing, not even the slightest breeze.

"Macala, is that you?"

The cowboy hat stopped swinging immediately, so I thought I had imagined the whole incident. Unsettled, it took me a long time to fall asleep. When I woke up the next morning, I found a sparkly Lip Smacker lipstick in the middle of my floor. I had given it to Macala several months prior to her passing, and I had not seen it since that day. There was no physical explanation as to how the Lip Smacker got to the middle of the floor where it most definitely had not been just hours before.

Shortly after the Lip Smacker incident, I was walking through West Edmonton Mall following a synchronized skating practice. Lying in the middle of the hallway was a dime. I picked it up and saw that it was printed in 1997, the year of Macala's birth. I slipped it into my pocket. Another dime appeared a few days later, and then another a few weeks later.

Soon, I was finding dimes everywhere—on the street, at restaurants and coffee shops, even during my nursing shifts at the hospital. Usually, they appeared when I was having a particularly difficult day or when I was contemplating a solution to a problem I encountered. I have since concluded that when the dimes make an appearance, they are Macala's unspoken guides. She is the angel on my shoulder, assisting me with decisions and providing me with reassurance when I need it.

The 2004–2005 skating season was the most difficult season for me. Macala and I loved figure skating. She had started taking lessons at age four so she could be coached by me. She loved watching me skate and would wave at me from the stands while I was competing. After I got off the ice, she would pout and complain that I didn't wave at her. To her young mind, I was an amazing skater, and she wanted to be just like me.

In March 2005, just five months after Macala's passing, my team-mates and I boarded a plane to compete at the Canadian Synchronized Skating Championships in Sarnia, Ontario. I found a dime at the airport going through security, another at the hotel before we competed for the first time, and one more dime at the arena before our second skate. We won the silver medal in the adult category that season.

I had a conversation on the plane ride home with one of my many skating moms, Nancy. I confided in her about the dimes. Nancy gave me a hug and said, "Angels leave silver for us to find. Macala is your angel now, watching over you and letting you know she is always with you."

I met my husband-to-be in spring 2005, and we started dating in 2007. I often thought about Macala and how much she would have loved Jonathan. He is great with kids, caring, genuine, and of Chinese heritage. Macala was infatuated with Chinese culture and people. She had a red Chinese cheongsam, which was her favourite dress, and she wore it at every possible opportunity.

When Jon and I took our first trip together to San Francisco in the spring of 2008, my dimes appeared. After getting engaged, we took our second trip together — to Cuba. I found a Cuban dime at the bottom of a swimming pool. I had to dive down multiple times to get it, but there was no way I was leaving my Macala dime behind!

On the day of our wedding, I found a dime at the hotel where the bridal party stayed while I was getting my individual portraits taken. I also found one after our wedding and at the reception. It seemed that Macala approved of our marriage! Our honeymoon took us to Fiji, Tonga and New Zealand. I have a dime from each of those countries in my collection. Jon and I have been fortunate to travel a lot over the past decade, and I have dimes from all over the world that Macala has left for me.

We now have three amazing children. They know about Auntie Macala and the dimes she leaves us. She has started leaving them for my children, as well. Each time they find a dime, they remind me, "Auntie Macala is watching!" Even though we cannot physically touch or see her, there is something reassuring in the knowledge that we have an angel in heaven watching over us and guiding us down our life path lined in silver dimes.

— C. R. Chan —

26

The Sign

Love recognizes no barriers. It jumps hurdles,
leaps fences, penetrates walls to arrive at its
destination full of hope.
~Maya Angelou

I hadn't known how excruciatingly difficult it would be to lose a parent, much less two, in the span of nine months. But here I was, at the age of fifty-nine, not feeling any less of an orphan than a young child would! Realizing this was just another one of life's "passages" didn't make it any easier. A part of me felt dead inside, knowing that I could never give my dad a big hug again, or even get one of those "looks" from my mom, reminding me of one of my recent indiscretions.

Dad had died quite suddenly on a snowy, cold morning in December 2008. A heart attack was the culprit, but I took a small semblance of comfort knowing that he passed quickly and did not suffer, just as he had desired. Mom tried to hang on, but they had been together for almost seventy years. I could see her struggling mentally every time I visited, and I heard the frustration and sheer sorrow in her voice as we spoke on the phone. Nine months later, she succumbed to an aneurysm.

Even though my folks were in their late eighties, I had always dismissed the possibility of their deaths. I guess, deep inside, I considered them to be somewhat immortal. It was indeed a classic case of denial!

But at least I knew they were now together in Heaven. Or did I? I held steadfastly to my faith, but I was slowly breaking apart inside. As the days passed and I struggled to find my footing and a direction to follow, I found myself looking for a "sign" from my parents. I needed to know they had made a safe arrival together at Heaven's gates. After all, I had read about many people having these experiences after losing a loved one, and I definitely wanted to be a part of this exclusive group.

I was absolutely clueless as to what type of "sign" I was searching for. I tried to remember something that might have some significance. Nothing jumped out at me as I had hoped it would. I was still so totally immersed in my grief that it was almost impossible to focus on anything.

After Dad's passing, I had started each morning by having a discussion with him. I kept a cherished photo on my bathroom vanity where I spoke out loud to him, talking about anything that was on my mind: my three children, whom he absolutely adored; my job issues; finances; my somewhat lackluster love life…. You name it, we hashed it over! Once Mom died, she became part of our elite group—just the three of us! Her photo was placed next to Dad's, and our conversations commenced. It was a cathartic release for me in numerous ways.

One morning shortly after my mother passed, I was feeling especially nostalgic and forlorn. It would have been her birthday that day. I told Dad that I urgently needed a sign.

Glancing at a small stack of magazines on the countertop, I noticed a magnificent buck deer with towering antlers on the cover of one of them. "There, Dad! That's it!" I exclaimed. "Please let a deer of this splendor and greatness cross my path in some way. Then I will know it is you, and all is well."

Then I found myself expecting instant results. Every day, I would search my surroundings desperately, waiting for a buck of great grandeur to appear magically. Autumn passed, and then the first snow of winter. I missed all the beauty of the seasons though, because I was only looking for one thing: that deer.

Christmas came and went, and I felt less emotional about the elusive deer. I was preparing to sell my parents' home, which was where I grew up. It was an arduous and emotional task. There were so many memories between those walls. Nevertheless, I hired a real estate agent and pushed the process along, hard as it was.

Previously, I had enlisted one of my folks' neighbors to keep an eye on the property since I lived about thirty minutes away. Bob had a direct view of their back yard and most of the house. He had adored my parents and considered himself to be the caretaker of the premises. I was very appreciative.

One day, Bob called to let me know he had shoveled the walks around my parents' house and was keeping watch in his usual meticulous manner. As we were chatting, he shouted suddenly, "Hold on!" and dropped the phone. Fearful that something was amiss, I waited in anticipation until he returned.

"You're not going to believe this, Gail!" he exclaimed with childlike wonder. "There is an enormous deer with the biggest antlers I have ever seen walking through your parents' back yard." I started to cry. I had never told anyone about my request of my father.

"Wait a minute," Bob bellowed. "There is a female deer walking right next to him. They are exploring the yard." Bob dropped the phone again as he hurried off to take pictures, leaving me to silently thank my fabulous father for not only coming home, but for bringing Mom with him.

— Gail Gabrielle —

27

A Time to Sparkle

*If angels rarely appear, it's because we all too often
mistake the medium for the Message.*
~Eileen Elias Freeman,
The Angels' Little Instruction Book

The first time, it was merely an inconvenience. I was reaching into my cupboards for my "good" bake ware, the kind I use when I'm making a dish for a holiday or birthday. In this case, we were going to my in-laws' for Thanksgiving. When I pulled out my Pyrex, I let out an annoyed groan. The bottom of the dish was coated in glitter — purple glitter, to be exact. Assuming my children had been rummaging in the craft drawer above and spilled an open packet, I thought, *That's all I need right now* — *one more thing to clean.* I scrubbed the dish and rushed off to get everyone dressed for the holiday.

The mysterious, sparkly annoyance didn't cross my mind again until Christmas. I reached for my roasting pan and, once again, the recessed lighting in my kitchen reflected a shimmer of violet. Roasting a prime rib for ten people is a time-sensitive business. I had not allotted an extra ten minutes for scouring glitter particles off the slats of my roaster. Fairly certain that my family would not eat beef that was both shining and lavender, I had no other choice. However, I was determined that there would not be a next time, so as soon as the pan was clean and the roast in the oven, I searched the drawer for the culprit glitter packet.

Indeed, there were glitter packets galore: red, blue, gold, and a multi-hued package that could only be described as unicorn dandruff. But no purple. Convinced that the package had fallen between the drawer and the cupboard below, I crawled partly inside and continued my quest.

"What are you doing?" My older son's voice startled me, and I jerked, cracking my head against the edge of the drawer.

Rubbing my skull and making a mental note to talk with my son later about the volume of his voice, I extricated myself carefully from the cave of crockery and answered him.

"I'm looking for the purple glitter packet that's leaking all over my good pans. You haven't been monkeying around in here, have you?" I asked, giving his ribs a poke.

He giggled and squirmed away.

"Nope. Maybe it was Calvin."

I shook my head. "Calvin can't reach the drawer. He's only two, sweetie. You sure you haven't used any purple glitter in the last month or two?"

Luke shrugged nonchalantly and wound around the island to procure a cookie from the pantry. Given that he had the worst poker face in the world, it was clear he was telling the truth. Taking a deep gulp of oxygen, I prepared to re-enter the recesses of darkness when Luke poked his head around the corner of the island again. Choking on my last inhalation, I made another note to self to put a bell on that boy.

"Maybe it was your guardian angel," he offered helpfully.

As he took his cookie into the living room, I started to call out to him to grab a napkin, but something about his words stopped my heart.

My best friend, Elizabeth, had passed away in October at the age of thirty-two after a brief and hard-fought battle with breast cancer.

Her favorite color — the color of the baby blanket she carried around our college dorm, and the color of the flowers in her wedding bouquet where I served as her bridesmaid — was purple.

The whole thing would have been fairly easy to dismiss as coincidental had she not told me she would do something like this. The previous spring, we had been eating lunch together at the sushi restaurant where we held our monthly "Mommies' Day Off" get-togethers. She had just been released from a lengthy hospital stay due to Cushing's disease, a complication that, while treatable, had come with a devastating diagnosis: the cancer that had been declared in remission just six months prior was back and spreading throughout her body. The doctors had given her only months to live.

In typical Elizabeth fashion, she continued to live her life to the fullest, playing with her kids in the yard, going out to dinner with her husband, and meeting me and our other two best friends from college for cocktails and sushi. Our friendships had survived over a decade of distance, marriages, motherhood, and anything that life could throw at us, and had grown stronger. It seemed unfathomable that now, just as we were settling into the main course of life, one of us was about to leave the party far too early.

"You guys know I'm coming back, right?" Elizabeth had joked between bites of California roll. "Not just in a generic, spooky-attic-noises, lights-on-and-off kind of way. No, I'll haunt you in the most irritating way possible, like short-circuiting your curling iron just as you're getting ready to go out or something."

Elizabeth was probably the only person in the world witty enough to make her own mortality hilarious. A former actress turned stay-at-home mother to two beautiful children, she had a dazzling kind of charm one doesn't see every day.

A sparkle.

When I got the text saying she was gone, my entire body went numb. They say denial is the first stage of grief, and I guess that was true for me, too. I simply couldn't believe that the world would dare go on turning without her. It seemed… wrong. At first, any reminder of her — the photos that popped up every other week as Facebook reminders, books she had given me, the sweater I had forgotten to give back to her the last time we saw each other — dug into the open wound of grief.

Then the glitter showed up, and for some reason, the searing pinpricks of memory subsided. Her chosen medium was as irritating as she had promised — having to scrub out my best pans by hand at the most inconvenient times. Once or twice, I found myself muttering out the window above the sink, "You couldn't have just sent me a cardinal or something, like a normal ghost?"

But then I would smile, remembering the way she lit up a room, and the way she lived and loved to the fullest every day of her life. When I'm feeling stressed about preparing for holidays or kids' birthday parties, I find myself peeking into the cupboard for that telltale glimmer of purple, and it never fails to lighten my spirits. It reminds me how lucky I am to be here for each and every one of those events, to take time to laugh and enjoy every moment.

That reminder is worth washing a few extra dishes once in a while.

— Laurie Batzel —

28

See You in Heaven

There is no expiration date on the love
between a father and his child.
~Jennifer Williamson

Our fifty-six-year-old father, physically one of the strongest people we had ever known, could no longer battle the unnamed sickness that overpowered him the last two years of his life. And there was nothing any of us could do to change it.

My siblings and I had reluctantly made the decision to end our dad's life support. I was driving my brother Bill that morning, and we were two exits away from the hospital when a car began tailing us. It seemed strange because I wasn't driving slowly. I commented to Bill that it was crazy how close the car was to my bumper, and he suggested I slow down and let them pass, which I did. The other car then pulled in front of us and slowed down — as if the driver were trying to teach me a lesson. It was a weird, rude thing to do, and it didn't make sense because I had actually been driving at the speed limit. But then something happened that made me think the other driver wasn't being rude; maybe he was just trying to send us a message — because just as we were about to exit to get to the hospital, we saw the license plate on the car. It said C U N HEVN.

As soon as we saw the plate, the car sped away and disappeared into the stream of cars on the freeway.

My dad knew I was a firm believer in signs, and I'm certain this was his way of saying goodbye to us that morning as we drove to the hospital to end his life support. Maybe he was telling us that it was okay, and that we were doing the right thing.

But there's more.

On the ten-year anniversary of his passing, I was heading home early from work and took a back way to get to my house. I was at a four-way stop to go forward, and the car to my left was turning right and had the right of way.

Waiting for the other car to turn, I was in deep in thought, thinking about how impossible it seemed that ten years had already passed since my father's death. We were all still heartbroken. Right at that moment, the car turned right very slowly, and then I saw it: C U N HEVN.

Ten years to the day we lost our dad, I was seeing that license plate again. It was the only other time I had ever seen the plate since the day he had passed.

I know some people will believe it's a coincidence, but not me. My heart knows this was a message from our dad. I'm sure that's why I was lucky enough to see that beautiful message twice.

— Kristi Allen —

29

Always a Father

*Being a daddy's girl is like having permanent armor
for the rest of your life.*
~Marinela Reka

I have had a fear of horseback riding for as long as I can remember. When I was a child and away at summer camp, my saddle slipped, spilling me to the ground. In my teen years my mom began dating and when my now stepfather thought it would be fun to take my sisters and me on a horseback ride, I had a full-blown panic attack. I decided then and there I would never ride a horse or anything with four legs again.

That was until last year. A friend and her husband decided to plan a trip and include my husband and me. The four of us were going to tour the Grand Canyon. Prior to the trip we had a "meeting" to determine what we would see and do on our road trip. One of the excursions they wanted to do was to ride mules around the rim. I made it perfectly clear I was not interested.

The trip started off great. We did some sightseeing along the way and then boarded a train to the Grand Canyon. We were having a ball. On day one, we took a small plane ride over the canyon, enjoying the beauty from above. Day two included a rafting excursion at the bottom of the canyon. The water and sights were amazing. Day three we hiked as far down and up as we could manage; we didn't make it all the way to the bottom but we were proud of ourselves for how far we got. The trip, up to that point, was just wonderful. However, I continued to worry about day four.

Day four we were to ride mules around the rim of the canyon. The other three in my group had great fun teasing me about what was to come and even went so far as to say, "If nothing else it will be fun watching D'ette do it!"

The morning arrived and I was a bag of nerves. I made it clear that there was a strong possibility I would not do it and would just wait at the barn for their return. Still undecided about going through with the adventure, I joined in on all the pre-check requirements: a weigh-in (yes… if you were too heavy you could not ride) and the purchase of a hat and scarf to cover the lower part of your face. (I am still unsure why these items were required, but whether or not I was going to go through with it I was going to look the part.)

The four of us arrived at the barn along with about fifteen other people. The handlers came out and lined everyone up against the coral fence. Person after person was assigned their mule. I don't remember the names of the ten or so people ahead of us but I know my husband was assigned "Big Steve," the largest mule they had. When the ranch hand got to me he said, "You will be riding Corky today."

My husband and I looked at each other and all I could say was, "Did you hear that? I am riding Corky." You see, my dad, who was always the protector, had passed away years earlier and although his legal name was Roy, everyone called him Corky his entire life. This had come about when he was a child and had a popular doll named Corky that had the same bright red hair as he had. His mother had found that he responded better if she called for his doll Corky to come, instead of him, and the name stuck. My father became Corky. I never once heard anyone call him anything but Corky.

As we waited for the mules to arrive I was stunned to see that "Corky" was a large "red" mule. I felt as if my dad was telling me, "I am here and you are going to be okay."

To my surprise, I got on the mule and felt no fear. The entire ride I felt so safe and protected — enjoying every second with Corky.

I didn't want the ride to end. I probably looked silly talking to Corky the entire time but I believe my dad came that day to help me conquer my fears and to let me know I would be okay.

—D'ette Corona—

Chapter 4

Angels in Disguise

30

Cardinal Red

We should pray to the angels,
for they are given to us as guardians.
~St. Ambrose

L ate one Saturday morning in May, I carried my supplies outside to begin my favorite pastime: sketching birds. The air was cool, and though the sun was getting higher, the grass sparkled with dew. The heavy fragrance of catalpa blooms and the songs of robins and vireos filled the air. In south Texas, there was always something for me to draw and that day, it was a mother cardinal gathering bugs for her nestlings.

I carried my sketchpad and a cigar box filled with pencils and crayons to my favorite spot: the back of my grandfather's old Packard. The car was ominously huge and black, but its shiny chrome bumper was roomy enough for me and everything I carried. Parked on the edge of the yard under a giant pecan tree, it was the perfect bird blind for a six-year-old. I pulled myself into a seated position on the wide metal bumper and waited for action.

We shared a large house with my grandparents. The giant fruit trees in our yard were a haven for birds near and far. I woke to their songs and fell asleep to their bickering as they nested at night. My grandparents and I would watch birds for hours from their second-story window. My grandfather taught me to tell males from females by the color of their feathers and to identify the types of birds by their songs.

That Saturday, my mother finished hanging the laundry and went inside. My little brothers rode their tricycles on the sidewalk. I watched the mother cardinal hop about in the grass, searching for food. I heard my brothers' voices and then saw them waving to someone.

I did not see my grandfather come outside or get into the car. It was only when I felt the car door slam and the bumper vibrate as the engine started that I knew what was happening.

My brothers abandoned their bikes and ran toward the car.

"Jump! Jump!" they both screamed.

I tossed the box and my sketchpad to the ground. I scooted forward, but part of my shorts caught on the bumper. Then the car started moving, and my fear took over. I couldn't move.

My brothers ran alongside the car, trying to get my grandfather's attention. As the car pulled onto the road, I screamed. Inside the car, my grandfather listened to the radio. And as my sketchpad and box got smaller and smaller behind us, I started to cry.

The sight of the black asphalt moving beneath my feet made me dizzy and nauseated, so I closed my eyes and held onto the chrome fins as tight as I could. My heart beat so loudly I could hear nothing else, so I prayed.

I prayed for what was happening to not be real and that this might be a dream. I prayed for someone to see me and help. I prayed for my grandfather to somehow see me in the mirror and save me. And I prayed that I would see my brothers and my mother again.

The road we turned onto next was smoother, and I felt calmer. I relaxed my left hand a little and felt two crayons slip from my fingers. I opened my eyes and watched them bounce on the road. I can still see them — one red and one orange. I tightened my hand around the fin again and heard a boy's voice.

"Hi," he said. "Are you out for a ride?"

I looked up slowly from the road and saw bike wheels, and then handlebars, freckled arms and a blue-striped shirt. Moving my head made me dizzy, so I looked back down at the road.

"What's your name?" he asked.

I closed my eyes and started to cry again.

"No one knows you're back here, do they?" he asked.

| Angels in Disguise

I tried to shake my head but couldn't.

"It's okay," the boy said in the most calming voice I had ever heard. "You're going to be fine. Just keep hanging on, and I'll help."

For some reason, I believed him.

"Do you know where you're going?" he asked. I looked up until our eyes met. His hair was blond. He wore glasses and smiled at me.

"Maybe," I said, startled by the vibration in my voice. "To the drive-in café where my grandpa has coffee with his friends…"

"Oh, good," he said. "That's just a couple minutes from here. I'll stay right with you."

He drifted to the right to look at the traffic ahead. His bike was cardinal red and new with the words "Western Flyer" written on it. I could hardly believe it. I had seen one just like it at my grandfather's hardware store. I couldn't wait to tell him.

We drove another block or so down the main road while cars passed us going in the other direction. No one ever came behind us, and no one seemed to notice a little girl on the bumper or the bicycle following her. Slowly, I began to relax as the boy continued talking and reassuring me that everything would be fine.

As we turned into the drive-in parking lot, we hit a small bump. I clutched the bumper fins tightly, and the boy rode up to the front of my grandfather's car. When the car finally stopped, I let go of the bumper. I looked at my hands, white and stiff and covered with cuts. I felt cold and started shivering. Tears streamed down my face.

Soon, I heard voices. When I looked up, my grandfather stood in front of me, white as a ghost. He picked me up from the bumper and carried me through a crowd of onlookers in the parking lot and into the café. He held me in his arms while he called my mother to let her know I was safe. Then we headed home with me next to him in the front seat.

I looked out the window and searched for the boy on the bicycle. I asked my grandfather if he'd seen the red bike that was just like the one in his store. But my grandfather had not seen a boy or a red bike. He told me that my mother had called the café as soon as my brothers told her what happened. As soon as he got out of the car, the manager came out and told him I was on the bumper.

As we drove up to the house, my mother raced to the car. My little brothers stood next to my grandmother, holding the crayons and notebook I'd dropped on the street. I could tell they had been crying.

Long after the babies had flown away I finished drawing the mother cardinal. My perspective changed when I was no longer allowed on the car or near the road. The view of our yard from the front porch included the sidewalk and part of the street. Those became the background. In the distance I drew a faint black tire and silver handlebars. No one else had seen the boy on the bike, but I couldn't stop thinking of him. Without him, there might have been no drawing at all.

—Karen Ross Samford—

31

The Lady Who Lived Over the Hill

How beautiful a day can be
When kindness touches it!
~George Elliston

My aunt was packing up her kitchen drawers in preparation for a move to a smaller home. "Oh, look at this cute pin," she said. "It must have been in there for quite a while. Do you even remember this?"

"How could I ever forget it?" I responded. Even though it had been buried deep in the drawer for years, the pin looked nearly the same as it had more than thirty years ago when a lady sitting behind my family in church gave it to my four-year-old daughter.

It was the first Sunday morning in December. My young children and I sat in our usual pew as we attended Mass. Everything was normal until the "handshake of peace"—a ritual in which participants greet those around them. On this particular morning, an unfamiliar woman sat in the pew behind us. I can't remember what she was wearing—not even the color of her coat—but I do remember the kind look in her eyes as we shook hands and embraced in the sign of peace. And I remember the Christmas pin on her coat lapel—the very one that my aunt was now holding in her hand.

My daughter had turned around to shake hands with the people behind us, and had been fascinated by the Christmas wreath pin on the lady's coat. "You like this, don't you?" the woman whispered to Katie, pointing to the pin on her lapel. Katie nodded. Her green eyes opened wide as the lady removed the wreath and gently placed it in her hand, carefully folding her little fingers around it.

I thanked her for the gesture, but assured her that it was not necessary to give my daughter the pin even though she had admired it. However, the lady insisted, so I pinned it on my little girl's dress and she wore it proudly the rest of the day.

As the service drew to an end, I felt a gentle tap on my elbow. A soft voice whispered, "Meet me in the parking lot when Mass is over. I have something for you in my car."

"Okay," I said, a bit confused. I had never seen this woman in my life. What could she possibly have for me?

"Look, Mom, the lady parked right next to us!" one of my children shouted as we headed to our car. I drew in a deep breath when she opened her trunk and I saw what was in it. There were exactly four presents, one for each of my children. They were so excited that they wanted to rip the gifts open right there in the parking lot, but I insisted that they wait until we got home. They thanked the lady and climbed into the car.

I thanked her for her kindness and asked how she knew us and where she lived. Her eyes twinkled as she replied that she had seen us each week at church, and that she lived over the hill behind our house. I was not aware of any homes over the hill, but maybe there was a new development in the area that I was not aware of.

All the way home, the kids shook, squeezed, and passed their boxes around in the car, trying to guess what was in them. When we pulled into the driveway, they raced inside to tear open their presents.

I could hardly believe what was in them. How did this lady whom we had never met before know that I had no money to buy Christmas outfits for my kids? How did she know their exact sizes and the right style and colors for each of them?

The kids couldn't wait to try on their new clothes, and I couldn't wait to find out who this lady was. So, dressed in their new Christmas outfits, we all climbed back into the car and headed to the hill where she had told us she lived. We arrived at the location, but found no existing homes and no new construction anywhere in sight. We looked at each other, shrugged our shoulders, and then stared over the hill again. The children's eyes were big and their mouths wide open, but not a sound could be heard. My seven-year-old broke the spell and summed up what we all were thinking.

"Maybe she's an angel," he whispered dramatically in his husky, little voice. After another brief moment of quiet, a chorus of soft sighs filled the car. And then silence all the way home…

Still trying to find a logical answer to this mystery, I had the children write thank-you notes, which we took to church the following Sunday. But our new friend was not there. I asked the people sitting around us if they knew the lady who had been sitting in the pew behind us the previous week. Not a single person remembered seeing any woman there at all. Not one!

But she had been sitting behind us. She gave Katie her Christmas wreath pin. She gave each of my children their perfect Christmas outfits. And now we were sure we knew who she was.

On the way home, we passed by the hill once again, looked up, and saw only a beautiful blue sky in the crisp, winter air. I'm certain our angel had found her way back home, her earthly mission complete.

— Kathleen Ruth —

The Writing Coach

*If you're not okay, you might as well not pretend you
are, especially since life has a way of holding us down
until we utter that magic word: help! That's when
angels rush to your side.*
~Glennon Doyle Melton

My blank computer screen glared at me accusingly. I had only an hour to write, and my mind was flooded with thoughts, but they weren't about my unfinished novel. My mother's recent diagnosis of Alzheimer's disease had upended my life. For the first time, writing — which had always been my passion and the way I coped with the world — had failed me.

"Why don't you just take a break?" my husband had urged me the night before. I certainly needed one. Caring for Mom was both exhausting and sad. Several days each week, I drove back and forth from my home in the San Francisco Bay Area to Mom's, a four-hour round-trip. Time to write had all but disappeared, but that wasn't the biggest problem. I'd lost my way and just couldn't seem to get back. Writing a book, *any* book, felt like an insurmountable task.

Still, I kept trying. After a draining and difficult morning with Mom, I wept as I drove the long miles home, despairing over this illness that was stealing Mom away. I dragged myself to my local bookstore, my favorite place to write.

I found a table in the bookstore's café and turned on my laptop, remembering how eager I'd been to start this novel a year earlier and how excited I was about the characters then leaping to life in my mind. But my energy for them was gone.

I ordered a cappuccino, listening to the whir of the machine in a brooding, distracted way. As I carried the coffee back to my table in the corner, I brushed past a man working intently on his own writing, head bent low over his laptop. A manuscript spilled across the cluttered table in front of him. He glanced up, caught my gaze, and smiled. Instantly, an intense surge of energy burst through me, exactly like an electric shock. The man's smile was dazzling. It lit his entire face and sparkled in his mesmerizing blue eyes, which twinkled warmly beneath his messy golden hair. *Wow,* I thought, *what was that?*

I settled in at my table and sipped my coffee. It tasted bitter, or perhaps it wasn't the coffee that was bitter but me. I wondered what I was doing there. I barely had time to get started before I'd have to leave to pick up my son from school.

I wanted to write, but it seemed hopeless. If ever there was a time I needed to write, though, it was then. But as I read over the last new scene I had written more than a month earlier, it seemed empty and flat.

"How's it going today?" The cheerful voice addressing me from the table across the way belonged to the man who'd smiled. Again, I felt a strange, exhilarating surge of energy, a powerful pull to turn and talk with him.

"Not so great," I answered truthfully, surprised to hear myself admit it.

"Some days, it's just one word at a time, isn't it?" Again he beamed a beautiful smile.

Any other day, I'd simply have agreed, but that day it felt impossible to say, let alone write, what was on my heart. "My mother has Alzheimer's," I wanted to blurt out. "I'm so worried and sad for her, and I feel overwhelmed. I need to write, but I can't." Instead, I remained silent.

"I come here every day," the cheerful man continued. "I just turn on my laptop and know that, no matter what else is going on, this is my hour to write. I let everything else go and give myself this gift of time, for me and my work."

Tears swam in my eyes. How could he know this was just what I needed to hear? I felt so drawn to this gentle man, to his kindness and infectious energy, so different from my own dark and depleted mood. He seemed oddly familiar, too, although I could not think where or when we could have met.

"That's the only way to get the work done," he added, nodding at his laptop. "Just write from your heart."

A shiver prickled the back of my neck. It felt as though he was reading my mind. Who was he?

"I'm Mark," he offered.

"Maureen," I responded.

"I'm here every day," he told me. "Here's my card." He reached across his table and handed me a white business card with a gold edge. As I took the card from him, I again felt a tingling, electric jolt of energy.

"Ah," I replied thoughtfully. "Maybe that's why you seem so familiar. I keep thinking I know you. Have we met here before?"

I'll never forget the look that flashed in his eyes then, one of pure amusement. It was as if he knew some delightful secret he couldn't possibly share. That was his only answer — that funny, knowing stare.

I glanced at his card, registering his name and noting he had a website before I tucked his card in my bag. Already, my mood had shifted. I felt more inspired than I had in months. We chatted a few moments longer, and then each of us turned back to our work. I pulled up a new blank page, setting aside the novel I'd been working on that felt so stale. I waited a moment, thinking about all that had happened since Alzheimer's had swept into my life. Then I wrote, "Let me tell you about my mother."

Words flew onto the page. When I looked up again a half-hour later, the table across from me was empty. I hadn't heard Mark get up, but he was gone.

That evening, I put Mark's business card on my desk at home, intending to contact him and thank him for our conversation. Swept back into the demands of life, though — a doctor's appointment for Mom the next morning, a meeting at my son's school — I didn't get back to my desk until the following night. The card wasn't there.

"I haven't seen it," my husband and son told me. Neither of them had even been in my office, nor had I since I put the card on my desk. I tried to remember Mark's last name or his website, but all I could remember was Mark. I returned to the bookstore several days that week and regularly for months afterward, working on a new book, but I never saw him again. I knew I wouldn't. He'd shown up that day to offer me the support and encouragement I needed to find my way again, to urge me to write from my heart—about Alzheimer's, my mother, an angel and me.

—Maureen Boyd Biro—

33

The Angels on the Train

*Angels assist us in connecting with a powerful yet
gentle force, which encourages us
to live life to its fullest.*
~Denise Linn

I was completing the nineteenth day of a twenty-day jail sentence. I had been through one of life's storms, and I had temporarily lost custody of my three daughters as a result of my poor choices.

Fortunately, I had been granted work release during my sentencing. As I rode the train to work that morning, I felt a true sense of accomplishment. I had almost completed something that I thought I would never have to experience: jail. I felt alive for the first time in a long time, and I was mulling over what I could do to complete my community service and give back. I knew I had a long road in front of me to get my children back, but I had just taken the hardest first steps.

In jail, I had read a book about Rex, a military dog. As I thought about that book, I glanced up and noticed an old blind man two rows up from me. A light bulb went off. I could work with service animals! I had always been a dog lover.

At that moment, the train came to its next stop, but unlike every other stop, the recorded voice did not announce the stop we were at. I saw alarm on the old man's face.

Quickly, I stood and walked over to him. I told him the station we were at and asked which stop was his. He thanked me and told me of his stop. We had two more to go, and I told him not to worry because I would make sure he didn't miss it. He thanked me again, and I sat back down.

I took this moment to look at the people nearby. It wasn't particularly crowded at this time of day, and everyone I saw was looking at their phones. Nobody seemed to notice the exchange between the blind man and me. I did see a lady at the far end of the train with a baby stroller. We made eye contact, and she gave me the slightest smile. She had a knowing look in her eyes. It was a brief moment we shared, but I felt strangely moved by it. My thoughts lingered on her look for the next two stops, but we didn't make eye contact again.

We arrived at the blind man's stop, and I informed him that this was where he should get off. He thanked me as I helped him stand and make his way to the train doors. I asked if he needed additional help, but he said he was fine. This was his normal stop, he said, and he knew where to go. I smiled and sat back down as I watched him walk down the steps slowly with the help of his walking cane.

He turned right and began to make his way down the track beside the train. I looked around again at the passengers on the train. As I glanced back at the blind man, my heart froze as he made an abrupt right turn and was about to walk between the train cars. In a split second, I realized he needed help. If I exited the train, I would miss my arrival time at work. I would miss my phone call into the jail and face the consequences of being late, which would mean extending my sentence.

Even as I thought of spending more time in jail after being so close to being finished, I found myself moving between the train doors as they tried to close. In an instant, I was out of the train and grabbing the blind man before he fell between the train cars. He appeared very startled and thanked me again for my help. It didn't occur to me at the time that if this had been his normal stop, he should have known which way to turn upon exiting the train. In that moment, I made a decision to get the man safely to his final destination and gave no more thought to the consequences I would face for being late.

It may well have been the first truly selfless act I had done in my life.

I got lucky, though. The conductor had seen the events unfold, and he had stopped the train and come to help. He asked if the gentleman was okay. The man replied he was fine, and I informed the conductor I was going to help him reach his final destination. The conductor made one final inquiry of the blind man's wellbeing before heading back to get the train back on schedule.

I guided the man to the elevator and asked where we were going. As he began to answer, a hand touched me softly on the arm. I turned to see the lady with the baby stroller. She gave me the warmest smile and said, "I have him now. You have somewhere you need to be."

She turned to the old man and said, "Sir, I have nowhere to be today. Let me help you get home."

He thanked her, and she gave me one last look and wished me goodbye. I raced back to the train and miraculously got back on before it pulled away. As I headed to work, on time, I pondered what had just happened. I never saw the lady exit the train; she just appeared beside me at the elevator. How did she know I had a pressing need to be on time? And how did she know I was planning to stay with the blind man? What new mother with a baby stroller has nowhere to be and offers her help to a stranger? It wasn't until later when I sat in silence that I realized what had happened and wept.

That old blind man and that young mother were sent to test me at the end of a long struggle; they were there to offer me a chance to prove to myself that I had truly changed. I had a spiritual awakening that day, because I had put a stranger's needs above mine in a totally selfless act.

I thank God every day for those angels on the train. That day marked my walk back into the love and light that I know now. And I'm happy to report that "The Angels on the Train" bedtime story is often requested by my daughters.

— Ryan Freeman —

34

Just What I Needed

Angels descending, bring from above,
Echoes of mercy, whispers of love.
~Fanny J. Crosby

I walked into the bedroom, and my husband stared at me. "Beth, you're as white as a sheet. What's wrong?" I didn't have to say much for Ron to guess... for him to know... the cancer was back.

Six months later, as I lay flat on the hard examining table in my paper cap, prepped for surgery, I prayed silently for my worried family, the doctors, and the surgical teams.

There would be two teams this time — one to perform the double mastectomy and another for the reconstruction surgery.

Maybe I'll wake up with a smaller belly since they're using abdominal tissue, I thought just before succumbing to the anesthesia.

They say an anesthetized sleep is the best slumber one can have. Perhaps it's true. Veins and arteries were moved and reconnected without my awareness throughout the twelve-hour procedure. However, that all changed when I awoke in the ICU.

"This is just the normal discomfort patients go through when they choose this surgery, honey," the RN explained. She assured us that the pain would subside. When I went home four days later with six drainage tubes going into the pouch that hung around my neck, nothing felt normal or routine.

Ron and our daughter, April, cared for me at home, giving updates to the visiting healthcare worker.

I winced. "Honey, what's wrong?" Ron asked.

"A pain in my abdomen comes and goes. I'm sure it'll be alright." But it wasn't.

"Dad, we need to call an ambulance. Mom's worse," my daughter said.

At 4:00 in the morning, my family thought an ambulance would be quick. Honestly, I didn't feel I had time. Hunched over my walker, I hobbled toward the front door. "I can't wait. I'm going to die."

April and Ron looked at each other in disbelief as I headed out the door and toward my car, moving as quickly as possible.

They drove me to the hospital in record time. When the emergency-room attendants saw me writhing in pain with all that gear around my neck, one said, "Lady, I don't know what your problem is, but I'll give you all the morphine you want!"

My family waited anxiously for the results of the X-rays and MRI. They called friends and family to pray. "Beth has been admitted to the cancer unit again." Prayers went up for me from across the globe.

Finally, the doctor came in. "We've discovered an intestinal blockage," he reported. Scar tissue from my previous struggle with colon cancer had been disrupted when the abdominal tissue was harvested for the reconstruction operation.

I had a tube going from inside my nose down into my stomach. It was taped to the tip of my nose and, combined with the tubes and pouch hanging around my neck, made me miserable. For several days, even water and ice were forbidden. I relied on sponge lollipops to moisten my lips. I needed to know God was there for me. I needed Him so badly!

"God, where are you?" Everyone pondered this question as the days passed and I found no relief. I began to doubt my decision to have the reconstruction.

Early one Sunday morning, frustrated, weary, in overwhelming pain, and irritated by the tube in my throat, I waited impatiently for the next shot of pain medicine. Ron called repeatedly, but the staff didn't come in or return the call as they normally did.

Then a new nurse came into the room. She was an attractive woman in her late forties with a medium complexion and long, dark hair. Her very presence brought comfort. We hadn't seen her before. She wore a white jacket over a light, olive-green blouse. Her long hair obscured her nametag. She didn't go to the computer to sign in as all the other medical personnel did but walked straight to my bedside.

"Don't be afraid," she said. "You're going to be so glad you had this operation. I had the same DIEP flap surgery six years ago for my breast reconstruction. You're going to be just fine."

She tended to my drains and told Ron to write down the amounts of fluid as she measured them. "Give these measurements to the regular nurse, and she will put the information into the computer," she said.

While she worked, she continued to reassure me. "You made a good decision to have this surgery. Don't be afraid." I felt my anxiety and frustration subside.

"I'll bring you a special bra that we will attach to your drains so you will be more comfortable. Then you won't need that pouch pulling around your neck."

She left and returned in a few minutes with the bra. She put it on me and folded the rubber tubes into it, attaching each one with Velcro strips.

Throughout the thirty minutes the woman helped me, she encouraged me and told me I had nothing to fear.

She walked to the door to leave, turned around and smiled at us. "You'll have a good night's sleep now. Your regular nurse will be here with your pain medication in a few minutes."

Just as the door closed, another RN came in.

"What was the name of the nurse who was just here?" Ron asked.

"I'm sorry it took me so long to get here," she said. "Another patient pulled out all his IVs. It took all of us to get everything back in place."

"That's alright. Who was the brunette nurse who was just in here? She said she had the same surgery as Beth six years ago."

She stared at us as if we were crazy. "All of us were working on that other patient. I don't think anyone was available to help you."

My husband and I looked at each other. The surprised RN continued,

"I don't know of any nurse who has had that surgery. I'm sorry. I'll check around, though."

She signed into the computer and entered all the information about my drains that Ron had written down.

That night, I slept the best I had since the surgery.

The next day, we asked every nurse we saw, even the Head Nurse of the Cancer Unit, if they knew the caregiver who had the same procedure. No one knew. Even my doctors didn't know. The Head Nurse said, "I asked around the hospital, and no one on staff here at this hospital has ever had the operation you had, Mrs. Crognale."

The mystery woman had brought physical comfort, emotional support, and spiritual peace straight from heaven to me when I needed it most.

After that, Ron and I both noticed a change in my spirit — a tranquility and confidence. Even the atmosphere in my hospital room had changed. We were in awe. "I think she was an angel sent from heaven," I concluded. Ron agreed.

Throughout the rest of my health challenge, I had a calm strength and assurance that had escaped me before the beautiful "nurse" with the long, dark hair visited.

— Elizabeth C. Crognale —

35

Chicken Soup for the Soul

The Flat Tire

*Today I choose to live with gratitude for the love that
fills my heart, the peace that rests within my spirit,
and the voice of hope that says all things are possible.*
~Author Unknown

O
ne minute, I was singing "A Groovy Kind of Love" along
with Phil Collins. The next, I was fighting the steering wheel. Pulling into the first parking lot I found, I
stopped the car and climbed out to assess the situation.
My heart sank as I discovered that one of my rear tires was flat.

I'd bought the secondhand car several months before, but it didn't
include a spare tire. Although I knew I needed to purchase one, my
schedule was so packed that I hadn't done it yet, because I was working
full-time in the emergency room at a local hospital and taking evening
classes at a university fifty miles away.

Now here I was, stranded forty miles from home. In those days,
cell phones were a luxury I couldn't afford on my tight budget. I had
no way to call for assistance.

My spirits grew darker by the minute as I checked the businesses
in the strip mall where I had pulled over. Each one was closed. The
only vehicle in the parking lot was a rusty, red pickup truck. It was
getting dark. I had two options: stay in my car until morning or start
walking in hopes of finding a convenience store with a pay phone.
Neither option appealed to me.

I was about to grab my purse and set off on foot when a man

emerged from one of the businesses. The sign over the door indicated it was a law office. Pulling a set of keys from his pocket, he locked the office door, and then turned and saw me standing next to my car. I must have looked scared and confused for he headed straight toward me.

"Can I help you with anything?" he asked.

His brown hair was cut short, his face clean-shaven, and his clothes stylish, so I decided I could trust him.

"I have a flat tire but don't have a spare," I said, relieved to see him.

I can help you remove the flat and then drive you to a tire shop to get it fixed," he said.

I remembered the cautionary words my parents had drilled into my head: Never get in a car with a stranger.

"That's okay," I said. "Thanks anyway."

The man shrugged, walked to his truck, and climbed in. My heart sank as I watched him pull out of the parking lot and onto the street. Kicking myself for procrastinating over the spare, I set out on foot to find the nearest convenience store. I'd barely walked ten steps when the red pickup pulled back into the parking lot.

The driver got out and walked over to me. "I can't leave you stranded like this. I'll take the flat to the tire shop and get it fixed for you."

"I don't have any cash on me," I said.

"Don't worry about that. I'll pay for it, and you can pay me back whenever you're in the area."

To say I was shocked by this man's generosity is putting it mildly. I watched in silence as he jacked up the car, removed the flat, and then tossed it into the back of his truck.

"I'll be back soon," he said as he drove off.

A half-hour later, he was back.

"The tire store was closing just as I pulled in," he said, lugging the tire over to my car. "I told them you were stranded, and they agreed to stay and fix it for you."

"Thank you so much," I said, watching as he replaced the wheel and tightened the lug nuts. "How much do I owe you?"

"It cost eighty-five dollars because they had to replace the tire itself. The hole was too big to repair."

Eighty-five dollars! That would put a serious dent in my budget. Yet I was grateful for all he'd done to help a complete stranger.

"I'm taking night classes, so I pass by this strip mall every Monday night. Would next Monday be okay for me to drop off a check?"

"Next week's fine. There's no rush," he said.

Suddenly, I realized I didn't even know his name. "What's your name? I'll need it to write the check."

"John Hackman."

"Thank you, John," I said, holding out my hand. "For everything." John glanced at his oily fingers, and then nodded rather than shake my hand. "You're quite welcome."

As I watched him jump back into his truck and drive off, I offered up a prayer of thanks and then headed off to class.

The next day, I bought a spare tire. The following Monday, I left work early so I could stop at the law firm where John worked. I had his check, plus a small box of chocolates as a thank-you gift.

"Could I please speak with John?" I asked the receptionist. "I have a check for him."

"John?" the young woman asked with a puzzled look on her face. "We don't have anyone by that name working here."

"I met him last week," I told her. "He helped me with a flat tire. John Hackman."

The receptionist gave me a blank look. "I'm sorry, but there's no John Hackman in this office. Can you describe him?"

"Average height, brown hair." Now it was my turn to look confused. "He drives a red pickup truck."

"I'm sorry, ma'am, but there's no one here who matches that description. Are you sure he doesn't work in one of the stores along the strip?"

"No, I'm sure he works here. He even locked the door behind him. I owe him eighty-five dollars and a huge thank-you for helping me with a flat tire."

The receptionist shook her head. "The only men in this office are the two attorneys representing this firm. Their photos are hanging on the wall right behind you."

I glanced at the pictures, but neither man looked anything like John.

"Can I leave this check with you in case there was a misunderstanding?" I said, confused. "He paid for a new tire, and I owe him the money."

The young woman behind the counter shook her head. "I can't take money. I'm sorry. You might check the stores along the strip. Maybe someone knows him."

Thankful I'd left early, I stopped in every business along the strip. But no one had ever heard of John Hackman or a brown-haired man driving a rusty, red pickup. Puzzled, I returned to my car and drove to class. For two months, I stopped by that same strip mall, looking for the truck. But no rusty, red pickup ever showed up.

I don't know where that man came from, but somehow I feel like he was sent to rescue me right when I needed it most.

—Renée Vajko-Srch—

36

The Perfect Companion

*Our perfect companions never have
fewer than four feet.*
~Colette

My grandma was an amazing lady. She was still driving and gardening well into her eighties. As she got older, she started using a cane for her daily walks around the farm where she lived with us, and she allowed my older sister to drive her to church.

Then one spring, things really started to change. Grandma's daily walks around the farm stopped. She spent more and more time sitting in her rocking chair, staring out the window. She was too tired to read to my younger brothers, check on her flowerbeds, or bake a loaf of bread. She began to lose weight. Even though I was a busy teenager, I knew we were losing her.

One day, on my way into the house, I noticed a half-grown stray cat standing by the door as if he belonged there. He was sleek and black with bright green eyes. We had several cats around the farm, but they dared not brave the yard full of dogs. This cat, however, showed no fear. I thought about picking him up and taking him out to the barn, safely away from the dogs. Then I heard Mom calling me.

Mom needed help with Grandma. I forgot all about the stray cat as Mom and I helped Grandma out of bed and then to the bathroom.

We helped her change and settled her into her rocking chair by the front window. She seemed so frail to me, not the spunky woman who had been such a big part of my life. I went to make her a cup of tea. When I came back, the black cat was sitting calmly on Grandma's lap, his big green eyes blinking as Grandma stroked his back. For the first time in months, Grandma was smiling.

Mom loved animals, but she did not believe they belonged in the house. In that moment, Mom made an exception — not because I begged, but because my dying Grandma was smiling. From that day forward, the cat spent all his time curled up in Grandma's lap. Where he came from was a mystery. We asked all the neighbors, but no one was missing a half-grown green-eyed black cat. Dad's hounds roamed the farm, and they didn't like cats, so how the stray survived was unknown.

The cat was attached to Grandma. In a house full of kids of all ages, he treated all of us with disdain. He spent all his days curled up on Grandma's lap. He spent his nights beside her in bed. I tried in vain to make friends with him. I was the biggest animal lover in the house. I was the one who had wanted a pet in the house for as long as I could remember. None of that mattered; he was devoted to Grandma.

Grandma began to fade, but the stray persisted. Grandma spent more and more time lying in her bed. There beside her, always within arm's reach, was the black cat. He curled up on one side of the double bed as Grandma slept. When Grandma was awake, he would stroll closer to purr and rub against Grandma's hand until she smiled. Some days, it was hard to coax either of them to eat.

One morning, we heard a thump and a feeble cry for help. We found Grandma lying in a pool of blood on the floor. We called the ambulance, and they took my now unconscious Grandma to the hospital. Through it all, the black cat stood on a tall dresser, its gaze knowing and unwavering.

Grandma died a week later. She had never returned to our house. Through all the busyness of neighbors, friends and family dropping by with condolences and food, the black cat stayed in Grandma's room. He sat on Grandma's bed and seemed so sad. I tried to comfort him, but he just stared at me with his big green eyes.

The day of Grandma's funeral was hectic. Besides the inherent sadness and grief of the day, there were practical matters at hand. Farm chores still needed to be done. Everyone needed clothes ironed for the funeral. We had our individual parts to practice for the mass. We rushed through our chores that morning, anxious not to be late. I remember taking care of Grandma's cat that morning, scratching him behind the ears as I left her room.

It was a long day and we were all exhausted by the time we got home. The first thing I did was to go check on Grandma's cat. I expected to see him curled up on a quilt at the foot of the bed. The cat wasn't there. We searched the whole room and then our whole property.

The cat had disappeared from our lives as suddenly as he had appeared. We never found out what happened to him. Some of the family came up with practical reasons for his disappearance. Mom and I knew the truth: He was sent to Grandma to help her make it through her last little bit of time on earth. He was an angel in a little cat's body.

— Theresa Brandt —

37

A Gentle Voice

Angels are all around us, all the time,
in the very air we breathe.
~Eileen Elias Freeman,
The Angels' Little Instruction Book

ll I wanted to do was start my day with a breakfast of lingonberry jam and toast. This was not to be. The only jar in the house was almost empty. I scraped the sides and bottom, praying for enough to cover at least half the toast.

I ignored the news report of bad weather coming our way and headed out to the market.

I could hear the distant sound of thunder as I waited in the checkout line. It wasn't until I went to pay that I realized my car keys were missing. I checked my purse and pockets, and then re-traced my steps. No luck. I went to the customer-service counter and asked if anyone had turned them in.

"Do you think you left them in the car?" the clerk asked.

As I rushed back to my car, I noticed the gloomy gray sky and the trees swaying in the breeze the way they do before a storm. Wham! I walked smack into the low parking-lot curb. I fell facedown and dropped everything I was carrying. My hands and knees hit the pavement.

While my situation was not earth shattering, at my age it was a catastrophe. With elbows and knees hurting, and storm clouds rolling in, panic overtook me. I sat on the curb, clutching my purse, the crumpled grocery bag at my feet. Tears streaked down my face.

"Please, dear God, I want to go home," I prayed.

"Let me help you," a gentle voice said.

I glanced up. A young woman stood by my car.

"I can't find my keys. They weren't in my purse. I looked everywhere in the store. I was on my way to look in the car." My words kept spilling out. "I fell," I ended in a whisper.

"No wonder you fell. You were worried about your keys." Her voice was so comforting that when she held out her hand, I forgot she was a stranger. I can still feel the warmth of her hands as she helped me up, brushing the gravel and leaves from my arms, hands, and knees.

"Look in your purse again," she said.

I wanted to assure her I had already looked several times. However, I examined the inside of my purse again, careful to check all the different compartments for my keys. To my amazement, I found them!

"Now sit in the car and take calming breaths," she said.

I got in the car and turned to thank her but she was gone! The parking lot was empty of people. There was no young woman with short, dark hair and soft brown eyes, dressed in jeans and a sweater, anywhere in sight.

I made it home as the storm hit. The rain poured down as I rushed inside. Changing my wet clothes, I realized my hands no longer hurt. I checked my knees. There were no scrapes or bruises, not even a scratch. I peeked into my grocery bag, expecting to find broken bits of glass covered in jam. Everything was intact.

It was a small, everyday kind of miracle, but a miracle all the same. Whoever that woman was, she was the angel I needed that day.

—Jeri McBryde—

Do Angels Carry Cash?

We are each of us angels with only one wing,
and we can only fly by embracing one another.
~Luciano de Crescenzo

"Hello, Violet," I said, when one of our customers entered the Christian gift and book store where I worked. A regular shopper at the store, Violet wore her usual powder-blue sweater, lace-trimmed blouse, and gray slacks. Her black handbag hung over her left forearm, and her white hair was combed in its natural wave. The only thing missing was her bright smile.

"You may remember my husband passed away two months ago," she said. "Our grandson has felt lost without him."

Violet told me her husband had prayed daily for their sixteen-year-old grandson, and they had shared a close relationship. With a catch in her throat, she said, "Joshua wonders who will pray for him now." His grief had brought Violet in that day. She was hunting for something to cheer him up.

We searched the store shelves for just the right gift to help ease his pain. "What about this?" I suggested, pointing to a framed painting of a boy carrying a backpack through a darkened forest. Light shone through the trees and radiated from an angel who watched over the young boy's path. Violet and I stood side-by-side and stared up at the

18x20-inch picture titled "Never Alone."

"Oh, that would be perfect," Violet said. "If only I had that much money."

I hesitated. Though we had no coupons advertised, I said, "For you, Violet... I believe there's a special twenty-percent discount today."

"That's nice of you, but it's still more than I can afford." With her head down, she confided, "I only have twenty dollars to spend — thirty if I dip into my household money."

On more than one occasion in nearly eight years of managing the store, I'd made up the difference when a customer fell short and had a real need. But this time I had no money to spare.

A chilly November wind swept through the front door and rattled the stained-glass sun-catcher display as a thirty-something man and a girl about eight entered the store. I greeted them with a smile and said, "I'll be right with you."

"No hurry," said the man, who was dressed in a long, tan trench coat. He stepped over and stood behind us while the girl waited by the counter. "Nice picture," he said to Violet. "You going to buy that?"

"Well," she paused, and then went on to tell him her dilemma.

He listened with a look of genuine compassion on his face. When she finished her story, he said, "I'll pay the balance."

Violet raised a gentle protest. "I couldn't let you do that. I don't even know who you are. And I certainly shouldn't have shared my troubles."

Pointing to the young girl whom I assumed was his daughter, he said, "We simply enjoy helping people. She's always giving food to someone. Besides, you said this picture is perfect for your grandson."

"Yes... it's true. I think every time Joshua sees the angel, it will remind him that he's not alone even though Grandpa is gone."

"That settles it then," the gentleman said. He reached up and removed the picture from the wall, handed it to me, and said, "Wrap it up, please."

He and the girl oversaw the whole operation while I retrieved a box from the back room and removed the price tag. Violet stood in front of the counter next to the pair, her hands clutched together as tears glistened in her eyes. "This is so good of you," she said to the stranger.

I rang the price into the register and subtracted the promised twenty-percent off. Violet set her twenty-dollar bill on the counter. "That leaves seventy-nine dollars," I said to the man, who paid in cash.

I handed the box to Violet, but the man said, "I'll carry that. Is that your blue car out front?" He told the girl to wait inside for him.

When he returned, I asked if I could help him with a purchase. He thought for a moment. He appeared to have no clear reason for his visit to the store. Almost as an afterthought, he decided to purchase a card. He snatched one from the card rack, barely giving it a glance. The girl took a forty-nine-cent metal Cross in My Pocket from a basket by the register.

"We'll take these," he said, pushing them across the counter. With a big smile, the brown-haired girl told me how they were always on the lookout for people who needed help.

I thanked him for helping Violet. He paid for their items, and they left the store. I glanced away for only a moment, and when I looked up I expected to see them on the store's walkway. Then I realized that Violet's had been the only car parked by the curb. With no sign of the man and the girl, I rushed to the huge windows that fronted the entire store. Puzzled when I still didn't see them, I ran out to the curb and looked up and down the sidewalk. They had simply vanished.

I had managed the store for nearly eight years and knew most of my customers by name or at least recognized their faces, but not this curious pair. I had never seen them before. Their only real purpose for visiting the store that day seemed to be to help an older woman encourage her grandson. Whether they were good Samaritans or angels, all I know is I never saw them again.

— Kathleen Kohler —

Angel Soup

When angels visit us, we do not hear the rustle of
wings, nor feel the feathery touch of the breast of
a dove; but we know their presence by the love
they create in our hearts.
~Mary Baker Eddy

I was ten years old when a sore throat and a dry, hacking cough turned into something much worse. Aching all over, I stumbled out of bed crying, shivering and calling for my mother. I remembered nothing else until I opened my eyes to find myself in my parents' bed with our family physician hovering over me. Back then, doctors still made house calls, and hospital emergency rooms were not visited lightly.

Even at that young age, I knew I had to be very sick for the doctor to be called. I understood little of what he said in his somber tone except that he "suspected rheumatic fever." I watched through dull eyes as he scribbled something on paper, insisting my mother hurry to buy whatever it was. He reached into a black bag, pulled out a glass bottle, tapped out two pills, and directed me to swallow them. I did and fell back asleep. About an hour later, Mama shook me awake. She was dressed in her worn winter coat and boots.

"Stay in bed," she ordered me. "I'll be back soon. I have to go to the drugstore for medicine. I tried to find someone to stay with you, but no one's home, and there's a bad snowstorm outside. I just filled the stove with coal, so you'll be warm until I get back."

"No, Mama," I cried, terrified to be left by myself. "Don't go!" I begged. I knew from past experience that she had to take a bus to get to the pharmacy and would be gone a long time.

"Stay in bed," she repeated in her no-nonsense voice, and I gulped back my pleas. "I have to get these pills for you. The doctor says you have to start taking them right away. I have no choice."

She left the room, and I heard the door close. My heart pumped twice as fast as I looked around me wildly, imagining monsters under the bed and ghosts in the closets. I pulled the covers to my cheeks and whimpered with fear. "I'm scared," I whispered to the empty room and began coughing uncontrollably. Then I heard footsteps. *She changed her mind,* I thought. *She's back!*

Instead, a young woman entered the room — a stranger. I should have been afraid, but her sweet smile and gentle eyes calmed me instantly. There was a glow around her, as if the sun was following her. She approached the bed and sat down beside me, leaning over to stroke my forehead. "You're not feeling well, are you?" she murmured softly. Her fingers were pleasingly cool against my brow.

"Who are you?" I inquired shyly.

"A friend. I was sent to watch you until your mother comes home."

I began coughing again — so hard that I had trouble breathing. As I gasped helplessly, the woman reached over and patted my back. The moment her fingers touched me, welcome air rushed into my lungs, and I stopped choking.

"Better?" she asked, and I nodded.

"Good. Are you hungry? Would you like some soup?"

I bobbed my head a second time.

"I'll just be a minute," she assured me. I leaned back against the pillows, closing my eyes.

I don't know if I slept, but it seemed she was back almost immediately with a mug of broth that smelled delicious.

"This will make you all better," she promised in her soft, melodic voice, tipping the rim of the cup toward my lips. At first, I swallowed slowly, surprised that it was just the right temperature despite the curls of steam that drifted upward.

It was even tastier than it smelled, and I drank loudly until it was gone. "Sorry," I apologized, embarrassed. "Mama says ladies should sip, not slurp, but it was so good."

"That's okay, sweetheart," she murmured. "I won't tell. How do you feel?"

I was amazed that, as she'd promised, my chest felt clearer than it had in days, and I was able to inhale through my nose. I gave a hesitant cough, and it didn't hurt. Even the pounding in my head that had been there for almost a week began to diminish.

"I feel fine," I announced incredulously. "The doctor gave me some pills. I think they helped."

"Possibly," she replied with a grin. "Or maybe it was the soup."

I doubted it, but agreed politely anyway. My mother always made soup, and though I loved it, it never gave me the sense of wellbeing I'd just experienced.

"Can I get out of bed?" I asked.

"I think you should stay put. You've been a very sick little girl, and you need to rest. We can play right here. I know you like cards. Would you like to play Go Fish?"

"Yes. It's my favorite."

"I know," she acknowledged, and she pulled a deck of cards from the folds of her gown.

It was only then that I noticed she was dressed in a white gown. I found it odd that she was wearing something so inappropriate for our Canadian winters. I was distracted quickly, however, and laughed with delight when she flipped the cards into the air, only to have them waft down again into a neat pile.

We played for a long time. When I tired of Go Fish, she entertained me with magic card tricks. She sang to me in a strange language, her voice lyrical and soothing. Twice, she went to replenish the stove with more coal. It was only when she turned on the light that I realized how late it had gotten. Mama had been gone for hours.

Finally, the lady stood up and announced, "It's time for me to go. Your mom will be home soon. She's coming up the street."

I wondered how she knew that, but asked instead, "Will I see you again soon?"

"I don't know, but I'll always be with you," she assured me quietly. "You're going to be okay now. It wasn't your time." With that, she bent to place a feathery kiss on my forehead and smiled. "Your fever is gone. Goodbye."

I didn't see her leave. She seemed to vanish. When I looked up again, I saw Mama at the bedroom door covered in snow, holding a small paper bag with my medicine. Her bus had gotten stuck during the storm, and that's what took her so long. She chided me for going near the stove and checked my temperature, astounded that it was normal. She clucked dismissively when I tried to tell her about the lady, explaining it away as a delirious dream because of my high fever. She never questioned the empty cup at my bedside.

The next day, the doctor pronounced me "miraculously and completely recovered." I never saw that particular lady again, but in times of trouble, others have come and gone just as inexplicably, touching my life and leaving me to believe that there are always angels who walk among us.

— Marya Morin —

Chapter 5

Guardians and Protectors

40

Someone to Watch Over Me

I guess I have never really doubted that we are all born
to our guardian angel.
~Robert Brault

When I was three, the lock broke on the passenger door and I fell out of our family car. A quick-thinking truck driver veered his vehicle away just in time, missing me by inches. I remember hearing my mother scream the second I hit the asphalt and the way she cried when she thanked the stranger who spared my life.

"Someone is watching over you," my mother decided. "There's no other way to explain it."

When I was seven, I was helping my mother unload groceries from the trunk of the car. The brakes failed, and our mean, green Mercury Cougar rolled down our driveway and pinned me up against a redwood fence. I walked away from the incident without a scratch on my body. After she stopped hugging me, my mother declared her theory again: I was being protected by something none of us could see.

When I was a college student, I watched the block I lived on catch fire, started by a van crashing into a parked car and igniting. I stood at my third-story window, looking down on the flame-filled street below. I remember hearing a voice — soft, gentle and feminine — say from behind me, "It's not going to touch you." The fire smoldered through the night, never once reaching the building I lived in.

Once I was old enough to understand the concept of a guardian angel, I embraced the fact that I had one. It wasn't long before I knew my protector was a woman. On several occasions, I've woken up from a deep sleep only to be surrounded by the strong scent of a sweet perfume. It dissipates just as quickly as it fills the air, gone within a matter of seconds. But each time I smell it, I know she is near. In fact, I welcome it, recognizing it as her way of making me aware of her presence.

Similarly, there is music. I don't know the name of the tune, but I recognize it the second I hear it. It's always the same instrumental section of the song. It sounds like something from a bygone era, like something that 1940s singer Frances Langford would've performed during one of her many USO tours. More than a dozen times, I've heard it coming from another room in my house. Once, it filled my ears seconds before my car nearly slid off the road in an ice storm — even though the radio was turned off.

The presence of my guardian angel was confirmed at a holiday work party. For the event, the company I worked for hired a psychic, who made herself available to anyone who wanted a reading. The second I sat down across from her, she looked at me and said, "There's a very strong presence that constantly surrounds you."

"Who is she?" I asked.

"You don't know her?" the psychic replied, surprised. "She seems to know you very well. She refuses to leave your side."

For that, I am grateful. Many close calls that have filled my life; I have escaped each of them with a deepening sense of gratitude for the angel who watches over me. Although I have yet to discover her identity, I know she is there and keeps me safe from harm. Always.

— David-Matthew Barnes —

41

Grounded

Alone is impossible in a world inhabited by angels.
~Author Unknown

I was in busy, chaotic O'Hare Airport in Chicago. People with briefcases were racing to make their flights. The air was filled with a cacophony of conversations, flight announcements, and people being paged. And to make matters even more overwhelming, it seemed that every five feet a bar was calling my name: "Gem, Gem, come in and drink here."

I hadn't felt the draw of alcohol like this since I was three weeks sober. I looked into one of the bars, at all the beautiful liquor bottles lined up against the lighted glass. I could feel the alcohol going down my throat and the calm assurance it had once brought. With just one drink, I knew the chaos would go away. I wasn't thinking of the hospitals I'd been in, the alcoholic paralysis, the jail, the flights I had missed, and the people I had hurt. All I wanted was a drink. I *needed* a drink. I had two hours before my flight to Los Angeles—plenty of time to skip into one of those bars for just one drink.

As I took a step into a bar, I stopped dead in my tracks. I had never had just one drink in my life. I had my first drink at age nine at my brother's party. I never stopped until all the booze was gone. I never met a drug I didn't like. I used poppers like nose candy. My friends had dropped dead from cocaine embolisms. Some committed suicide. A young addict I tried to help one evening suffocated the next day on her own blood from a broken blood vessel in her throat.

I pleaded, "Please, God, I cannot do this by myself. Please help. Please help me."

Suddenly, a young woman ran up behind me, put her hand on my shoulder and spun me around breathlessly. "Aren't you Gem from the Radford AA Clubhouse in North Hollywood?" Stunned and shocked that anyone from my home group in Los Angeles would find me in Chicago, I answered weakly, "Yes."

She grabbed me harder and said she needed desperately to talk. She begged me to sit down and help her with a horrible problem she was having. I wasn't very confident in my 12 Steps nor that I had anything to give, but all recovering alcoholics know the 12th Step — it is part of our program to help those who still suffer. I had to listen to her. I had to do my best to help her. And so we sat down in the black leather and chrome chairs, and she began to talk.

The loud hustle and bustle were still around us, but all I could hear were her words — as if they were the only words in the world. Sitting on the edge of the chair, she spoke on and on. She was so upset, worried and frantic. I was glued to every sound she made, trying to read her face to see how I might help. What step might help? But I don't think I said a word. I just listened.

Finally, she took a breath, and I heard the loudspeaker above us announce, "American Airlines to Los Angeles is now ready for boarding." I looked up at the speaker to make sure I had heard correctly. I turned back to ask if she was on that flight, but she was gone. The chair was empty.

I stood up, searching everywhere for her, but she was nowhere to be seen. I ran down the concourse, circling to find her, but she had simply vanished. The speaker above bellowed, "Last call for American Airlines to Los Angeles." I searched one last time, and then picked up my briefcase and ran to my gate for the flight home.

When I boarded the plane, the flight attendant told me that my seat was next to a man who was quite drunk, but that the flight was full. She said she was sorry, and if there had been an extra seat she would have moved me. I told her it was okay. I'd been on plenty of flights drunk myself.

The man was in his thirties, drunk as could be. He kept telling me that his girlfriend was the reason he was so drunk, so I asked him where she was and if she had poured the alcohol down his throat. He gave me one of those drunken looks. He knew I knew. He was too drunk to buckle his seat belt so I did it for him. The whole flight home, I knew I was looking at my former self sitting next to me.

The next morning, I went to my Radford Clubhouse and told my story from the podium. I asked if anyone knew this woman whom I had met at O'Hare. No one did. At every meeting I went to for the next five years, I asked the same question. The answer was always the same: "No."

Over time, I realized that my prayer had been answered. God had sent an angel to be with me in that airport. By helping her, I had been saved.

That was thirty-five years ago. Today, I am still sober by the grace of God, one day at a time. Life is not always easy, but I know with all my heart that with "my God as I understand him," I am never alone.

—G. E. Mimms—

42

Heavenly Escorts

Prayer enlarges the heart until it is capable of
containing God's gift of himself.
~Mother Teresa

My mother was a full-time caregiver for my father, who was diagnosed with multiple sclerosis early in their marriage. Confined to a wheelchair for many years, he required around-the-clock care. My brother, sister and I tried to help out as best we could, but our lives and schedules became more demanding over the years. Although we hired support for my mother, she typically worked right alongside each provider to ensure the best possible care.

Our entire family was so focused on my father's health that we rarely considered the health of any other family member. However, a day came when my mother's doctor insisted on a series of tests in an outpatient wing of our local hospital.

My mother was instructed to arrive with a companion since it was not advised that she drive herself home. Being fiercely independent, my mother did not want to disturb any of us. I had just had my first baby, my sister worked at a very demanding job, and my brother worked different shifts so his schedule was always uncertain. Although she was told not to come alone, she called a taxi and went by herself that day.

When I called my parents' house, the healthcare aide revealed her secret. Holding my new baby in one arm and the phone in the other, I tried desperately to reach my mother. Calling the hospital to check on her produced no results due to patient confidentiality. Nervously, I paced the floor. I felt so guilty knowing she already bore the heavy burden of caring for someone ill. I became filled with regret that I had not asked more specific questions about when her tests were scheduled. The minutes ticked by slowly as I waited for the phone to ring. The only thing that gave me solace was the prayer I whispered to God asking that he watch over her.

Finally, the call came. "Mom," I said rather sternly, "how could you not tell me, or anyone for that matter, that you were going for tests by yourself?" I knew I should not have spoken so harshly, but the moments of worry had taken their toll. "Sometimes, you need to ask for help," I continued. "There was no one there for you!"

"That is not actually true, dear," she said serenely. "I was not at all alone." A wave of relief passed over me. Perhaps another family member, friend, or neighbor had heard about her plan and accompanied her.

"Thank goodness, Mom," I said breathlessly. "Who was with you?"

After a long pause, she said, "That is what I have to tell you!" My mother's eyes always shine when she tells this part of the story to anyone who has not yet heard it. It is like the experience plays out before her eyes every time she describes it.

"When I stood to walk over to the nurse," she told me, "I felt the presence of two angelic beings on either side of me. I glanced to my left and my right and saw the glowing arch of their wings. As I walked, they measured their steps to mine. I was escorted lovingly right to the door. I was never alone, after all!"

She could not see my falling tears on the other end of the phone. My prayer had been heard in the most extraordinary way. That day, I received the greatest gift of reassurance in the face of fear, loneliness and despair. It was the peace of knowing that if I believe, I never face anything alone.

Several years later, I received a call in the middle of the night that my father had passed. As I drove to the hospital to meet my mother, I knew she would be inconsolable. I prayed for the strength to be able to say goodbye to my father and comfort my mother in a way that would make a difference. When I saw her, the knowledge came to me in one sudden rush. "Mom, your angels were here to take him back home! He had your heavenly escorts, too!" She smiled through her tears and acknowledged what I said with a small nod.

Since that day, as a wife, mother, teacher, and friend, I have called upon these heavenly beings countless times. I think of these angels as family friends, just waiting and watching for when we need their divine assistance. Their introduction to my life has given me the blessed assurance that I need never walk alone. I only need to ask for an escort.

—Elizabeth Rose Reardon Farella—

43

How Did She Know?

When we are touched by something, it's as if we're
being brushed by an angel's wings.
~Rita Dove

I have eight beautiful grandchildren. My memories of my own dear grandmother, Lila, make me strive to be as good an example to my own grandchildren as she was to me.

Several years ago during the Christmas season, one of my daughters, her husband and children came to visit my husband and me during the holiday season.

Feeling the Christmas spirit, I took great joy in decorating our home with both sentimental items from years past and a few new treasures in preparation for their visit.

One of the newer decorative items was a lovely ceramic angel that stands almost a foot tall and was designed to be displayed on a mantle or tabletop.

Her wings are spread open, and she holds a harp with delicate hands. Her long, wavy auburn hair frames her dainty face with a loving expression.

The edges of the angel's wings are covered with transparent fiber-optic tubes so that when she is plugged in, her wings light up in a plethora of colors that change and alternate every few seconds in breathtaking fashion.

When other lights in the room are dimmed, she casts a mesmerizing glow. It almost seems that she is watching us, no matter where we are in the room.

I decided from the moment I first took her out of the box that she would represent my guardian angel.

So when my seven-year-old granddaughter became transfixed with the beauty of this angel, it gave me a chance to have a meaningful dialogue with her about angels and how they watch over us throughout our lives.

"What is her name, Grandma?"

"Well, you know, dear, I hadn't really thought about it. What do you think I should call her?"

She thought deeply for a few seconds without saying a word.

"What name do you think would best suit her?" I prompted gently. "She's so beautiful, she must be given a beautiful name. Don't you agree?"

Suddenly, without hesitation, and with a twinkle in her eyes, my granddaughter exclaimed, "LILA! I think you should call her Lila!"

I froze, at first not believing my own ears, but I agreed quickly. "Yes, Lila is a lovely name for her, my dear! Did you know that Lila was the name of my grandmother?"

I didn't understand how she could have known. I had never spoken about my grandmother in her presence. It made the hairs on my arm stand up to think that of all the names she could have chosen, Lila was the name that came out of her mouth.

"Lila she is then," I said softly. "She will be my guardian angel from now on."

— Melody R. Ringo —

Jadyn's Guardian Angel

Angels represent God's personal care
for each one of us.
~Andrew Greeley

I t had been a fun morning with my grandkids, and now it was rest time. All was quiet until a bloodcurdling shriek broke the silence, coinciding with a mighty crash directly above us. Jadyn's room! Five-year-old Caleb and I sprang off the couch and headed for the stairs. We had been enjoying after-lunch down time, watching his favorite Ninja Turtles movie while his two-year-old sister, Jadyn, had her afternoon nap upstairs.

I don't think Caleb knew that Grandma could move up the stairs that quickly. To be honest, neither did I. We were both terrified to open Jadyn's door. The shrieking had reached an ear-piercing pitch. All kinds of ghastly images flashed through my mind.

We rushed through the door to see a heavy oak highboy lying on the floor while my sweet, little Jadyn stood screaming and shaking with fright in the corner of the bedroom. Exactly what had happened was evident at a glance. She had pulled out all of the dresser drawers in an attempt to climb to the top, resulting in the horrendous crash. This was not something any of us would have expected Jadyn to try!

A quick scan assured me she was uninjured. She must have jumped clear before the highboy hit the floor. But how? She was only two.

As I breathed out a prayer of gratitude, the answer soon became obvious. All of the items on top of her chest of drawers — her "pretties," as she called them — lay scattered across the floor from corner to corner. A little porcelain dish lay in pieces. However, the angel I had given her at her birth lay wedged under the top edge of the highboy, holding it above the floor and making just enough room to protect her from being crushed under the weight of the dresser. This explained how she escaped without severe leg injuries or much worse. I attempted to move the chest off of the angel, but I couldn't budge it.

Fully expecting her angel to be chipped and broken, I kneeled down to see how she could possibly be supporting this huge wooden piece of furniture. I couldn't believe my eyes. The angel was totally intact, and though I assumed there would be cracks and chips, she too miraculously didn't have a mark on her.

Jadyn's angel is a stone-art creation about eight inches tall. It may look delicate at a glance, but it had just proven to me it was stronger than a solid wooden highboy. She has wire wings and is delicately sculpted, holding a beautiful baby in her arms. Every detail has been captured to reflect the love between this angel and her beloved child.

The caption around the bottom states, "Grandmothers are angels following you through life." This grandma didn't feel like she had followed her grandchild very successfully that day, but thankfully her guardian angel had taken charge and managed to spare my precious granddaughter.

When my son and daughter-in-law returned from work a short while later, and Ryan lifted the furniture off the floor, even he had to admit that the little stone angel had kept his baby daughter safe. There simply was no other explanation. Although the impact of the chest on the angel had left deep gouges in the wood of the highboy, no other damage could be found to either chest or angel.

Recently, I went into Jadyn's room to revisit her angel and was still in awe of the delicacy of this stone-art creation. As I read the caption, I offered my thanks again to the angels for their miraculous rescue. Noticing my son had now attached the highboy to the wall, I smiled and offered up another thanks, knowing this would never happen again.

There is no doubt in my mind that Jadyn's guardian angels protected her that day. By positioning that little angel as they did, none of us could doubt their role in keeping my granddaughter safe. They even took the further step of making sure that Grandma was present to experience it.

—Yvonne Hall—

45

Airborne

*The most glorious moment you will ever experience in
your life is when you look back and see how God was
protecting you all this time.*
~Shannon L. Alder

A s my best friend and I walked out of the gymnasium
doors and into the parking lot, the sky opened up and
rain poured down. I was a sprinter, so I took off running. Neither of us had umbrellas, and the last thing this
black girl wanted was to deal with wet hair! I was running parallel to
the parked cars but perpendicular to the driving lanes. I was having
a great time zipping through — until I saw the headlights. My first
thought was to try and outrun the car. The problem was that I was
fast — but not *that* fast!

My best friend shouted with everything she had in her,
"SONEAKQUA!"

I was in a full sprint with my arms above my head to hold my jacket
over my hair so it didn't get wet. I had too much forward momentum
to stop completely. But then I felt a pull on the back of my shirt collar.

I was being held back, and it was amazing! It was like being
suspended in mid-air, as if I were literally hovering over the car. If
my feet had been planted on the ground, I would have been eye-level
with the top of the car. Instead, it felt like I was a whole head length
above it. It passed in front of me about two inches away from my face.
If my eyelashes had been just a bit longer, I would have given that car

one of the longest, wettest butterfly kisses ever! It was as if time had shifted into slow motion because I could actually see the couple inside.

Immediately after they passed, I nearly fell flat on my face into the spot where the car had just been. I turned around to look at my friend, laughing and squealing with excitement that I didn't get hit. Even better, my hair wasn't wet! As I started to thank my friend for grabbing me, I realized that she was standing more than twenty feet away. (I was a sprinter, but she wasn't.) She had stopped in her tracks the minute she screamed my name. She hadn't touched me, and there was no one else in sight.

I never asked her what she saw. I only know what I experienced. I know that someone grabbed me and held me over that car. I should have been pulverized, but I wasn't. We walked to the car in silence, drove home and never spoke of the incident to anyone. I had been in church since I was six years old and had always heard about angels. But at seventeen, I learned firsthand what it was to be saved by one.

— Soneakqua J. White —

46

The Angel Who Saved My Daughters

If the only prayer you said was thank you
that would be enough.
~Meister Eckhart

While I was a child, my parents told me how angels are all around us, helping us when we need them most. Angels would keep my loved ones and me safe.

I imagined an angel with long, shimmering golden hair. Her eyes were crystal blue like the sky, and she wore a long, flowing white dress embellished with pearls and rhinestones. She was beautiful. I was about eight years old at the time, and my angel became my friend and constant companion. I felt comforted to know that she was by my side when I was sick or at school. She became a big part of my childhood.

As the years rolled by, I felt my angel many times. She was there to protect me in my teenage years when I didn't make wise choices. Throughout my adult life, I felt her presence when I had mishaps that could have been tragic. I will never forget one particular day when a very special angel helped save my two daughters from drowning.

At the time, we were living in Arizona in the Phoenix area. My husband Harold and I decided to take our children up to Oak Creek in the mountains for a day of relaxation and swimming. I was eight months pregnant with our fifth child. We found a nice spot to sit along the creek of Slide Rock State Park, while two of our daughters waded in the water. There were many families out swimming that day, enjoying the last warm days of summer. Everything was calm. The only sounds that could be heard were the rushing water and children's laughter.

The silence was suddenly broken by a woman's shrill scream. "Those girls are drowning!" I looked over in horror as I watched my own two girls bobbing up and down in the water as the current pushed them under. They tried to grab onto a rock, but it was too slippery. Each time my daughters popped back up from the water, their eyes were wide with terror. My heart nearly stopped. I screamed to my husband, "Hurry, get them, get them!" I felt so helpless in my advanced stage of pregnancy. I cried out for someone, anyone, to please help my girls.

Harold jumped into the water fully clothed to get to our daughters. Going against the current made it difficult for him to go as fast as he needed. Out of nowhere, I saw a woman, strangely familiar, sprint into the water from the other side of the creek. She got to my daughters a moment before Harold. The young woman lifted my girls safely onto the rock where they sat until my husband got to them.

Aside from a few scratches and a missing water shoe, my daughters were okay, but shaken. "Thank goodness that woman got to you quickly before Dad was able to help," I said to my daughters.

Harold and the girls looked at me oddly. "What woman?" my husband asked.

"The lady who ran into the creek, the one with the long, blond hair," I said as I scanned the area to see if I could find her in the crowd to thank her. I looked at my daughters and said, "You know, the woman who picked you up and set you on the rock."

"Mom, there wasn't a lady. The water sort of lifted me up!" my older daughter said.

"Me, too, Mommy. The water pushed me up," my younger daughter piped in.

As we walked back to our car, I couldn't stop thinking about the blond woman who helped my daughters. Then I realized why she looked familiar. She had the same long, flowing blond hair as the angel I had imagined many years ago. Silently, I thanked her and asked for a sign to let me know it was her.

As we approached the parking lot, my daughter blurted, "Look, my shoe!" She pointed to the hood of our car. Then it was clear to me what I had witnessed. There was no way the water shoe could be on our car since it had washed down the creek in the current. If it happened to be retrieved, how could someone get it to our car before we did? We had left immediately after the incident. How would anyone know it was my daughter's shoe or our car? I didn't need to solve the mystery. I already knew. It was the sign I asked for from my angel to let me know of her presence.

That night, as I tucked my girls into bed we said a prayer of thanks. "I want to thank the angel for protecting us," my younger daughter said. As I kissed her cheek, I whispered to her that it was very nice that she would thank the angel for protecting her and her sister earlier that day. Only seven years old at the time, she looked up at me and said simply, "You know what, Mommy? I think the angel has long, blond hair and wears a pretty, white dress!"

Like mother, like daughter, I thought to myself. I smiled as I brushed back my daughter's hair from her forehead.

As I shut off the lights to the bedroom and closed the door, I said my own thanks to the blond angel who saved my girls that afternoon.

— Dorann Weber —

Doctor's Orders

*Children often have imaginary playmates. I suspect
that half of them are really their guardian angels.*
~Eileen Elias Freeman,
The Angels' Little Instruction Book

My daughter Allie was only about three weeks old when she had to have life-saving surgery to remove half of her colon following a premonition I'd had about her health. She had peritonitis, but because the doctors were not able to identify the cause, they recommended she be followed for the first five years of her life.

Although Allie recovered quickly from her first surgery, some stages of her development were delayed. One of these was speech. It is every parent's joy the first time they hear their child utter the words "Mama" or "Dada." Surprisingly, Allie's first word was "angel"!

It was a relief to watch her grow and thrive following such a traumatic event in her life. As she did, she spoke about her angel more and more. Not only did she always say he was right beside her but he became her favorite playmate. We just believed he was an imaginary friend until strange occurrences started happening around our house.

One day, I was looking for a book for my son Daniel, who is three years older than Allie. Daniel and I searched everywhere for his favorite book, but we couldn't find it anywhere. As we were coming up the stairs from the basement where there were still some unpacked boxes from a recent move, two-year-old Allie came to me with the book in her hands. "Here, Mommy," she said. "My angel told me you were looking for this and showed me where it was!"

I pulled her aside and asked her to tell me more about her angelic friend. What did he look like? Did he have a name? Her face lit up as she responded, "Oh, yes, Mommy! His name is Bummer, and he's huge! Up to the ceiling!"

Bummer's presence in our house soon became the most normal thing in the world. We all got used to Allie playing with and speaking to Bummer daily.

On another occasion, I drove to the drugstore with my mother and Allie in the car. I asked my mother to wait in the car with Allie as I was only going to be a few minutes. When I returned to the car, I noticed that Allie's back window was wide open. When I asked my mother about it, she told me she hadn't opened it and hadn't noticed that it was open. When I asked Allie, who was strapped in her toddler car seat, she said, "Mommy, Bummer opened the window! I can't reach it!" And, sure enough, her short, little arms could not reach the window from her car seat in the middle of the back seat.

One evening, I put both kids to bed upstairs and went back downstairs to relax. About an hour later, I heard two sets of footsteps running across the hardwood floors in Allie's room. I ran upstairs thinking I would catch the kids in the act of sneaking out of bed, but Daniel was fast asleep. Allie was just getting back into her bed.

"Allie!" I said. "What are you doing? Who were you running with?"

She responded, "Bummer, Mommy. But then he told me I better get back to bed, or we were going to make Mommy upset."

Bummer continued to make his presence known every day. Late one afternoon, Daniel was upstairs doing homework while I was cooking dinner downstairs. Allie was in the playroom next to the kitchen. I was accustomed to hearing her talking and laughing out loud to herself, but suddenly I heard a deep male voice respond to her. I ran into the playroom, but no one else was there except Allie! When I asked whom she'd been talking to, she responded, "Bummer!"

My husband remained skeptical about this, but he heard the same deep male voice coming from the playroom several days later when

Allie was playing there alone.

When the kids were young, we enjoyed taking them to Florida in the winter to visit their grandparents and get away from our cold Michigan weather. They enjoyed playing on the beach and swimming in the ocean. We also celebrated Allie's birthdays there.

One particular January morning, I went into her room to wake her up and get her special day started when I found she was already wide awake, but deeply upset and sobbing. I tried to console her. Had she had a bad dream? Did she hurt herself?

"No," she said, shaking her head and still crying.

"Then what, Allie?" I asked as I pulled her onto my lap.

"It's Bummer," she sobbed. "Bummer told me he had to leave!"

"What?" I responded. "What do you mean he had to leave? Where did he go?"

With her little index finger, she pointed upward and told me, "He said it was time for him to go, but he would always stay close by!" As I continued to console Allie, wiping the tears from her face, I reminded her it was her birthday, and we were going to have a party for her later that day. And then it struck me. It was her fifth birthday, and the doctors had said she needed to be watched the first five years of her life.

Bummer did come back to Allie a few more times in the months that followed, and that left her feeling more at peace. Years later, Allie remembers Bummer as a dream she had. But I'll never forget how real and comforting his presence was when she needed him most, and how he said goodbye with the reassurance that he would "always stay close by."

— Lynn Darmon —

48

A Brief Encounter

The golden moments in the stream of life rush past us,
and we see nothing but sand; the angels come to visit
us, and we only know them when they are gone.
~George Eliot

I was young and very naïve when I signed up to study abroad in France. I thought that bad things only happened to other people and I was invincible, ready to take on the world with my friends.

It just so happened that the host family I was placed with lived in a very nice place, but it was close to a questionable part of town. There were four tall apartment buildings that were filled with dangerous people. Some boys showed me a gun when I walked back from school. I watched as others threw a Molotov cocktail onto a car and burned it to the ground.

Still, I wasn't smart enough to be scared. To get to the center of town where my friend was staying, I had to take a bus. To get to that bus, I had to walk past those buildings.

One Friday night, my friends were gathering for a night of festivities. Of course, I wanted to join them. After my multiple-course Alsacian meal, I ran out to catch the last bus into the main part of town. I didn't even think of the dangers that were out there at 10 p.m. All of a sudden, a little old lady in her bathrobe and slippers came shuffling toward me and sat next to me on the bench waiting for the bus. I still remember her worn floral robe. Her slippers scuffled as she walked.

She was slightly bent over and walked as if in pain. I thought it was strange that she was out and about at that time of night dressed like that, but I didn't question it. "Different" made life interesting. How boring it would be if we were all the same.

She didn't speak English, and my French was horrible, but we attempted to converse. She leaned over and took my hand. She told me she had been lying in bed when she knew suddenly that the bus would be late. She put on her bathrobe and came down to sit with me until the bus came.

As we struggled through small talk, she suddenly patted my hand. Four young men were coming down the road, obviously looking for trouble. They headed straight for us. Then I got nervous. What could a nineteen-year-old and an old lady do?

But that old lady stood up very slowly and turned toward the boys. I held my breath, thinking she was just bringing attention to us. They stopped, talked amongst themselves, and then crossed the street and went back the way they had come. She never said anything; she just sat back down. Five minutes later, the bus pulled up. I smiled, gave her a hug and told her I enjoyed our chat. I fully expected her to get on the bus with me, for who would sit at a bus stop late at night for an hour chatting with a stranger?

I got on, the doors closed, and she waved goodbye from the street. After I sat down, I turned around to see where she was going. She was gone, completely vanished in the night. I firmly believe she was an angel sent to protect me.

— Karleen Forwell —

49

The Day I Got My Own Angel

*You should never feel alone there's always someone
to turn to, it is the Guardian Angel
who is watching over you.*
~K. Sue

My dad had warned me not to go to work. But at seventeen, I thought I knew it all. So, despite the weather reports, I ignored him and every meteorologist and left to travel the three miles to my first real job.

The going was fine. Then the weather began to change abruptly, and my supervisor decided to close shop and send us home early for safety's sake.

I could have called my dad. He would have gladly come to pick me up, and the return trip home would likely have included hot chocolate and corn muffins at the diner.

But when you're seventeen, you know it all.

I started the car and worked a good twenty minutes scraping ice off the windows of my eleven-year-old jalopy.

The rear defroster wouldn't defrost.

The wipers were frozen in the upright position.

I should have called my dad.

I eased out of the parking lot and skidded gracefully onto the main road.

Guardians and Protectors | 157

It looked awfully deserted. Snow was blowing sideways, so visibility was near zero, as the weather forecast had predicted.

I rolled down my driver's side window and hung my head outside to locate lines on the road.

There were none.

I turned down what I thought was a familiar street, but I had lost my bearings.

My car shimmied and fishtailed, turned slightly sideways, and then landed on the wrong side of the road.

I tried to back up. I tried to go forward. My tires would have none of it.

I needed to call my dad, but this was before cell phones, so I couldn't.

Normally, I didn't cry easily. But I was sobbing.

I left the engine running because I was afraid I'd freeze to death.

I figured a police car or snowplow would be by any second, and I would be rescued. Then I realized with dread that I had gone down the road leading to an old, abandoned factory.

There were no streetlights.

There were no houses.

There was no through traffic.

The radio was issuing warnings to stay off the road. It was too late for me to heed them.

I had seen enough buried-alive movies to know that I shouldn't stay in the car, but also enough scary movies to know that the result could be disastrous if I ventured out.

I hoped I wasn't getting delirious and starting to hallucinate because I swore I heard a rap on the window.

I huddled low in my seat and blasted the heat.

The rap grew louder.

I put my hands over my ears.

"Young lady, are you alright?"

Someone was trying to pry open my door.

I was too scared to budge.

Then I screamed and must have scared him because he backed away.

A flashlight shone on my dashboard and then back upon the stranger's face.

"I'm Bernard Schaefer. I live on Livingston Place. I was driving home when I saw your headlights beaming through the trees. We've got to get you out of here."

Prying open the door, he yanked me onto the snow bank and then scooped me up into his pickup truck.

I was shivering and couldn't talk, although I remember feeling grateful.

Mr. Schaefer never asked me for my address.

Within minutes, we were parked in front of my house, and my dad came racing out. He hugged me so hard, and then he yelled at me. "I told you it was too dangerous to go to work."

I was only seventeen. I knew everything.

When we turned around to thank Mr. Schaefer and invite him in to thaw out, he was gone.

The next day, my dad and I drove to Livingston Place and searched until we found a mailbox marked "Schaefer."

We knocked on the door, and a young gentleman answered.

"Hi, we're looking for Bernard Schaefer. My daughter and I wanted to thank him for his heroic efforts last night. If it weren't for him, I don't know what might have happened."

"I think you're mistaken," the young man replied. "My grandfather, Bernard, died more than three years ago." I had never seen my dad cry until then.

Sometimes in life, not everything makes sense.

Maybe it's not supposed to.

— Lisa Leshaw —

50

Prayer Card

*We give thanks to God, who delivers us
from great distress.*
~Lailah Gifty Akita

On the last day of kindergarten, my teacher handed me a prayer card. The block lettering read: "Day by day, prayer by prayer, the Lord will always get you there." Next to the words was a cartoon of an angel lifting a little boy wearing roller skates. At dismissal, I ran down the steps of Holy Trinity Elementary holding the prayer card close. I waved it at my mom, who waited for me by our van with my little brother.

"Look!" I handed it to her. As she read it, I said, "I don't want to lose it."

Mom smiled. "I know exactly where to put it."

Once she buckled us into our car seats, she got into the driver's seat and opened the overhead sunglasses compartment She tucked in the prayer card and clicked the door closed.

"Fits perfectly!" Mom said. After that, every time she popped open the door, I checked to make sure the prayer card was still underneath her glasses.

A few years later, my brother and I walked down to Mom at the same van after dismissal. She was in a hurry. Quickly, she buckled my brother into his car seat as I settled into mine.

She told us, "I'm running behind on some errands I have to do before we go home. But if you two are good, we'll pick up dinner on the way home." We were on our best behavior that afternoon and, as promised, we stopped for dinner before heading home. We got past the rush-hour traffic and began picking up a normal speed when a car turned onto the road going the wrong way and hit our van head-on.

On impact, the airbags went off, knocking the wind out of my mom. My brother and I didn't understand why she couldn't respond, but I could see her head moving. I unbuckled both of us from our seats as the sound of sirens surrounded the accident. First responders ran to the driver's side, and my mom was able to tell them the doors were stuck.

While they pried open the driver's side door, my brother attempted to climb over Mom to climb out her window, but her collarbone couldn't handle the weight. Later, she learned it was broken. The shattered passenger-side window was the only other way out. My brother and I were small enough to crawl through; Mom needed to be cut from the seat. Police officers took me aside while my mom and brother were strapped onto stretchers. Soon enough, the three of us were in the back of an ambulance.

We spent a long night in the hospital where saltine crackers and Popsicles substituted for a meal. The recovery process was painful, but our injuries weren't as bad as they could have been.

The morning after the accident, my dad went to the junkyard to pick up our personal items from the totaled van. The crushed hood had been pushed all the way into the dashboard like an accordion, leaving no legroom. If the crash had happened only a few inches to the left, my mom's legs would have been crushed. Dad mentioned that it looked like a bubble had formed around the driver's seat. Then he looked over at the passenger seat, where he saw the prayer card lying there as if a guardian angel had left a business card. Finally, Dad looked toward the overhead compartment. It was shut, and Mom's sunglasses were still inside.

I do believe a guardian angel protected all three of us that night, but not because of the prayer card. Someone was watching over us, and the card only served as the perfect object to remind my family of that. Now, I drive a car of my own, and I keep that same prayer card in the overhead case. I know that someone will always be by my side.

—Hayley Pisciotti—

Chapter
6

Answered
Prayers

On Angel Wings

*The prayer that begins with trustfulness and passes
on into waiting will always end in
thankfulness, triumph, and praise.*
~Alexander Maclaren

It was one of those beautiful spring days when everything should seem a little brighter. Yet, from where I sat, everything was bleak. As I sipped my coffee, I stared at the empty page in my journal. I looked over at my dog, Jack, who lay at my side, loyal and comforting.

"You're such a good boy," I told him before bursting into tears. Immediately, he sat up and leaned into my hand. A Golden Retriever can break one's heart with a simple look — an expression of love, concern, sweetness and beauty rolled all together. Jack was giving me that look.

But my heart already felt broken. Only I wasn't sure why. I just knew that a weight had enveloped me like a wet wool blanket, heavy and uncomfortable. Common sense told me it was part of the mourning process. My brother had only been gone nine months, his battle with cancer a brief, valiant one fought with dignity and courage. But for all my sorrow over losing him, I'd felt his presence regularly. As a result, my faith had strengthened. I would get through whatever came my way. Or so I believed.

A large part of my endurance included turning to angels for assistance. Shortly after Neal passed, I'd stumbled upon angel cards and began to review them daily. The words were comforting and often seemed to speak directly to me. Asking the angels for help and guidance became routine; I felt certain that God had opened my eyes to them at a time when he knew I could use the additional support. If I was wrong or crazy, what did it hurt? So my mornings became my time to journal and spend meditative time with God and the angels.

That morning was different. I didn't want to pray, didn't feel thankful and didn't want to ask for help. What I felt, and had been feeling for several days, was anger, fear and pain. Up until that point, I'd been resilient, which I knew was due in no small part to my faith. But life seemed to be playing some manic game, comprised of non-stop curve balls being lobbed my way. One thing after another was piling up — things I couldn't control, let alone understand. My twenty-one-year-old daughter had just experienced the Boston Marathon terrorist attack and was showing symptoms of PTSD. My parents mourned the loss of their son, while their own health declined. I was trying to take care of everyone while juggling a stressful job in a toxic workplace. Additionally, I had recently endured my second major surgical procedure in a year.

I missed my brother. I mourned with my parents. I worried about my daughter. I felt weary and a burden to my husband. I resented the ugliness at work. At my wits' end, my prayer was simple: "I need your help, God. Please surround me with your loving angels and help me through this."

Within minutes an overwhelming sensation of peace came over me. Never before had I felt anything like it. I no longer felt fear, sadness or anger. It was an amazing, beautiful feeling, and I didn't dare move for fear it might go away. Quietly, I sat in peace, finally able to appreciate the resplendent morning outside my door. I marveled at what I was feeling, knowing full well it was a gift. I remember saying "thank you" over and over. And as I did, I continued to stare outside, basking in my newfound comfort.

Then I saw it... Falling slowly from the sky, swaying back and forth in a big Z pattern, was a big, downy white feather. It wasn't the typical narrow bird feather that we often see on the ground or find in a nest. The biggest feather I'd ever seen was falling from the sky directly in front of me. I watched as it drifted lazily downward before disappearing from sight beyond our deck. No sooner was it out of sight than a second feather — similar in size and shape — also appeared, zigzagging a descent. In stunned silence, I watched as the second feather mimicked the journey of its predecessor. Before it disappeared from view, I jumped up and ran to the door, down the steep stairs of the deck and over to the area of the yard I imagined the feathers would have landed. Looking up, I saw nothing but blue sky.

Glancing down again, my eyes went straight to the place where the feathers had landed. They were side by side on the ground, among the new crocuses, themselves a sign of spring and renewal, as they are the first perennials to appear each year.

My "angel feathers" sit in a china bowl on a shelf in my bedroom now, a reminder that I am never alone. I've received numerous signs from above since that day, but none quite as striking. And to this day, several years later, I have yet to again experience the remarkable, all-consuming peacefulness that came to me on that beautiful spring day — delivered on the wings of an angel.

— M.J. Shea —

How God Took My Burden

Hope is like the sun, which, as we journey toward it,
casts the shadow of our burden behind us.
~Samuel Smiles

Many years ago, I was a guest at my aunt's wedding reception. As people finished their dinners, they began to light up. As I lit my cigarette, the woman sitting next to me asked me why I smoked.

"Can't quit," I said, taking a long pull. "Want one?"

"No, thanks," she said, waving me off. "I quit."

"How'd you do that?" I always asked people how they'd managed to quit because I never could.

She didn't miss a beat. "I asked God to take my burden," she said. She stared at my shocked expression and said, "You should try it." Although I've always had a deep faith, I just couldn't believe this woman's solution would work for me.

I'd been smoking for twenty years, since my best friend offered me a cigarette on the beach during the summer before Grade 9. It seemed that nearly everyone smoked in those days. I started with a cigarette now and then, and gradually grew my habit into three packs a day.

I'd tried every smoking-cessation product and method available, with no success. I worked a stressful job as a court reporter. The more stress I had, the more I smoked.

After another twenty years, when I quit reporting, my smoking dropped to a pack and a half a day. I thought I'd gradually wean myself. I'd even stopped inhaling after a bout of bronchitis, but withdrawal symptoms still plagued me if I tried to quit altogether. After two smoke-free hours, I'd be shaking and headachy, and unable to breathe.

The craving held me like a vice. I'd read somewhere it was similar to a heroin addiction. I couldn't go anywhere without my pack of smokes and a lighter. Now without a job, my funds were limited, so every cent of my spending money went to cigarettes.

It was difficult enough to admit that my late husband and I were both smokers, but it was worse knowing that our son was asthmatic. That's why I kept a standing ashtray outside my kitchen door. I spent a lot of time walking back and forth from that door. One day as I came back into the house, I was struck by an overwhelming fear I couldn't name. I remember as I looked back at the doorway, it seemed like some kind of enormous evil was pulling me back to those cigarettes, as if some monstrous power was drawing me into its dark world. Terror filled me. Would I die of cancer?

That night, I was so afraid that I prayed, begged, wept and pleaded with God to take my burden of nicotine addiction. I vowed I would do anything He asked of me if only I could be free of it. I was so afraid that if I lit a cigarette when I awoke the next morning, some irreversible disaster would befall me, and this nameless thing would consume me.

The next morning, I awoke feeling very ill. I stayed in bed that day and most of the next as the room whirled around me. I couldn't focus or walk without falling, so I crawled to the bathroom and back with my eyes closed. It was an ordeal I'd never before experienced.

Finally, a day and a half later, I began to feel better. I sat up, swung my legs over the edge of the bed, and was about to stand when I became aware of something — a presence behind my left shoulder. I sat absolutely still because, although there was nothing visual or audible, I was being given information that this presence would stay with me for eighteen months. I thought of it as a holy presence, a Spirit from God.

The Spirit made me aware that I had nothing to fear, and nothing would bother me. I'd be able to go forward with no worries or concerns because the Spirit would protect me. Although it said nothing about smoking or quitting smoking, I knew somehow that I would never smoke again. I thanked this invisible presence, rose from the bed and went forward into life. After that, I had not the slightest desire for a cigarette, never a craving, and no withdrawal symptoms at all.

About a year later, my mother and I were having lunch, and she told me about a time when she became very ill when I was just a child. "I prayed and asked God to allow me to live until you were eighteen," she said. "I wanted to see you grown, a young woman ready to start your adult life." Having lost one daughter, she was fervent in her wish. We both knew she'd survived that severe illness, and I wondered why she'd brought it up all these years later. Then she told me. "Now I'm praying for something else. I pray that I'll see you stop smoking before I die." She hesitated, eyeing me. "What's so funny? Why are you smiling?"

"I've quit," I said. Astonishment is the only way I can describe Mum's reaction. She laughed and cried and hugged me all at the same time.

In the entire year and a half after I first encountered the Spirit, it never again addressed me. But one afternoon while I was in the kitchen speaking with my husband, I became aware of the Spirit's presence. It indicated it was leaving, that I would be on my own but would be fine. Everything would be just as it had been when the Spirit was with me, except now it was up to me. I accepted the challenge. "Thank you," I said, knowing that what it said was true and how blessed I had been. Then, in an instant, it was gone.

Three years ago at a family event, I heard a woman mention something about God taking her burden. I asked if she'd attended that long-ago reception and if she'd possibly told me how she'd quit smoking. She didn't remember me, but had attended the event. She'd told her story many times to people who wanted to quit, so my question didn't surprise her. I told her what a difference it had made in my life, how it was the only thing that worked for me, and I thanked her. She accepted none of the credit. "It wasn't me," she said. "You know that."

As a smoker, I was always afraid of running out of cigarettes and being unable to obtain any. At the time I stopped smoking, I kept an unopened package of cigarettes with my lighter and ashtray in case of relapse. They were, collectively, my security blanket.

It's been eighteen years since I stopped. Through all of those eighteen years, I've had no desire to smoke. Now I see the cigarettes, lighter and ashtray that I held onto as symbols of pain, fear and entrapment, but at the same time and far more important, as symbols of how God answered my prayer.

—Darlene Grace Peterson—

53

The Parking Lot Angel

Prayer does not change God,
but it changes him who prays.
~Søren Aabye Kierkegaard

A few years ago, I joined an online writing group on a whim. Every day, we wrote our thoughts about the day's assigned topic. If we wanted, we could share our work with the group.

That was my first attempt at writing about my feelings. Sometimes, I wrote with a combination of excitement and dread at what my words would reveal.

Writing and then reading about the experiences of others changed my perspective. I realized that we all struggle sometimes. I met a wonderful group of supportive people, and some of them have become great friends. They are committed to sharing their thoughts and experiences with each other. I've learned a lot and really appreciate their friendship. We talk almost every day and support each other in our daily lives.

The subjects of our conversations vary widely, from raising children to the nature of Spirit in the universe. For a while, the subject of guardian angels came up, and several people said they often asked their angels and guides for help.

I'd never imagined that I had guardian angels. It wasn't something I considered. Once in a while, I did notice positive signs when I made a good decision, but I didn't think much about it. The idea intrigued me, even though I wasn't aware of any angels by my side on a daily basis.

When I tried to communicate with them, it felt strange. I wasn't sure how to talk to an invisible being that I wasn't sure existed.

Several friends shared that they were using angel cards to connect with angels. I was curious and wondered if they'd work for me. The cards are larger than a regular playing deck, and their purpose is to answer specific questions in a supportive way.

I decided that I needed some so I ordered a deck online. The cards came in a lovely box with an image of a beautiful woman with soft, white wings. A small booklet of instructions was inside. Each card represented a specific angel and had a supportive message on it. The beautiful artwork and message highlighted the individual angel's talents.

I followed the instructions carefully, lit a white candle and shuffled the deck with intention. Each day, I drew a card and read its message, bringing it into my awareness and trying to remember it during the day. While I enjoyed the inspiration, I still felt that I wasn't doing it right.

In frustration, I asked for help. One night as I was preparing to go out for dinner with friends, I stood in front of my bathroom mirror and said, "I don't know how to do this. I need your help. Please bring me a sign to let me know angels exist. Help me figure this out. Please show me what I am not aware of."

When we arrived at the restaurant, I opened the passenger door and saw a small china angel on the pavement. I picked her up and admired the fluffy, white feathers glued to her back. Then I discovered that she had a switch, which turned on a glowing light inside her.

The softly changing light gave me a feeling of peace. As I watched, the lights cycled through blue, yellow and pink.

"This is so lovely," I said, turning to my friend. "But this angel isn't for me. Someone else needs this angel more than I do." I left her light on and gently set her on a small ledge that faced toward the street.

We walked toward the restaurant for dinner. Just before we turned the corner, I glanced back and saw the angel glowing in the darkness.

Several times during dinner, I thought of her, hoping she was all right and had found the person she was meant for. Then I started questioning my judgment. Finding the angel had been such a surprise that I became confused and tried to give her away! It was a typical move; I usually put other people first. I couldn't get her out of my mind as it occurred to me that she might be the angel I had asked for. By the time we finished dessert, I was anxious to see if she was still there. I decided if she was, I would claim her.

When we turned the corner to the parking lot, I felt a flutter in my chest when I saw the softly glowing light. I realized that she was my answer. I had asked for an angel, and there she was.

—Tree Langdon—

54

Never Give Up

Do you think the universe fights for souls to be
together? Some things are too strange
and strong to be coincidences.
~Emery Allen

Despite the fairytale beginning of our relationship, my husband and I found ourselves straining to hold onto the magic when real-life challenges tested us. The worry from chronically ill children and dwindling financial resources wore down our patience with one another. Because neither of us is perfect, our character flaws began to make situations even harder to deal with. We became easily agitated with each other, and the constant conflicts made us distant.

One night, after yet another argument, I felt there was little hope for our marriage. But I didn't want to hurt our three little children so I felt trapped. I was so angry with my husband for putting me in this position, and I fell to my knees in desperation and prayed to God. All the angst-ridden contents of my heart spilled out as I pleaded with Him to help me.

"Dear God," I prayed. "I don't know what to do with this man. He is so stubborn and selfish. No matter what I do, he won't listen."

Between sobs, I pointed out how my husband fell short, how he angered me, how he disappointed the children or neglected to live up to his responsibilities. When I was emotionally and spiritually spent, I fell silent, not really expecting an answer. I was at a complete loss as to what to do next. I needed God to help me with this man or our precious family was going to be destroyed.

Then a vision appeared before my eyes. A man was on his knees praying to God, just as I had been only minutes before. A bright beam of light shone down upon him. This was no mortal man. He had a magnificent presence that is hard to put into human words. A perfect specimen of creation. Beautiful and radiant. An angel of God. Curiously, he wore a sort of breastplate type of armor, but there was no mistaking his divine nature. The air around him felt clean and pure yet energized with a palpable peace. Yet, it wasn't his appearance that stunned me most, but what he said.

He didn't speak to me, but with hands clasped and eyes gazing upward, he prayed in a gentle and anguished voice: "Dear Heavenly Father, I don't know what to do with this woman. She is so stubborn and selfish. No matter what I do, she won't listen." My heart stopped. I recognized those words. They were the very words I had cried out in my complaints about my husband. As the angel continued, he spoke every single word I had spoken against my husband. Exactly.

I gasped. My own guardian angel was not only complaining to God about me, but he was ready to give up on me—just as I was ready to give up on my husband. I felt mortified. A Bible verse came to mind: "For by your words you will be acquitted, and by your words you will be condemned" (Matthew 12:37). I was being condemned by my own words spoken against another person.

The angel faded away slowly, leaving me in silence to reflect. God had answered my prayers, and that answer was to reflect upon my own shortcomings that I wasn't seeing. And I did so, long into the night. Many incidents replayed before my eyes. I saw the times when I had been stubborn and selfish, and I saw how I had failed to practice patience, understanding, and forgiveness. I wasn't working on my own flaws because I was focusing on my husband's.

It was the most humbling experience of my life.

And as I sat there in remorseful silence, I heard the tender whisper of my guardian angel. "Things aren't always as they seem." My husband was not really a selfish, stubborn man. I wondered if I were being selfish and stubborn by insisting he be the one to change instead of simply loving him the way God loves me — unconditionally and "as is."

That night, as my husband sat in his chair, I wrapped my arms around his shoulders from behind. I whispered in his ear how sorry I was for always pointing out his faults instead of working on my own. "I love you unconditionally, just as you are," I told him. He looked startled at first, and then his whole body softened. He reached around for me to sit in his lap, and he embraced me long and hard.

"I love you, too. More than you'll ever know. Warts and all."

"Hey, I don't have warts!" We laughed.

"I know I'm not perfect," he said.

"You're far closer than I am," I interjected, putting my head on his chest. "I am so thankful that you're patient with me. I'm so sorry, and I will try harder."

"You don't have to try so hard. Perfection is overrated. Our faults and quirks make us who we are as individuals."

I began to see where my guardian angel was right. My husband, even with those traits I saw as shortcomings, is a very good man. He loves me unconditionally, and I believe he is with me to teach me how to love in the same non-judgmental way.

There were many sweet moments to savor even though life continued to get harder for us. We had to say goodbye to one of our darling children when he died at the age of twelve. Another child was diagnosed with the same terminal genetic disorder. Yet, through it all, we became stronger. Together.

I never forgot that vision of my guardian angel praying to God about me, and for years it really tore me up with guilt. But one night, my angel returned to whisper more guidance in my ear: "Life is to teach you, not torment you. Forgive yourself for you have been forgiven."

My fairytale marriage remains "happily ever after" because of that angelic visit, and I am eternally thankful. I will always remember his divine lesson: Be humble. Focus on my own faults and shortcomings. Love unconditionally as I hope to be loved. And never, ever give up on others the way I hope my guardian angel — and God Himself — will never give up on me.

— Lori Phillips —

55

Prayers and Positive Thoughts

Prayer is the best weapon we possess,
the key that opens the heart of God.
~Padre Pio

"**A**re you praying?" In many circumstances, this question would be deemed intrusive and inappropriate. But considering the source — my mother — I didn't take offense. If anything, I was embarrassed to admit that prayer was the furthest thing from my mind.

Over a month had passed since the oncologist had delivered the diagnosis: Inflammatory Breast Cancer, Stage IIIB. While I had shared the stage, I had kept those first three words to myself. I didn't want family and friends Googling IBC and discovering the seriousness of the diagnosis. In 2004, the five-year survival rate for IBC was 30 percent. As for the ten- and fifteen-year survival rates, the percentages were in the single digits and not even worth considering.

My mother's maternal instincts must have been on high alert. She wasted no time in soliciting prayers from her relatives and friends across Canada, Italy, and the United States. Whenever any of these people would call me, they would end the conversation with some variation of "Stay strong! We're praying for you."

At the same time, I struggled to respond to the many offers of help that I received. Friends and colleagues were more than willing to drop off prepared meals, drive me to appointments, buy groceries, and run errands. I didn't want to appear ungracious, but I didn't really need that kind of help. If I even caught a whiff of tomatoes, garlic, onions, or any other strong odors, I would have to run to the nearest bathroom. As for driving me to treatments, I found it easier to book a driver through the Canadian Cancer Society, especially on those cold, blustery days when the roads were treacherous.

To my surprise (and theirs), I said, "I'd appreciate your prayers and positive thoughts."

They — along with my mother's posse — delivered.

My mother and her friends in Sudbury attended mass regularly and offered many prayers on my behalf. The staff at St. James Catholic High School in Guelph gathered in the library to pray for me several times during my cancer journey. Many of them also included me in their morning and evening prayers. A group of relatives visited Lourdes and prayed for a speedy recovery. When a family friend visited Italy, she made a special trip to the shrine of Padre Pio.

My mother had spoken often of Padre Pio, a favorite saint among Italians. A strong believer in prayer and meditation, he is well known for the following mantra: "Pray, Hope and Don't Worry."

While I did experience many of the side effects associated with chemotherapy, including fatigue, hair loss, nausea, and tin mouth, I maintained a positive attitude. This both pleased and surprised me. I'm not a Pollyanna by nature, nor am I a pessimist. I consider myself a realist, parked somewhere between those two extremes.

In early November, I received an unexpected gift. As the oncologist felt my right breast and used a ruler to measure the size of the tumor, she stopped and glanced at her notes several times. Then she smiled and said, "It's gone. Your cancer is in spontaneous remission."

Taken aback, I didn't know what to say.

She continued examining both breasts. "They're exactly the same."

I glanced at my breasts, something I hadn't done in a while. That first month, I must have touched my right breast hundreds of times. But as more and more health professionals examined my breasts, I distanced myself from them. I avoided mirrors and averted my glance whenever I was in the shower. At some level, I felt that my breasts were no longer mine.

But today was different. It was definitely a day for celebration. My right breast had shrunk to its original size, and all the puckering and redness had disappeared.

At home, I took some time to process the information. It was good news, but I wanted to tread slowly before calling everyone. After spending several hours researching on the Internet, I discovered that spontaneous remissions are extremely rare: about 1 in 100,000 cancers. While there was no overt mention of miracles in the articles, I concluded that the scientists were both fascinated and baffled by the phenomenon.

When I shared the news with family and friends, the word "miracle" came up in every single conversation. Even more interesting were the initial reactions from the rest of my healthcare team. Each of them gushed, or did the medical equivalent of gushing:

"Miraculous!"

"This is a first!"

"I can't tell the breasts apart without looking at your chart."

"They'll be writing about this case for years to come."

I basked in their praise and felt that warm, inner glow of accomplishment. It was not the usual feeling for a cancer patient, but then cancer doesn't follow formulas. Instead, it defies all human logic, throwing monkey wrenches into otherwise well-organized lives. Very rarely do breasts and lives revert to their original pre-cancerous states.

Encouraged by this miracle, I asked, "Does that mean I don't need a mastectomy or radiation?"

The medical guns emerged.

"Your breast is compromised."

"We can't take any chances, especially with IBC."

While their tones were clipped, there were flickers of doubt and uncertainty in their eyes. I suspected that they didn't really know how to proceed. Staying on course appeared to be the safest alternative.

In my heart of hearts, I knew the cancer wouldn't come back, at least not in the right breast. My mother agreed and reassured me that

God does not take back miracles. And this was a miracle. The breast was completely normal. No pain. No redness. No *peau d'orange*. No excessive warmth.

But whenever I spoke of prayers and pilgrimages, the oncologists would smile politely and say nothing. Disappointed at first, I soon realized that many different points of view exist regarding prayer and health. As a devout Catholic, I believe in the power of collective prayer, and that faith laid the groundwork for healing to occur.

After much deliberation, I decided to "lock in" the miracle with the mastectomy and radiation. In November 2019, I will celebrate fifteen years of cancer-free living.

— Joanne Guidoccio —

56

The Day the Wind Stood Still

He got up, rebuked the wind and said to the waves,
"Quiet! Be still!" Then the wind died down
and it was completely calm.
~Mark 4:39

When I discovered the money was missing, I was panic-stricken. Four hours ago, my husband had given me grocery money. I had developed a bad habit of putting money into my pocket instead of in my purse. Now I was suffering the consequences for my carelessness.

The money could have fallen out of my pocket almost anywhere from the house to the supermarket, where I now stood. I had to retrace my steps. We had company coming for dinner that evening, and I needed that money. How could I ever explain my carelessness to my husband?

In the course of retracing my steps, I returned to the post office where I had dropped off several mailbags. I had just completed a 5,000-piece mailing for our ministry. Could it have fallen into one of the mailbags?

When the postal clerk said, "Lady, as high as this wind is, that money is long gone by now," it was nearly impossible to choke back my tears.

My next step was to return to my office where I had spent some time working that morning. As I continued retracing my steps throughout the building, one of my co-workers joined the search. The extra eyes didn't help. The money was nowhere to be found.

"Please stop and pray with me," I said to the other half of my search party. "I'm in big trouble if I don't find this money." We prayed, and I left for my next destination.

When I got in my car, I couldn't hold back the tears any longer. Between sobs, I heard myself crying out to the Lord, "Father, I'm so scared. How will I ever explain this to my husband? Forgive me for my carelessness. I have learned an expensive lesson from this experience. If you get me out of this jam, I promise to be more careful. Wherever the money is, please surround it with angels."

Almost immediately, I felt the peace of God enter my heart and heard Him instruct me to go home.

As I drove down the street and turned into my driveway, I could see it — the grocery money! It was on my next-door neighbor's lawn next to our driveway.

The wind was high, and yet in four hours it hadn't blown away the money.

Do I believe in prayer? You bet I do. Did I learn a lesson? You bet I did. Do I believe in angels and miracles? Absolutely!

— Dr. Mary Edwards —

57

The Handkerchief

*The life of the dead is placed
in the memory of the living.*
~Cicero

I had never planned a funeral before, so when my mother died I was lost. But I did know one thing. Other than during her last few years, when strokes and Alzheimer's changed her, she never left the house without looking put together.

My mother was born in the early part of the twentieth century and there were rules among women of that age. Going downtown meant wearing a hat and carrying a handbag. A lady always carried a handkerchief. On many occasions, she would ask, before we left home, "Do you have a hancha?" Hancha was her own contraction for handkerchief. If I didn't have one, she would go to her drawer, which was always neatly arranged, and give me one. Although my mom could be bawdy with the best of them, her delicate side always showed in her manner of dress, her home décor and the white lace handkerchief she always carried when she was dressed up.

After her death, Daddy was in no condition to handle the details, and we had to get started with the funeral plans. I made arrangements for the funeral home to pick her up, and I went about finding an appropriate outfit to bury her in. She had lost so much weight, and I didn't want to buy anything new as there were so many clothes in the house. This would be her last show. She had to be perfect. I moved from closet to closet trying to find something pretty.

Something told me to look in the room where many of my clothes were stored. I saw a suit that belonged to me, but was now too small. Mama had seen the suit and admired it. It was formfitting and stylish. I searched through her jewelry box and found a pair of clip-on earrings that matched the suit. When I put the outfit together, I felt a sense of relief. I gathered her wig, underwear and shoes, feeling really good about what I had chosen.

When we went to the funeral home the next day, we chose the casket and made arrangements for cars and such. Daddy appeared dazed until he was asked what type of flowers he wanted for the family spray. "Red roses," he answered quietly.

The private family viewing would be the next day. My oldest sister, Jackie, would arrive in time to attend. Time seemed to move at a snail's pace for the next twenty-four hours.

Finally, it was time for the viewing. We walked into the front door of the funeral home, and I went to the desk to let them know the Smith family had arrived. Our funeral director, Pernella, greeted us and escorted us down a long hallway. Mama had been embalmed, and I was about to look at her. I like to think of myself as strong, and throughout Mama's last days, I had been able to approach her care with an almost clinical distance. But this moment I was about to experience was not something I had thought about. I was terrified.

Pernella put her hand on the doorknob and turned it slowly. It was as if she was approaching the room of a sleeping person, and she was being very careful not to wake her up. I fully expected her to say quietly, "Ms. Rosie, your folks are here to see you." Her gentleness made the moment of entry almost reverent. We walked in, and I saw Mama to the right.

She looked beautiful and Pernella had done a fantastic job of making her look "alive." She appeared to be in a deep, comfortable sleep. I looked at her from head to toe. As my eyes drifted down her body, I was caught off guard by what was neatly tucked inside her folded hands. There, spread open like a blooming lily whose petals had nearly reached their peak, was a white lace handkerchief.

"Pernella, where did this come from? I didn't bring it. How did you know?" I asked anxiously.

"Know what?" she answered, looking puzzled.

"How did you know that when my mama dressed up, she always carried a white lace handkerchief?"

She looked me in the eye and replied calmly, "Well, when I prepare someone, I always pray before." I smiled. Something or someone had inspired Pernella to put that white lace handkerchief in Mama's hands.

There will always be incidents that occur on this earth that rational thought cannot explain, and skeptics write off as coincidence. The phone rings, and it is someone we are thinking about at precisely that moment. We stumble upon a relative's picture and then realize it is the anniversary of their passing. I know occurrences like these can easily be written off as pure chance.

I believe that Mama wanted to make her exit the same way she made an entrance: dressed to the nines, well groomed, and carrying her white lace handkerchief. I had forgotten it; she remembered.

— Deborah J. Konrad —

58

Divinity on Seventh Street

Prayer is the principal means of opening oneself to the
power and love of God that is already there,
in the depths of reality.
~Bishop James Albert Pike

When I had abdominal pain and post-menopausal bleeding, I made an appointment with my gynecologist. Initial testing revealed that I had four neoplasms within my womb, a strong indication that I had endometrial cancer. Surgery was mandatory.

After I got the news I sat in the doctor's office stunned and fighting back the tears.

On my way home, I stopped at a local park with an expansive view of the Rocky Mountains. The reality of cancer totally engulfed me. I sobbed in the privacy of my car for a solid hour. Luckily, I was the only one in the parking lot.

After dinner, I told my husband. In the days that followed, we camped out on our laptops, researching the world of cancer.

While Joe worked in his office on the other side of town, I worried and prayed. Walking helps me calm down, so one morning I grabbed my wooden cane and embarked upon a stroll through my neighborhood. Little did I know I had a divine appointment to keep.

During my walk, I spotted a young man in the distance. I turned a corner and went on my merry way. Fifteen minutes later, I turned onto Seventh Street and the young man was walking directly toward me from the other end of the block. A friendly conversation started between us when we met. He introduced himself as Pablo.

Pablo noticed that I used a cane when I walked. He asked me if he could pray for me, and I told him about my potentially cancerous tumors. With my permission, we held hands while Pablo prayed earnestly for my restoration to good health. We prayed for ten minutes, and then I thanked him as we went our separate ways. That was the first and last time I ever saw Pablo.

Two months after my shocking doctor's visit, I was scheduled for surgery at our local hospital. Joe took the day off from work. We arrived at the hospital at 6:00 a.m. for an 8:00 a.m. procedure. I was at the precipice of receiving a frightening cancer diagnosis, but a profound sense of peace filled my soul.

Before I knew it, I woke up in the recovery room, and Joe was by my side. A half-hour later, the doctor appeared by my gurney with a surprised look upon his face. In his hand, he gripped my medical reports, which were complete with color photos. Joe and I braced ourselves.

The doctor dropped the bombshell that I was completely clean inside. The original report showed that I had four neoplasms within my womb; the doctor didn't find anything. He had the authentic images of his procedure to prove it. Eventually, all the laboratory tests were completely normal. Joe and I were astonished.

The best explanation that I could muster was that I encountered an angel on Seventh Street and the power of our joint prayer wrought this real-life miracle.

— Gail Walkowich —

59

The Day I Met an Angel

Through the eyes of gratitude, everything is a miracle.
~Mary Davis

I was a single mother of three in 1978, living through the recession. I lived close to my mother, so I didn't have to pay for childcare when the kids were out of school. I worked as a waitress for $1.05 an hour plus tips and managed to squeak out enough for the necessities, but as the recession worsened, so did my tips. I couldn't really blame the customers, but it sure made things tough.

Nonetheless, my faith kept me going. I knew that God had a plan, even if he hadn't let me in on it.

One morning in August, I sent the kids outside while I neatened up the house. I was thinking about the upcoming school year. They really needed clothes, especially my two boys, ages five and seven. My younger son, Dave, was wearing his brother's hand-me-downs, but they weren't new when his brother, Thomas, got them, and some of them were unusable now.

Suddenly, Thomas ran in to tell me that someone was outside waiting to talk to me. I wondered who it could be since we didn't get a lot of visitors. A new white Cadillac was parked in the street and a slim, twenty-something woman with blond hair was on our porch. I greeted her, and she asked if I would accept some boxes of clothing.

She explained that her son had recently outgrown them, and she was looking for somewhere to donate them when she saw my children playing in the yard. I agreed, figuring that if they were trash, I could just throw them away, but maybe I'd get a few things we could use. She brought in two big boxes of clothes. Before I could thank her or even get her name, she was gone.

We started looking through the boxes. None of the clothes looked worn — no holes, stains or evidence that any child had ever worn them. Everything was the size each boy needed. In the bottom of one box, we found three coats. The largest fit my daughter perfectly. It buttoned either way, so it could be worn by a boy or a girl. When my daughter put her hand in the coat pocket, her face lit up — she pulled out three silver dollars!

I will never know who this woman was or why she had two boxes of clothes that appeared to be brand-new and were perfect for my children. She may have just been a very kind and generous woman, but I will always believe she was an angel sent by God. Whether He sent her from heaven or from across town, I'll never know. Either way, she helped us when we needed it most.

— Jackie Eller —

Divine Messengers

I Met My Angel at Dog Point

And tonight I'll fall asleep with you in my heart.
~Author Unknown

The plan was to pack up my broken heart and my dog, Wally, and hit the road for a few months. We would live in my truck camper and explore those hidden places in the creases of the map that fuel the imagination and feed the soul. Twenty miles down a double track in the desert, or watching pronghorn antelope next to a lake in the grasslands, or sitting streamside in the cool shadows of the mountains, I would invite the opportunity to rediscover my rhythm with a sense of adventure and gratitude.

My sweet wife, Linda, had passed away only three months earlier at age fifty-seven from early-onset Alzheimer's. I had a few months to get my affairs in order and purge the vast majority of my physical possessions, including my business, home, furniture, clothing and anything else that wasn't pinned down. As someone who relishes the outdoors, I would seek solace and understanding where the quiet of wide-open spaces could provide the backdrop for my own transformative healing. I wanted more than anything to give birth to a newer, healthier version of myself with joy and contentment born from the perspective of what the last eight years as a caregiver had taught me.

One of my goals was to camp out on the North Rim of the Grand

Canyon. Linda and I had visited the crowded South Rim many times, but now I yearned to sit on the desolate cliffs on the far side of the Colorado River and let my legs dangle over the precipice, looking down on hawks and crows as they whistled and cackled below me. But after weeks of travel, it became clear that the constant moving was taking a heavy toll on Wally. He had already been through so much upheaval — the loss of my wife, and the dismantling of our home.

Wally was growing increasingly agitated and erratic in his behavior. I didn't have an exit strategy — my home being one of the things I had purged — so it wasn't like we could just drive back home and unwind. I had no idea how long we would be on the road; it could be months.

With Wally worsening, I came to the heartbreaking conclusion that if he didn't have stability soon, he wouldn't survive. I decided to detour to Kanab, Utah, which is home to the very special and respected Best Friends Animal Society, where they took in Wally with a truly heartening welcome. It would only be a matter of time before he could be with a family that would provide him with the stability he needed to find his own rhythm again.

In truth, Wally, who had crawled into Linda's lap at the dog shelter four years earlier, was more Linda's dog than mine, but I loved him dearly. I sat in the parking lot of the Animal Sanctuary for about an hour and wept fiercely, my shoulders heaving from the weight of the last eight years like a yoke that was trying to unshackle itself. I was chafing with the thought that Linda would be upset with me, and I implored her to show me somehow that she understood why I had to do this for Wally.

I drove on, feeling like I was swimming in a puddle of my own tears. From the Animal Sanctuary, it took a few hours to arrive at the North Rim of the Grand Canyon. I slept in the truck until morning before I could speak to a ranger about finding a remote place to camp alone.

The ranger station didn't open until 8:00, and I arrived a few minutes early to wait. It's important to note that until now, every ranger in every park I had visited had worn a nametag with a first name only. I had never seen a nametag with a full name. At 8:00 promptly, a middle-aged woman wearing a green National Park ranger uniform showed up to open the door where I was waiting. I looked at her soft and open face and noticed her nametag. It said Linda Davis. Not Linda, but Linda Davis. Stunned, I told her about my wife, also named Linda Davis, and how I was traveling the country looking for some solace.

This Linda Davis put her hands on my shoulders and looked into my eyes, and we both erupted in tears. She pulled me close and whispered in my ear that I was going to be okay, and she had the perfect spot for me to camp. Pulling out a park map, she directed me to a twelve-mile dirt road at the end of which I could camp on a promontory overlooking the canyon. I would, she assured, have the place to myself. I mentioned nothing to her of Wally, only of my desire to find a place to process my grief. She repeated that this spot was exactly what I was looking for.

Still disheartened from leaving Wally behind, and deeply troubled by the thought that my wife was upset with me for doing so, I began to drive up the dirt road to my little camping spot on the rim of the canyon. I arrived after an hour or so of slow, dirt-road driving. As I reached the promontory, I spotted a U.S. Forest Service sign that designated this place as Dog Point.

Linda Davis had sent me to Dog Point less than twelve hours after I asked her to forgive me for what I felt I had to do. I could feel nothing else but the recognition that my beautiful wife wanted me to know that she completely understood and was still behind me with the full measure of her heart. I felt a shift in the trajectory of my life that day. Linda had been my wife, and now she had become my angel. With that, my pilgrimage began to ease, as I felt the soft rhythm of my soul find a new cadence, and the dark corners began to fill with light.

—Dr. David Davis—

61

Divine Comfort

Where flowers bloom so does hope.
~Lady Bird Johnson

Cleaning, organizing and other last-minute preparations for my parents' arrival from out of state had distracted me from the cloud hanging over me. But the reality of my hurriedly scheduled surgery rushed back in when I thought about the tears my technician tried to hide during my ultrasound. She had been horrified by what she saw, and she knew what I was going to hear: incurable cancer.

As I vacuumed the hallway, I looked at the smiling faces of my grandsons, four-year-old Christopher and two-year-old Quinton, whose photos lined the walls. It was devastating to realize that my grandsons were too young to sustain any lasting memory of me.

I turned to modern technology. I set up our video recorder and tripod in the sunroom at the back of the house. Next, I spent close to an hour mentally rehearsing the words for what might become the only keepsake my precious grandchildren would have of me as they grew up. It had to be just right — not maudlin, but maybe not too cheery either. I wanted them to see me, to know me and how very much I loved them. I realized the biggest challenge might be to make sure no trace of my fear came through in the message. It was what a grandma should do, what I needed to do.

When I was as emotionally ready as I'd ever be, I prayed for the wisdom and composure to say the right words, and then headed toward my place in front of the camera. On the way, I noticed a toy within camera view. While stooping to move it, something outside caught my eye. Straightening up, I peered out the window and took a few steps closer for a better look. Just inside our tree-fringed back yard, a yellow star danced atop its stem as if nodding at me in the light breeze. The daylily hadn't been there the day before, nor the day before that. Frozen in place and staring at that flower, I realized I'd never seen one in our yard, or any other yard in the neighborhood during the two and a half years we'd lived there. While I was pondering this odd sight, a soft voice startled me.

"You don't have to do this," it declared. Unaccustomed to hearing voices other than mine while home alone, I looked around uneasily. No one was there.

Nerves, I thought, questioning whether I'd truly heard something or my trepidation had gotten the better of me.

The soothing voice repeated its simple proclamation. "You don't have to do this."

This time, the words flooded me with calm and the understanding that my guardian angel would be there to safely guide the surgical team and hold my hand. I took a few moments to embrace my release from fear and then shut down the camera, unscrewed it from the tripod, and put them both away. There was no longer any need to leave a message for my grandsons. I would be right here with them.

I am so blessed to have received that inexplicable message, followed by successful surgery. I cherish the time given me to enjoy those two grandsons, as well as the five additional grandchildren who arrived afterward.

In the eighteen years since that day, I still have never seen another daylily anywhere in our neighborhood. One might say that's a real mystery, but I know the truth. That star was an angel's virtual knock on my troubled soul to deliver her message.

— Barbara Bennett —

62

No! Don't Take It!

For he shall give his angels charge over thee, to keep
thee in all thy ways. They shall bear thee up in their
hands, lest thou dash thy foot against a stone.
~Psalm 91:11-12

I left the doctor's office, got in my car and cried. It was a cold November day, but I sat there with the engine off, too distressed to even remember to turn it on.

I'm not usually a complainer. When I go to a doctor, it's because I know there is a problem. The last time a doctor told me "nothing is wrong," I had cervical cancer. It cost me the opportunity to bear the children I so desperately wanted. Now, fourteen years later, living in a different town, I was severely sick.

I will never forget the conversation with the gynecologist. "How long have you been in Maine?" he asked. My southern accent made it obvious I wasn't from Maine.

"Three years," I responded.

"It must be stressful being away from your family," he said.

"Of course I miss them, but it isn't stressful."

He proceeded to tell me all my symptoms were due to stress. This medical doctor didn't know me. This was the first time we had met. He didn't know my ability to handle stress or even if my life had stress. With no further tests, he gave me a prescription for a drug to stop my bowel problems.

I went to the drugstore and got the prescription filled. At home, I got a glass of water, opened the prescription bottle and took out a pill. I had the pill at my lips when I heard a voice say, "No! Don't take it!"

I was home alone, but I turned to see who was talking to me with such authority. I saw no one and didn't recognize the voice, but I *had* heard a voice.

I put the pill back in the bottle, put the bottle in my purse and never took any. I sat in a chair to think and pray. I realized the pills might alleviate my symptoms, but they wouldn't solve the underlying problem.

The following four months I continued to lose weight. At times I was in such pain I couldn't stand up. One day, my husband Rick came into the store where I was the manager. I was sitting on a crate bent over in pain. There were no customers, and I had no idea where my employees were. I was "out of it" due to the pain. He helped me get up and walk to the car, then took me to the emergency room.

The emergency room physician examined me and felt something. He called in a gastroenterologist who said it was a tumor. He set me up for a CAT scan. Rick and I were to be at this doctor's office in a few days to get the results.

On my thirty-seventh birthday the doctor said, "You have cancer."

I looked at Rick. He looked frightened. I'd never seen him look like this. I reached out and took his hand. The doctor was a kind man. It was obvious by the look on his face he felt anguished about giving us this diagnosis. He told us I had a grapefruit-sized tumor. The doctor's assistant set appointments for me with radiation and chemotherapy oncologists.

Before we left, I showed the doctor the bottle of medicine prescribed by the gynecologist. He looked at the bottle, and a horrified look came across his face.

"If you had taken this, you would have died. Your waste is breaking down to liquid because it cannot get past the tumor. If you had taken this, the waste in your body would have built up and poisoned your entire system. It would have killed you!"

I hadn't known what was wrong with my body, but my guardian

angel did and demanded I not take the medicine. Hearing that voice with such authority and clarity saved my life.

—Sara Schafer—

63

The Unexpected Messenger

*Speak when you are angry, and you will make
the best speech you will ever regret.*
~Ambrose Bierce

On a brisk April morning, my husband and I were arguing in the living room. We seemed to do little else lately. I don't recall what started the whole thing, but I rambled on incessantly. My husband's face was a picture of sheer frustration.

Suddenly, I announced, "I'm getting out of here!"

"Go," Stan said, shrugging his broad shoulders. "Do whatever you want to do."

Still muttering, I stomped to the pantry, grabbed an old loaf of bread, stalked to the car, and drove to the duck pond twelve miles away.

This particular duck pond sits in the center of a cemetery. For some reason, the pond drew me during difficult times. *Maybe it will hold an answer today,* I thought.

A parade of ducks waddled to greet me. While I reached in the back seat for the things I'd brought, they nosed around my feet, searching for whatever treats they could find.

"Just old bread, you guys," I said, shooing them out of the way.

The entire flock trailed me to the small cement bench next to the pond. Hungrily, they eyed me as I unwrapped my meager offering. In minutes, the bread was gone.

As the ducks dispersed, I sat under the Texas pines thinking about the argument I'd walked out on. All my life, I'd heard that the seventh year of marriage was the toughest — the seven-year itch. I had to acknowledge that my marriage had tarnished over the years. The reasons varied, but my tendency to drone on when enough had been said didn't help matters. I always wanted to have the last word — at any cost.

Often, I vowed to be different, spending weeks with the words from Ecclesiastes 3:7 — "a time to keep silence, and a time to speak" — taped on my bathroom mirror. But before long, I'd find myself stuck in the same old rut: talking when silence was in order. Inwardly, I longed for change.

Watching the ducks in the pond, their reflections a kaleidoscope of colors, I had a thought. If only I could behold my own reflection, like the ducks in the water. If only I could see myself. Breathing a silent prayer, I asked God to let this miraculous thing happen.

While I prayed, I heard a car approach. The engine sputtered a time or two, and then died. Turning, I saw an elderly man emerging from an ancient, ramshackle Cadillac, with a peeling vinyl roof.

Tall and lean, the man moved briskly around the front of the car, swinging two loaves of white Wonder Bread in his hands. Quickly, he laid the bags of bread on the hood of the Cadillac, opened them and began flinging whole slices through the dazzling sun like tiny, white Frisbees.

"You come here often?" I called across the lawn.

He cupped a hand to one ear.

"Do you come here often?" I said, louder.

Tossing the final slices, he stuffed the plastic wrappers in a garbage bin and walked to where I sat.

"I'm sorry, ma'am," he said, squatting beside me. "I still didn't hear you."

"I just wanted to know if you come here often," I said, suddenly wishing I hadn't said anything.

"When the weather's nice and not too hot," he said. I found it unnerving that he didn't look directly into my eyes when he spoke, but stared curiously at my forehead.

With nothing better to do, we gazed across the pond while a cluster of ducks gathered at our feet, quacking so loudly that it was annoying. I considered jumping up and yelling, "Shhhh!"

I glanced at the old man. He smiled, but said nothing. I wished he would leave.

As if reading my mind, he sprang to his feet and said, "I gotta split." Then he pointed a bony finger at the noisy ducks and said in an irked voice, "You know, them crazy ducks just don't know when to hush."

With that declaration and a wave in my direction, the old man sauntered to his car, brought it to life and clanked off into the distance, a flurry of leaves chasing after him.

What did he say? Did he say those crazy ducks just don't know when to hush?

Suddenly, I recalled my earlier prayer — my desire to see myself. Had God sent that man as an answer to my prayer? Did I sound much like the quacking ducks?

I knew I did. And I had the strangest feeling that I had just entertained an angel.

A gust of wind whipped around my legs as I hurried to the car. The little ducks stood quiet now, like statues scattered across the ground, their silence speaking volumes to me.

When I arrived home, my husband lay sprawled on the couch looking worried. "Hi," he said, his voice even. "Where've you been?"

I hesitated. "I went to the cemetery."

"Cemetery!" He half-laughed. "Are you planning on killing me?"

"Nope," I said, planting a kiss on his puzzled face, "but I sure got some great pointers on keeping you alive and happy."

— Dayle Allen Shockley —

64

Go and Get It

*Angels are not merely forms of extraterrestrial
intelligence. They are forms of
extra-cosmic intelligence.*
~Mortimer J. Adler

I had two things left on my to-do list before returning to work after a two-week vacation. Lying in bed, I debated whether I should paint the accent wall in the family room or go for my scheduled mammogram. I really didn't want to do either, but both were long overdue. I rolled over to look at the clock, and then rolled back over and continued thinking about my dilemma. I settled for the painting and decided to reschedule my mammogram — for the third time.

I showered, dressed and went downstairs to fix my breakfast. "Well, good morning, Sleeping Beauty. What are you planning to do today?" my mother asked nonchalantly as she turned a page from the morning paper and slowly sipped her coffee.

"I thought I had settled it, but I'm still not sure if I want to paint and get that over with or go for my mammogram," I said. Standing in the pantry pushing cans and boxes of food aside while looking for the oatmeal, I heard a firm but soft-spoken voice say, "Go for your mammogram."

"No, I'm going to reschedule," I said loudly while being quite aggravated that I couldn't find the oatmeal.

"Don't put it off any longer!" I heard.

Stepping out of the pantry, I said, "Ma, why are you talking like that, and where is the oatmeal?"

Looking puzzled, my mother said, "What are you talking about? And the oatmeal is on the counter."

Later, pulling into a strip mall, I decided to stop in the gift shop next to the paint store to pick up some cards. While browsing, I observed a shelf stocked with statues of angels. One dressed in pink really caught my eye. As I reached up to get her down, a woman who was standing to my right said, "She's a beautiful breast-cancer angel."

Too busy examining the angel to look at the woman, I said, "Yes, she is. I collect angels, but she's a little pricey. I only stopped in to pick up some cards, and I have to go next door to get some paint."

Putting the angel back on the shelf, I stopped short as a sharp pain ran from my shoulder down my arm. The woman came around to my left side and placed her hand gently on my shoulder. I wanted to step away from her, but I couldn't. I wanted to say, "Hey, lady, don't touch me," but I couldn't. In that split second, I only felt calm, peace and a warmth that seemed to cover my left side. Then she said firmly, "Honey, get the angel and your mammogram. You'll be fine." Then she turned quickly and walked away.

It all happened so fast and unexpectedly that I was stunned. I stood for a minute before walking around the small store looking for her. I wanted to ask her how she knew I needed to go for a mammogram. And why did I feel a wave of warmth when she touched me?

I had questions, but she was nowhere to be found. On the one hand, I was surprised, but on the other hand, I wasn't. I knew I needed to take her advice.

Walking over to pick out my cards, I couldn't stop thinking about the strange lady. Her voice sounded like my mother's voice earlier that day — but had it been my mother's? As for the warmth, maybe I had a one-sided hot flash. My mind tried to explain the unexplainable.

I walked back over to the shelf of angels. I reached up and took down the one dressed in pink. I had to buy her, and then I had to get over to the hospital to get my mammogram. Painting the wall could wait.

After the mammogram, a sonogram and a biopsy, I was scheduled for surgery a week later. The diagnosis was Stage II Ductal Carcinoma Breast Cancer. The tumor was so far back in my breast that it was impossible to see or feel, but that explained the sporadic pain in my shoulder and arm. For several days, all I could do was cry, pray and be thankful that I had listened to the voice and that strange lady.

The chemotherapy was ruthless. I lost my appetite, weight and hair. I became dehydrated, anemic and nauseous. I was in and out of the hospital on a regular basis for one thing or another. I became tired of being sick and tired, but I never gave up hope. The image of my beautiful breast-cancer angel and that strange lady's three little words, "You'll be fine," were constant reminders that I would be.

I have believed in angels since I was in parochial school, thanks to my third-grade teacher, Sister Maria, who always quoted Psalm 91:11: "For He shall give His angels charge over thee." She taught us that we all have guardian angels to help protect, lead and guide us in the way we should go. I never forgot her strong belief in angels and angelic activity. However, as I grew older, the childlike faith I had in them waned even though I collected angels and have them in every room of my home. Nevertheless, I did feel that I might have experienced their divine intervention and protection several times in my life.

Now, I have no choice but to believe. Had I not heard that voice or met that woman, I probably wouldn't have gotten my mammogram in time.

I was declared cancer-free nine years ago. As much as I loved my beautiful breast-cancer angel, I gave her to another breast-cancer patient with hope that she would believe in angels, have faith in their divine intervention, and someday hear the voice of her own guardian angel, the way I heard the voice of mine.

— Francine L. Billingslea —

A Dream Come True

Faith is not only daring to believe;
it is also daring to act.
~Wilfred Peterson

My husband and I dated in the early 1950s while he attended California Open Bible Institute on his way to becoming a pastor. During the nearly sixty-two years of our marriage, which included fifty years of full-time ministry, we witnessed and were amazed by the many and varied ways that God works in the lives of people every day.

My husband's family was no stranger to miraculous interventions. As soon as I was introduced to some of his extended family, I learned the inspiring story of my husband-to-be's grandmother, Elizabeth Jane (Robb) Douglas, and how her simple faith was rewarded in a spectacular way through an angelic visitor. That visitation transformed the lives of the Douglas family for many generations to come.

Sixteen years before the 19th Amendment to the United States Constitution awarded American women the right to vote, forty-six-year-old Elizabeth Douglas was about to create one of the longest-lived election-related patents in history: the collapsible voting booth. This unique invention would also launch a manufacturing company that would be owned and operated by the Douglas family for 105 years.

It all began at Grace Methodist Church in the small town of Crete, Nebraska, in 1904. Dr. Albert Shelton, a visiting missionary on furlough from his mission assignment in the Far East, made a plea for donations in order to build a fifty-bed hospital in a remote area of Tibet. Elizabeth Douglas was moved by his request and greatly desired to share in this effort, which she felt sure was directed by God. When she stood and made a faith pledge of $20,000, she imagined that the eyebrows of some in the sanctuary that day might have been lifted in astonishment, but no one was more surprised than she. This was an incredibly large amount of money. (Today's equivalent figure would be greater than a half-million dollars!) Elizabeth and her husband had both been schoolteachers, and she had no idea where she could possibly come up with such a huge sum.

Elizabeth knew it would take a miracle to fulfill the pledge. But she had felt a burning compassion in her heart for the people in Tibet who needed a hospital in their area.

Reflecting on the events of the day as she drifted off to sleep that night, she had a very vivid dream in which she saw a man with a long, white beard and heard him say: "Make what I show you, and you will have the money to pay your pledge and much more." She was careful to memorize everything he showed her in the dream, and with a piece of cardboard and pins, she made an exact replica of the invention in the morning when she awoke.

Elizabeth asked their two sons, Bill and Bob, to make a prototype of the unique voting booth she had created using metal and canvas. Thus, the first collapsible voting booth was fashioned. A patent for the Douglas Collapsible Voting Booth was granted in 1906, and the Douglas Manufacturing Company was born.

Although production started immediately, marketing proved difficult and only produced a few sales in their home state. Soon, a decision was made to take their product to the largest voting district in California, the County of Los Angeles.

After the presentation at a city council meeting, and a few questions answered regarding the cost, delivery date, and state and local voting regulations, an order was placed to provide booths in all the voting precincts. The resulting $40,000 sale was paid in full to Douglas Manufacturing in silver.

Elizabeth's compassion for the needs of Tibet, her pledge of a tremendous amount of money, a miraculous vision by what she guessed had been a ministering angel, and her ability to act on that vision had resulted in one sale that was double the amount that she had pledged!

Of course, the story does not end there. As the bearded man had told her, her pledge would be paid, and there would be much more.

The Douglas Manufacturing Company was the oldest producer of election equipment in the country. It is astonishing to think that fourteen years before women were granted the right to vote, a woman with a vision established an election supply company. The company she had formed went on to produce not only voting booths but ballot boxes, election signs, media storage and flash-drive containers over the next 100 years.

On December 30, 2015, Douglas Manufacturing Company closed its doors for good. Roger Douglas (Elizabeth Douglas's great-grandson) noted: "We had very good loyal employees that were here for a long time." He said his wife's involvement in the company continued their long history of female management and concluded, "The company has been dominated by very capable women for over one hundred and five years. It's been a great run. It's history."

I learned so many valuable lessons from this inspiring true story of American success and ingenuity. Grandma Douglas didn't need the "right to vote" in order to create a product that would help people exercise their right to vote. She didn't need a large bank account in order to help people halfway across the globe when she heard of their plight. However, she did need the faith to believe that God is willing and able to use her as part of His plan to bring good to the world. Although Douglas Manufacturing Company has closed its doors, the story of Grandma Douglas's simple faith and willingness to follow God's direction in spite of unusual circumstances continues to inspire us all to this day.

— Ruth Douglas —

66

An Angel's Whisper

Believe in miracles. I have seen so many of them come
when every other indication would say that hope
was lost. Hope is never lost.
~Jeffrey R. Holland

We had lost our house in California. Therefore, my wife, four young daughters, and I packed up and moved to Texas, hoping our family there could help us. We rented a four-bedroom house that we shared with one of my wife's sisters and her family. It was very tight living, but it was what we could afford.

I found a job right away, but it was only part-time. There weren't any full-time positions available for me. My wife was only able to find a part-time job as well. We were struggling, but we had to keep it together for the girls. Every night, I prayed to God and the angels for guidance. I needed something with benefits to support my family.

Months passed with no success in finding a stable job. I'd had various interviews that went well, but as soon as I had bought the uniform and shoes necessary for the job, I would receive a call or show up to the workplace and be told, "I'm sorry, the job was canceled at the last minute," or "The position was dropped." It broke my heart every time. Regardless, I continued with my prayers every night, always asking for help in getting work.

Soon, my youngest daughter's Head Start graduation was approaching. During my nightly prayer, I thanked God for Cynthia's first year of school. She had learned so much and made many friends. Once again, I asked for direction on where to look for work and was thankful for the small income I had for my family.

The next day, my wife, mother-in-law and I went to my daughter's graduation. It was wonderful seeing her smiling face among all the other children. After the ceremony, Cynthia pleaded, "Daddy, please. It's my graduation. I want McDonald's. Can we go?"

"Of course, sweetie," I said. I was just glad I could afford it.

We had just picked up the food we ordered and were heading to a table when Cynthia ran up to a boy who looked about her age. He was dressed nicely in khaki pants and a green polo shirt.

"Hi, Pablo," she told him. She looked at me and yelled, "He's my friend! From school!"

Standing next to the little boy was his father, a tall, strong-looking man. He smiled at me while extending a hand.

"Nice to meet you," he said. "I'm Pablo, Junior's father. Why don't you come join us at our table?"

My wife responded quickly, "That'd be nice. I'm Maria. This is my husband, Sergio, and my mom." She was always more outgoing than I was. Usually, I sit back and let her do most of the talking.

We sat at a table near the play area inside to keep an eye on the kids, and Cynthia and little Pablo rushed off to play. Honestly, I don't remember much of the conversation. My wife did most of the talking. All I could think about was where else I could apply for work. Again, I sent a silent prayer toward heaven asking God to help me find something stable. I didn't know how much longer I could last in my current job. I tried to focus on the conversation that was going on, but then my wife and mother-in-law stood and excused themselves.

As I watched them walk away, I heard a whisper in my right ear. "This man can give you work." Immediately, I turned to try to identify the speaker, but I saw no one. I thought I had imagined it, so I simply shrugged it off.

Louder, I heard again, "This man can give you work." I didn't even try looking for someone this time. I said to myself, *All right, God or the angels, if this is you, I'll listen to your advice.* I looked at Pablo and asked casually, "So what work do you do?"

Strangely, he replied, "Are you looking for a job?" He dug into his pocket and pulled out a business card. "Here's my card. Go to the company and fill out an application there."

"Thank you," was all I was able to say. He offered it so effortlessly that I was surprised. I had struggled so much, and now this man was offering me something I desperately needed.

My wife and mother-in-law came back and sat down again.

"Well, Junior and I need to get going," Pablo said as he stood up. "It was very nice to meet you." He shook everyone's hands. "Let me know if there's anything you need," he told me as he went to fetch his son from the play area. Then they both walked out the door.

We left McDonald's not long afterward. I took my family home and decided to pursue this job opportunity. I slipped into more business-like attire and drove to the address on Pablo's card. I had no idea what this job would offer. He never even mentioned what his work was, and I didn't think to ask at the time. I walked into the building and asked if I could apply for any job they had. The secretary mentioned that there weren't any openings at that time. I couldn't believe it. How could this be happening again? I walked out and decided to call Pablo to thank him for trying to help.

As soon as he picked up, I let him know who I was and that they weren't hiring, but thanks anyway. He told me to wait a few minutes and hung up. Not even two minutes later, he called back.

"Go inside and tell them your name. There's an application waiting for you," he said.

I went back inside the building and did as he said. I filled out my application and was hired on the spot. It was so surreal. Excited, I drove home and explained everything to my wife, even about the whisper in my ear. We felt so blessed that we both prayed together that night to give thanks.

Fifteen years have passed since that day, and I am still working at the place I was guided to by God and the angels. I have even been promoted in the company as an assistant to the engineers. Because of this job, I was able to support my family and find us a better place to call home. Today, I continue to pray every night, and I never forget to thank God for all my blessings.

— Sergio Jauregui —

67

Someday

A ministering angel shall my sister be.
~William Shakespeare

Steam hissed as I ironed a blouse for work the next day. I pushed the iron back and forth, back and forth, while I thought about my sister. She had died unexpectedly of complications from surgery several weeks earlier, and I was staying with my mother because I didn't want to be alone.

We were only fifteen months apart. Rosemary had been my playmate, confidante, guardian, and bossy big sister. Blinking back tears, I continued to push the iron back and forth, immersed in a flood of childhood memories.

I had always believed in an afterlife, but I had never lost anyone close to me. "I want to believe that we'll be together again, Rosemary," I whispered, "but will we really? How can I be sure?"

I felt a tug in my heart, as if someone was urging, "Put down that iron. Come over here." Dismissing the silent voice as a silly fantasy, I continued to glide the iron.

"Stop. Put down that iron and come over here," the voice insisted.

Shrugging, I turned the iron on its end and walked over to "here" — Mom's sewing machine. A pile of bills and papers lay atop the maple cabinet. Lifting the pile uncovered a small, black, leather-bound book. *What's this?* I wondered.

I picked up the book and stared at the title, *My Way of Life* by Saint Thomas Aquinas. Opening the cover, I found a small, typewritten label taped inside: "Sr. Mary Lenore." Early in her life, my sister had been in the convent and had taken my name.

Curious, I pulled the thin, green-silk marker, and it opened on page 600, "The End and the Beginning." As I skimmed a couple of paragraphs, the last sentence on the page caught my eye. I read the sentence again, blinked, and then read it a third time: "They (saints) will live in the company of their loved ones, their relatives and friends, who have also died in Christ and in the grace of God."

That little, black book now sits on my nightstand, still marked at page 600, with that sentence underlined. When I am thinking of loved ones who have gone before, I often pick up the book, read the quote and smile, remembering.

Whether my heart's whisper that day was from my sister or my guardian angel, I'm not sure. What I do know, though, is that the whisper came from someone in heaven to reassure me that Rosemary and I will someday live and laugh together again.

— Lenore Petruso —

Heeding the Angel

We shall find peace. We shall hear angels. We shall see
the sky sparkling with diamonds.
~Anton Chekhov

The grumpy old man in Room 1143 — that's how most people described Mr. Wolfe. He was wheelchair-bound from a stroke. His deeply wrinkled face was painted with a permanent scowl buried beneath a messy gray beard. His dull, blue eyes squinted through thick lenses. When he wasn't complaining, he was grumbling. According to his chart, he had no family or church affiliation. No friends came to visit, and his contact person was listed as the nursing home.

When staff offered a cheerful "good morning," his response was always the same: "What's so good about it?" If we wished him sweet dreams at bedtime, his response was always the same: "Never have 'em."

Eventually, we got used to Mr. Wolfe. He would venture out of his room on occasion, but only so he could find more things to complain about. I would often hear him say, "My food's cold; the pudding's runny; my coffee's too hot; it's drafty in here; the sun's too bright; the music's too loud." Mr. Wolfe wasn't a mean-spirited person; he was just miserable, but we didn't know why.

Mr. Wolfe's medical chart offered very few clues. When volunteers tried to engage him in conversation, or the recreational staff tried to enlist him in an activity, he would grunt and dismiss them with a wave of his hand. He was essentially an enigma, and obviously wanted to stay that way. We respected his privacy, accepting his predictable moans, groans and daily complaints. Loving Mr. Wolfe was a challenge, but he became very endearing to many of us who cared for him. Maybe some of us saw a little bit of ourselves in Mr. Wolfe, or maybe it was empathy. But not even a brightly lit Christmas tree or a hug from a staff member would bring a smile to his face.

Early one morning during nursing rounds, I overheard one of the nursing assistants call out a cheery "good morning" to Mr. Wolfe. I smiled in anticipation, expecting to hear his usual reply, but to my surprise he replied with a cheerful "good morning." I was a little startled, not sure what I had heard. It didn't take long for the nursing assistant to come hastily out of his room with a surprised expression.

His behavior that day continued to be curious. He wheeled himself up and down the hallway, patting people on the back and apologizing or offering words of comfort. He told the nurses how pretty they looked and even told the cafeteria staff that the food was excellent. He said "good day" and "goodbye" to people coming and going, and he wore a smile for the first time. He had even allowed the nursing assistant to shave his beard. He had a nice face, and his blue eyes popped with excitement. It was an amazing transformation.

He told the nursing assistant and a few other people that he had had a visit from an angel during the night. The angel had told him that today would be his last day on Earth and he should get things in order. It became the topic of discussion throughout the day. Some people said he was too mean and grumpy to be visited by an angel. Other people surmised, like me, that it was a dream or maybe a shadow he saw from the moonlight flickering when the window blinds swayed. Some said it was early dementia, but most of the staff laughed, stating that tomorrow he would be back to his same old grumpy self. But today he was smiling. It was the first time we had seen his face light up with contentment and peace. I was hoping that he would stay pleasant and agreeable in the days to follow.

The next morning was typical at the nursing home. Staff rushed from one room to the next getting residents up for breakfast and passing out medications. Everyone had forgotten about Mr. Wolfe's prediction the day before. When the nursing assistant walked into Mr. Wolfe's room, she offered a pleasant greeting, expecting to hear his usual grouchy response. However, sometime during the night, Mr. Wolfe had passed away peacefully in his sleep. He was right. He told us that the previous day would be his last on Earth, and it was. How did he know? Did a celestial being, a divine messenger, actually come and tell him that he was going to die the next day?

Whatever occurred, I was grateful for Mr. Wolfe's angel. I had the blessing of sharing his last day with him, to see him smile and know he was going to be happy in his next life. His angel encounter wasn't just for him; it was for me as well.

— Dana D. Sterner, RN —

And the Angels Sang

Music is well said to be the speech of angels.
~Thomas Carlyle

When my best friend's father was admitted to hospice, we knew he didn't have much time left. I offered to babysit when the time came for her to say goodbye. After I hung up with her, I settled in to go to sleep. I heard a low, melodic sound. As I tossed and turned, the sound grew louder, and I realized it was a choir of voices singing.

As I strained to hear the voices, I discovered I could hear each separate voice if I concentrated on the words they were singing. If I shifted my focus to a different voice, I would hear again the words and music for the song they were singing. Each angel was singing its own song, different words and different music. But when I focused back on the choir as a whole, the mixture of songs and music was the most beautiful sound I had ever heard. I couldn't understand how so many different songs and words could become such a beautiful chorus when they came together as one.

Finally, my husband asked why I couldn't stop tossing and turning. I told him he'd think I was crazy if I told him why I was still awake. I explained I was unable to go to sleep because the angels were singing too loudly. I'm not sure he believed me.

I lay quietly and listened to the beautiful song. I felt a peace come over me, and my fear turned to admiration. I also felt deeply that my friend was about to call and ask me to stay with her kids while she said goodbye to her father.

When the phone rang, I picked it up and quietly said, "I'll be there in a few minutes."

The next day, my friend asked me how I knew she would be calling. She said she could tell by my voice that I had been waiting for the phone to ring, and I hadn't seemed surprised.

I smiled and explained that I had heard the angels singing and knew they were welcoming him home. Like my husband, I'm not sure she believed me, but she accepted my explanation.

When my mother was dying, I arrived at her room at the nursing home to wait for my sister. Mom's breathing was shallow, and she was not awake. I was afraid she would pass before my sister arrived.

Once my sister was there, we asked the nurses to provide care to reduce Mom's breathing difficulties and ease her pain. To our surprise, Mom rallied and woke from her deep sleep. She asked us to play music for her. Our mother and father both loved music, a gift they shared with all of us.

We put her favorite country gospel CD in the player, and as she started to sing along with her favorite song, we joined her. As our voices blended together, the room grew brighter, and we could hear many more voices joining ours. When the songs were done, she grew quiet and went back to a deep sleep. She rested peacefully and didn't awaken again.

Several hours later, she passed away quietly. The next day, we gathered together to make decisions on scriptures and music for the funeral. My sister, who had spent Mom's last day with me, asked, "When we were singing with Mom yesterday, we weren't alone, were we? Several other voices were singing with us. It sounded like a choir."

I smiled and said, "No, we weren't alone. We got to sing with the angels. They came to help us sing her home."

I've heard the angels a few other times since then. I'm no longer frightened when I hear them. I choose to say a prayer, asking for comfort for whomever they are singing home. I ask for peace for their families. And I always thank God for giving me the gift of his angel choir. I listen to their song, and I feel a deep inner peace in my heart and an abundance of unconditional love. I know that when my own time comes to leave this world, the angels will come to sing me home, too.

— Sheryl Hutchinson —

**Chapter
8**

Miracles
Happen

70

Faithful Fingers

*The miracle of self-healing occurs when the inner
patient yields to the inner physician.*
~Vernon Howard

I held my hand in front of my face and stared in disbelief at the damage I had done. Mindlessly, I had reached for my hot curling iron and wrapped my fingers around the heated part. In the split second in which this happened, I realized that it would land in the sink full of water if I dropped it. So, in that additional split second of contact, my fingers turned bright red, and my arm began to throb.

Gasping with pain, I considered going to an urgent-care facility near my home. This accident had occurred because I was running late for church. I had slipped into a sweater and slacks, put on a dab of lipstick, and thought I could quickly put a couple of curls in my limp hair.

Perhaps I was in shock, but as I held my lobster-red hand in front of me, I decided not to go to urgent care. I wanted to be in church. I felt compelled to go as though pushed by something beyond my control. I covered my aching fingers with large Band-Aids, took some ibuprofen, and drove to church, elevating my right hand to alleviate the pain. It didn't help.

At church, I slipped into the last pew, cradled my hand under my jacket, and tried to focus on the hymn, prayers, and Psalm reading without success. Then the Gospel reading grabbed my attention. It was my favorite story — about the woman who had been suffering for twelve years. She believed that if she could only touch the hem of Jesus's garment, she would be healed. When she reached out, "Jesus realized that power had gone out from him" (Mark 5:30), and healed her.

Whenever I hear this story, I am awestruck by so many elements of it. I identify with the woman, and through times of pain, I have drawn upon the inspiration of her faith. On that Sunday morning, I was drawn back into the story once again and found myself drifting away from my pain.

When I left church, I noticed that my arm wasn't throbbing anymore, and I gave a silent prayer of thanks. In my car, I looked at the five Band-Aids cushioning my burned fingers and wondered what to do next. Get medical attention? Wait for the blisters to come? I'm right-handed, and it was going to be difficult to do daily tasks with all my fingers essentially useless. I fussed at myself about being so foolish as to grab the curling iron in the first place.

I decided to take a look and gingerly removed the Band-Aid on my thumb. There was nothing to see, and I assumed it had been the least burned. But as I unwrapped each finger, I was astonished to see no indication of injuries! I flexed my fingers. No pain. I touched each finger one by one with my other hand. No blisters. No redness. It seemed impossible, but I knew from previous little burns on the stove that the blisters might come much later. That didn't happen, and as the days went by, there was no sign of injury at all.

I was healed. I don't know how my burned fingers had healed completely in an hour at church. It remains a mystery, but I think my complete absorption in the story of the woman who believed so strongly is perhaps an explanation for the unexplainable. For a little while, I became that woman, and we were both healed.

— Caroline S. McKinney —

71

The Invisible Life Saver

I think miracles exist in part as gifts and in part as
clues that there is something beyond
the flat world we see.
~Peggy Noonan

My fiancé Raymond was driving my SUV down the interstate highway at the speed limit when our right front wheel fell off. It flew high up into the air, and then bounced somewhere into a deep canyon on the right side of the narrow mountain road. Our Ford Explorer was headed for the dangerous sharp left curve ahead.

Sparks flew as we careened out of control. Raymond and I looked at each other, thinking we were doomed.

Then, everything seemed to move in slow motion. Somehow, our vehicle was lifted up miraculously and then set down gently exactly in a one-car-length parking space on the otherwise shoulder-less mountain road. We came to a peaceful, silent halt. We sat there looking at each other in shock.

How did we go from sure death to a safe stop?

We gathered ourselves and prayed together. "Thank you, God, for saving us. Now, can you please find our tire?"

The canyon must have been fifty feet deep with nothing but huge, immovable rocks as far as the eye could see. It was an amazing view, but a very difficult hike.

How on earth would we get our lost wheel back in this rocky mountain canyon? I told Raymond I would pray for direction. "Dear God, please help him find our wheel," I pleaded. Even if he did find it, which seemed impossible, how would he get it back to the car? He wouldn't be able to roll it up that steep incline covered with jagged rocks.

I prayed as Raymond climbed down the steep slope, walked about thirty yards, and went directly to the runaway wheel behind a giant boulder. Raymond hoisted it up on his wide shoulders and carried it back. I was dumbfounded. The wheel was not at all visible from where we had been standing on the highway. Yet he walked right to it. Our prayers had been answered.

Raymond was an auto mechanic, so he quickly removed one lug nut from each of the remaining three wheels and used them to secure the fourth wheel onto the front of our car. Then we continued our long drive to Phoenix to visit my beloved daughter, grateful for the help we received. We even arrived on time.

— Carolyn Jaynes —

72

The Angels Are a Little Deaf

Miracles come in moments. Be ready and willing.
~Dr. Wayne Dyer

I plunged my hands into my suitcase, searching the pockets of all my clothes for my wallet and passport. Then I realized I had left them in a taxi the night before. In the lobby of a boutique hotel in Italy near Lake Maggiore, sitting on a rose-colored sofa surrounded by majestic mountain views, I was on the verge of a panic attack.

At that moment, Adrianna, the conference organizer for the business event I was attending, approached me and asked if everything was all right. I let out a long huff of air and told her I had lost my wallet and passport. I was due to catch a flight back to the States in about four hours.

She joined me on the sofa. Using her phone, she contacted the taxi company. To nobody's surprise, no American passport and wallet had been turned in. I could feel panic creeping back in when she grabbed my hand and looked me in the eyes.

She told me there was a solution. She instructed me to repeat an angel prayer after her. We had to be loud, she explained, because the angels are a little deaf. The disbelief must have been etched all over my face because Adrianna started laughing. However, she reassured me she was not joking. I only knew her as a no-nonsense businesswoman, and here she was praying to deaf angels. Then again, I was in no place to argue with the one person who had appeared out of nowhere to help me.

We sat up straight, and with her hand over her solar plexus, she belted out an angel prayer in Italian. The entire lobby of people stopped dead in their tracks and looked at us. Then I repeated the prayer as best I could in my broken Italian, which was met with giggles.

Imagining angels with horns in their ears listening to me beg for help in Italian made me laugh and lifted my mood. Adrianna explained that we needed to go the police station to file a report so I could submit it to the consulate for a temporary passport. After the police station, she arranged for a taxi to take me directly to the American Consulate in Milan.

My heart swelled with gratitude until I saw the driver. He must have been eighty-six years old and stood barely five feet tall. His head was engulfed by both a newsboy cap and a large, push-broom moustache. I reminded Adrianna that I needed to get to Milan fast, and I wasn't sure this was the solution. We'd be going through steep mountain terrain. She laughed again, assuring me that Mario was the best.

He guided me to his tiny Fiat Panda hatchback. After stuffing myself into the back, he told me not to worry about anything because we had angels with us. I froze. Had he spoken to Adrianna? Did he know about our angel prayer?

To my utter shock, Mario drove like lightning. The car seemed to be locked onto the ground as we glided through the mountain roads. He shared with me that he had spent his whole life in these mountains and hills and knew them like they were family. He knew all the shortcuts. This was another huge gift, as we arrived in Milan early.

My head began to spin when I saw the large crowd of people surrounding the Consulate entrance. I thought of Adrianna, placed my hand on my heart and said, "Angels, please help me. I need to get home."

Mario turned and said, "Tell everyone you are American, and they will let you pass."

I followed his advice and was surprised to find the chaotic jumble of people clearing a path for me to go inside. Not only that, but the prayer seemed to work in even better ways by expediting the process for getting a passport and replacement credit cards in a matter of a few hours. The only remaining obstacle was getting a new flight. I had missed my original one and was on standby for the next day.

The following morning, I reached the airport and found the ticketing area crowded with at least two hundred people. Then I heard a woman's voice over my shoulder calling for me, "Hello! Excuse me, sir. I can help you."

I turned to see a young woman standing behind the ticket counter with a radiant smile. Apparently, she had just arrived, and I was the first person she saw. Quickly, I hurried over, giving her my old itinerary. I explained I was on standby and would be grateful for any help. I remember saying, "I would even sit in the lavatory if that was an option." We both laughed, and she assured me it would not come to that.

She began to type furiously on her keyboard, all the while keeping her smile. I explained what had happened, and she nodded with empathy. She had lost her passport only six months earlier, and it had been filled with exotic travel stamps from locales like Mozambique and Bhutan.

"I'm sorry, Mr. Guard, but it appears that every single flight back to New York is booked," she said, pausing before clacking the keyboard again.

"Wait," she said, looking at me with her radiant smile. "I found you a ticket that will take you to Paris and then to New York."

I let out a chuckle. Maybe there was something to Adrianna's angel prayer after all. Without knowing about the prayer, the agent then said, "When I lost my passport, I learned that we all have an army of angels waiting to help us. All we have to do is ask."

Her words left me frozen. I could feel my stomach tingling and a pulse of electricity zipping through my spine. This was the third person who had said as much about angels, and it made me think about how horrible this process could have been. Instead, I had been blessed with good luck at every turn. But there was more to come.

She handed me the new tickets and advised me to hurry. Then she apologized for not being able to get me the same kind of seat. That confused me. I was in economy and thought she meant there were no aisle seats available. I was grateful to have any seat. Then I looked at the ticket: She had booked me in First Class. I had never flown in First Class. I looked up at her and thanked her quickly, feeling my eyes well up with tears of gratitude. She said simply, "Angels are with you, Mr. Guard."

I laughed, adding, "And they can hear me."

— Jeffrey Guard —

73

A New Start

The Lord is my strength and my song;
he has given me victory.
~Exodus 15:2

My world was full of adventures, and very little could slow me down. That is why I didn't think twice when I felt I might be coming down with a cold.

As the morning hours passed, the symptoms worsened. I tried extra coffee to no avail.

Around noon, my friend popped in with lunch. She discovered me slouched over on the kitchen table, barely able to speak. In a panic, she called 911. I remained unconscious for days with my husband by my side. Eventually, doctors determined I had a serious case of myocarditis, an inflammation of the heart muscle that can lead to heart failure. I spent twenty-one days in intensive care fighting for my life, heavily sedated and hooked up to multiple machines.

Weeks went by before I started to respond to treatment. My care team was amazed by what they saw as my determination and positive spirit. However, I believed that something else was at play. I tried to explain that I had a sense that something greater than us was making its presence known in my hospital room. I felt a powerful sense of connection. It added a lightness to the room that was more spiritually felt than physically seen. I knew that presence was there for a reason, seeing me through those days in the hospital.

Adjusting to life with heart failure included slowing down and giving up many things I enjoyed. I began educating myself and making lifestyle changes to support a healthy heart, but healing continued to elude me.

Two years later, I sat quietly in my doctor's office waiting for test results. When he walked into the room, I began to quiver because his face said it all. I was in end-stage heart failure. He started to discuss options, but when I heard the words "heart transplant," the room went cold and dark. It was not an easy decision. I considered the quality of life that awaited me. Following the complex surgery, I would need to deal with things like being immune-suppressed and taking a lot of medications for the rest of my life. Although a heart transplant is not a cure, it was the best option if I wanted to see my two little girls grow up. The following day, I was referred to the cardiac transplant center at Duke University in Durham, North Carolina.

As days turned into weeks, I waited patiently for an appointment. As I worked hard not to fall into a pit of hopelessness, I got on my knees and prayed. "Lord, I am listening. Please talk to me. Help me. Give me a sign. I know you have a plan that is not fully known to me. I am trying to have patience, but I just need something, anything, to know you hear me."

Later that day I was at a store and something caught my eye on a display of pumpkins. It was a shiny, silver-painted rock. I couldn't help but think I was supposed to pick it up. A message was painted on it: "When you are down to nothing, God is up to something." I gasped and nearly fell over with astonishment. It was my sign! God had heard me. I looked around, and not a soul was in sight. The next day, the transplant clinic contacted me to set up an appointment.

After completing a weeklong transplant evaluation process, we received the news that another prayer had been answered. I was put on the heart-transplant list. Now the potentially long wait for a matching donor heart began, but my condition deteriorated quickly as the weeks passed. I struggled to do simple tasks. Some days, I could not get out of bed. My heart needed more support to keep beating, so the decision was made to admit me into the hospital and have me wait there.

My husband and I arrived in Durham the night before my scheduled admission. While finishing dinner, I collapsed. I already had a defibrillator implanted, but it had never gone off before then. As my husband called 911, my defibrillator continued to go off repeatedly, delivering forty shocks in forty minutes. I arrived at Duke University Hospital screaming in horrific pain as my defibrillator continued to send shock waves through my body. I believed I was going to die, and I thought about my family going on without me. The trauma room was filled with medical personnel feverishly trying to stabilize me as the sedatives began to take effect. I woke up the next day back in intensive care.

Four days later, settled in to wait for a donor, my transplant coordinator shared the news a heart had become available. I was overcome with emotion. As I waited through a long and restless night for the surgical team to arrive with the heart, I said a quiet prayer for the donor family and the donor. I could not imagine what they were going through, and I was grateful to all of them. Before entering the operating room, I kissed my husband and then raised my fist in the air and sang out, "I got this!" Three other lives were saved that night by my donor, my hero. My prayers had been answered.

Slowly, life came back together, although it would never be the same. There were new norms to adjust to, but I was alive. I dreamed about all the things I would be able to do and started to make plans again. I held tighter to the belief that we can get through anything, especially with faith by our side. With my strong, beating heart, I had a new start.

—Renee C. Houghton—

74

A Divine Bug

Never drive faster than your guardian angel can fly.
~Author Unknown

A native Coloradoan, I had been driving in treacherous weather conditions ever since I got my license at age sixteen. By the time I was twenty-eight, I had made the long trip, 250 miles each way, between Denver and my hometown on Colorado's Western Slope at least fifty times. Though I had moved to attend college in the Mile High City years earlier, my parents and my Poodle, Sage, were still back in Grand Junction, and I took every opportunity to return for a visit.

On this frosty day, I was making my way back to Denver from one of those trips, even though my aged Volkswagen Super Beetle was hardly an appropriate car for heavy-duty mountain driving. Its weary old engine could barely power the car up the steep mountain passes, but the Bug usually picked up more than enough speed on the downhill side to propel itself up the next incline.

There's something about old Beetles and Super Beetles that makes them seem like they have their own unique personalities, even if they are just hunks of cold steel. So, I had named my bright yellow Bug "Guenter."

With the break in the winter weather, I was glad to finally switch off Guenter's windshield wipers, loosen my death grip on the steering wheel, and relax a bit. Yet as I came over the crest of a hill, already picking up speed on the descent, I was horrified to spot two smashed-up cars in the middle of the road directly ahead. They were stopped across both lanes at the point where this particular hill ended, and another uphill climb was about to begin. The drivers and passengers were huddling to the right side of the road.

Quickly, I realized exactly what had caused the accident, as this part of the highway was now a virtual skating rink. Gently, I pushed on Guenter's brake pedal, which unexpectedly propelled the Bug's front end toward the concrete barrier on the passenger side. Quickly, I recovered from the spinout, but realized I had no way to slow down my car without losing control.

I saw that if I continued in the right lane, I would plow directly into the two cars at the bottom of the hill. If I could get into the left lane, I might hit only one of the cars. So I nudged Guenter in that direction as gently as I could while maintaining traction. Once in the left lane, however, the frozen road took control. Every attempt I made to steer from then on was met with no cooperation from the Bug. Black ice dictated my path.

Time seemed to slow down as I wondered whether I was about to be killed or severely injured by the impending impact with the wrecked cars. A VW Super Beetle with nothing but a spare tire and a suitcase full of clothes in the trunk at the front of the car was not going to afford much protection. I was praying without words, just silently hoping for divine intervention to see me through this looming disaster.

Suddenly, I had something else to worry about. A sports car with two young men in the front seat crested the top of the hill behind me at high speed. They were in the right lane, and I saw their car slide to the left and then the right as they careened on the black ice. Before I knew it, the sports car nearly caught up to me and was just to the right of Guenter's rear bumper.

Spying the wreck at the bottom of the hill, the sports car's driver slammed on his brakes, sending his vehicle into a tailspin. The sports car slammed sideways into the concrete barrier on the right side of the road and then ricocheted left toward me. I braced for impact, but somehow the sports car's driver managed to keep his vehicle out of my lane.

However, at this point, neither one of us could adequately steer our cars on the unforgiving ice, nor could we brake to slow them down without spinning out of control. It appeared that our mutual fate was to hit both crippled cars blocking the highway ahead.

As I neared the wreckage, I suddenly felt as if someone else was guiding Guenter. I still couldn't get the car to respond when I tried to steer on the ice, but Guenter was drifting ever so slightly to the left, aiming for a wee gap between the disabled car in front of me and the concrete median along my driver's side.

I felt a slight spark of hope, thinking that I might simply sideswipe that damaged car with the passenger side of my Bug, leaving most of my car, and me, relatively unharmed. As I got closer to the immobilized automobile, my Bug seemed to be driving itself, expertly floating on the ice to move me out of harm's way.

Abruptly, Guenter shot out of the only opening where a VW Bug could possibly squeeze through. Somehow, my car and I had sailed past the wreckage utterly unscathed.

The sports car just behind us was not so lucky. The driver had managed to slow down somewhat, but as I glanced in my rearview mirror, I saw his car plow into the middle of the two damaged vehicles.

I couldn't stop to see how the occupants of the sports car had fared as Guenter and I were still at the mercy of the ice. I hadn't regained control of my car and braking to stop was out of the question, so momentum kept us skating further down the frosty highway.

How did I avoid near-certain disaster that day? Did Guenter possess a sentient spirit that somehow kept me out of danger, or did a guardian angel step in to protect me? All I know is that, many years later, I'm still here to tell the story of how I survived a perilous trip through the Rockies in a very "Super" Beetle.

— Tammy Parker —

75

Midnight Stranger

Impossible situations can become possible miracles.
~Robert H. Schuller

"You're burning the candle at both ends," I said to our seventeen-year-old son, Ben. "You can't keep going like this. Your body is not a machine."

"Oh, Mom, I'm fine." Ben waved his hand through the air to brush aside my concern. "You worry too much," he added as he headed out the front door for work. I watched him climb into his pickup and barrel down the driveway in a cloud of dust.

"Lord, please watch over him and keep him safe," I whispered.

Ben acted no different from other teenagers his age who think they're invincible. Besides school, he had started a landscape business two years earlier that kept him busy on weekday afternoons. When he bought his truck, he took on a weekend job at the movie theater to help pay for insurance.

At 12:30 that night, my husband Loren snored beside me while I listened for the sound of Ben's truck. Eventually, I fell into a light, restless sleep. When someone banged on the front door, I bolted upright in bed. Maybe Ben had forgotten his key. It was 1:30 a.m. I wondered why he was so late as I made my way to the front door.

From the living-room window, I could see that the bulky figure on the porch was not Ben. In fact, I recognized the uniform of a Washington State patrolman. My throat tightened, and my heart pounded. My hand shook so hard that I could barely grasp the knob to unlock and open the door.

The officer verified our address from Ben's driver's license. We lived down a rural road, twenty-two miles from town, and he'd had a difficult time locating our house in the dark.

"Yes, I'm his mother," I heard myself say as if watching a movie clip in slow motion. "Is he okay?"

"Your son's alive, but he's been in an accident," said the patrolman. Though he didn't know Ben's condition, the trooper assured me he'd arrived at the hospital.

"From the looks of the tire tracks, he made no attempt to stop," the officer said.

Through tears, I managed to choke out, "I'm sure he fell asleep."

"He's one lucky boy. If he'd gone off the road fifty feet in either direction, he'd be dead for sure."

From the officer's description, I knew the location. A solid wall of 150-foot fir trees edged both sides of the highway except for a short patch of swampland. Luck had nothing to do with it.

Loren and I hurried to the hospital, imagining the worst.

When we found Ben stretched out on a gurney in the emergency room, he reassured me, "I'm okay, Mom."

"He's stable," a nurse said. "He just needs to be stitched up."

"Someone was watching out for him," the ER doctor said to us as he entered. "Another fifteen minutes, and he would've bled to death."

After the doctor stitched the gash on Ben's head, we took him home.

Later, we learned from Ben what we had already suspected. Exhausted from long work hours, Ben had dozed at the wheel and his truck had careened off the dark road and plunged into the swamp. As the bottom of the pickup scraped down the steep gravel bank, the gas tank gave way and tore from its mounts. The truck bed detached and landed upside down several yards away.

Ben had reached up with his right hand to wipe what he thought was oil on his face, but it had been blood that was pouring from a four-inch gash on the right side of his head. He knew he needed help and realized no one would find him. The truck was on its side, so he struggled against gravity to push open the driver's door. It wouldn't budge, so he lay on his back across the bench seat and kicked the sunroof until it broke free. Then he crawled from the vehicle and splashed into the water-filled swamp grass and tall stands of cattails. Blood ran down his face and soaked into his jacket as he clawed his way up the bank and onto the highway.

Ben stumbled down the road toward the unmanned fire station five miles away. A car passed him and then made a swift U-turn and crunched to a stop on the gravel in front of him.

"I'll go for help," the man said, and then hesitated as he assessed Ben's injuries. He assisted Ben into his car and drove him to the volunteer firehouse where he sounded the alarm. The stranger left Ben seated on the ground outside the building and drove away. Firefighters rushed to the station and eventually Ben was transferred from one group of first responders to another until he was delivered to the closest hospital, thirty minutes away.

Several days later, we tried to locate the man who had driven Ben to the fire station so we could thank him. We asked around the area to see if anyone knew who had picked him up that night. But in a community of fewer than 300 people, no one could identify the man.

One of the firefighters suggested we inquire at the local mom-and-pop store a short distance from the station. He assured us that the store's owner would know. But neither the storeowner nor the locals recognized Ben's description of his rescuer.

We never did discover the man's identity. All we know is that Ben's rescue was nothing short of a miracle.

—Kathleen Kohler—

My Icy Miracle

*Miracles happen every day. Not just in remote country
villages or at holy sites halfway across the globe,
but here, in our own lives.*
~Deepak Chopra

School had been canceled due to a snowstorm the night before, but the sun was shining brightly. I bundled up the children — six-year-old Kevin and four-year-old Tanya. We were going out to celebrate this sunny yet snowy winter day. As we headed out the door, our small black Lab puppy, Stormy, followed us.

The back yard of our apartment building was huge and bordered a local millpond that was covered with a thin layer of ice. The ice was covered with a layer of snow so one couldn't tell where the yard ended and the water began. We built a snowman and ran in circles. Kevin and Tanya thoroughly enjoyed their mid-week break from school.

As we played in the snow, Stormy began to pick up his paws, signaling to me that his feet were cold, and he needed to go inside. I picked him up and headed to our apartment, hollering back to the kids, "Stay in the yard!" Then I went upstairs to our apartment.

I removed my coat, boots and wet socks and stood at the kitchen window that overlooked the back yard. I filled the sink with soapy water and began to wash the breakfast dishes.

After only a moment, I noticed Kevin run across the yard toward the house. I heard the downstairs door open and then him stumbling and banging on the stairs, making strange noises. I opened the door and looked down the stairs to see what was wrong. Kevin was soaking wet and crying. His face was bright red, and he was slurring his words.

"We fell in the water, Mamma! Tanya is in the water!" he cried.

Running past Kevin down the stairs, I didn't even stop to put on shoes. I tried to see Tanya through the trees, but I couldn't find her. "She's over there, Mamma!" Kevin pointed, and I began to run. "Go get the police, Kevin!" I managed to blurt out as I ran. When I finally saw her, Tanya was under the ice on the pond, and she wasn't moving. Her little purple coat hood kept her head afloat against the ice, and I could see her eyes open under the water. Like a slow-motion nightmare, I ran out to her on the ice, forgetting all the safety rules, and promptly fell through the ice myself.

I became instantly uncoordinated the second my body hit that ice water. I couldn't move correctly, and my legs wouldn't do what I asked them to. I struggled to pull myself out of the water.

Kevin had run across the street where the Town Office and Police Department were located. By the time I had managed to pull myself out of the ice, a few police officers had shown up in the yard. Not long afterward, fire trucks and ambulances arrived. It was a struggle to reach Tanya, as her body had started to drift toward the dam. They tried many ways to get her out, and a brave off-duty firefighter finally grabbed a boat oar and began smashing the ice. He swam in the frigid water to reach her. Those on shore pulled the fire hose that had been tied around his waist, and he held onto her as they were pulled ashore.

Tanya was finally pulled out of the water, but she had been dead for quite some time. She was transported to the local hospital and then transferred by ambulance to a larger facility after they managed to get a heartbeat and brain activity. I was in shock and barely remember the ambulance ride with her. She fought the attendants on the ride there, and I learned afterward that it was a good sign. I felt horrible watching my child thrash and scream for the half-hour ride to the larger hospital.

Two days later, on my birthday, Tanya woke up from the medically induced coma she had been put under by the doctors. After hearing me repeat that I loved her while she was asleep, she said, "I love you, too, Mamma. I love you, too!"

It was a miracle. She had been in the water almost a half-hour by the time they were able to free her from the ice. She woke up and smiled at everyone. She accepted a Popsicle and loved all the attention she was getting. Her two lower baby teeth had been knocked out by a breathing tube, and the doctor worried that the foreign objects in her lungs might cause pneumonia. Fortunately, she didn't get it. They did tests and warned me that she might have some difficulties or minor brain damage from being clinically dead for so long. Her tests showed that she had suffered no long-term injuries. Tanya came back as perfect as she had been the morning she fell through the ice.

It was as if that awful day had never happened except in our memories. My son, whom I was so very proud of, had looked both ways before he ran across the street to get help. He had fallen through the ice with Tanya, but thankfully had pulled himself out to come get me. Everything that day worked in our favor. Kevin is going to be thirty-five this year; Tanya will be thirty-three. They are two continual reminders to me that miracles do happen.

— Donna Keenan —

77

Your Daughter Is Alive

It was possible that a miracle was not something that happened to you, but rather something that didn't.
~Jodi Picoult, The Tenth Circle

I was relaxing in the warmth of my car as I waited for my ten-year-old daughter to finish her chores at the horse farm. A rattling noise got my attention, and I glanced in the rear view mirror to see a Jeep hauling a large flatbed trailer loaded with hay bales. Perched on the highest bales were the four girls volunteering that afternoon. I could see they were smiling despite the cold. I settled back into reading as the clatter of the trailer faded into the distance.

Shortly thereafter, my phone rang. The caller ID showed it was the lady who ran the farm. Why would she be calling?

When I answered, her cheerful voice seemed at odds with her words. There had been "a bit of an accident" involving my daughter, but she was alive. I tried to process those words. My daughter was alive. I sped down the gravel drive to the pasture.

She was lying on the gravel path with tears streaming from her eyes. I bent down, spread a plaid blanket over her, and then smoothed back her long, russet hair. A bloody mixture of gravel, dirt and tears was smeared across her left cheek. Bloody scrapes marred her chest, right eye and forehead. She asked, "Am I going to be okay?"

"Yes," I replied, and I meant it. Relief washed over me as I saw more and more that she was truly going to be okay.

She *had* to be okay. Fifteen months earlier, I had made the choice to let her volunteer here, despite my concerns. I couldn't resist her pleading eyes. I had told myself that this would be good for her. After all, hadn't she wanted an opportunity to be around horses, to find other girls to spend time with and make new friends?

Now, the unthinkable had happened.

Urgent decisions had to be made. Did I want her loaded up in the farm Jeep and taken to the local clinic? Did I want an ambulance instead? Conflicted over the extent of her injuries, I decided on the ambulance.

Activity buzzed around us immediately upon arriving at the emergency room. Her temperature was taken, pulse and blood pressure checked, urine sample collected and scans scheduled.

In the midst of the organized chaos, a nurse approached.

"There's a policeman on the phone wanting to talk to you," she informed me.

Puzzled, I followed her to the phone, wondering why a policeman was calling me.

"Hello," I answered hesitantly. I was met with a volley of questions.

"Your daughter is alive?"

"Yes, of course."

"Does she have a fractured skull?"

"Not that I know of."

"Is she conscious?"

"Yes."

"Does she have any broken bones?"

"Apparently, only a tiny hairline fracture across her pelvic bone."

In an incredulous voice, the policeman circled back to his second question. "So, she doesn't have a fractured skull?"

"No, sir. Not at all."

"Amazing," he said simply.

I wondered at his disbelief, but in my dazed state, rather than ask him questions, I simply said goodbye.

Many tests and hours later, we arrived home, grateful the tests showed only minimal injuries. Exhausted after the late night and emotional strain, we crashed for the night.

The next morning, I picked up the bag containing the clothes she had been wearing and pulled out her shirt and jeans. A wave of shock ran through me. I laid the jeans flat on top of the washing machine and stared at them, cold chills running up and down my body.

Going up the back left leg of her jeans was a muddy tire track. The enormity of what had happened began to dawn on me, and my eyes filled with tears.

Taking the jeans to my daughter, I showed her what I had found. "Do you remember anything that happened?" I asked.

"It's coming back to me," she replied as she stared at the jeans.

For the next five minutes, she shared the memories of those moments as they slowly emerged from the depths of her mind.

She had been sitting on top of the hay bales with the other girls. As they bumped along, she noticed that her hay bale was beginning to shift. The other girls told her to stay where she was. At the next big bump, her bale began to slide, taking her with it. She tried grabbing at something, anything, to stop her fall, but to no avail.

She blacked out and woke to find herself on the ground, with a trailer wheel coming up her body and toward her head. As she watched the wheel roll over her, she felt the pressure of the tire against her face, and then it was gone. The rattling of the trailer continued on. She turned her head and watched it roll away.

Words could not express how I felt as I listened to her. I understood more clearly the import of the words, "Your daughter is alive?" and the disbelief of the police officer.

The full weight of what should have happened hit me like a ton of bricks. I sank to my knees beside her bed and gathered her in my arms, my heart swelling with gratitude for the miracle we had experienced.

Surely, angels had acted swiftly, lifting the trailer as it lumbered across my daughter's body, saving her from serious harm.

— Sandra Hesler —

78

Mavis's Ladybug

The bond between friends cannot be broken by chance;
no interval of time or space can destroy it.
Not even death itself can part true friends.
~John Cassian

O ne of my dearest friends lay sleeping in her bed at the nursing home where she'd lived the final two months of her life. Mavis Vitums was in hospice care and knew she had only days left with us.

I sat on the edge of her bed, took her hand, looked into her eyes and said in all seriousness, "Mavis, we have to work out something here and now. What are you going to send me to let me know you're all right once you pass over?"

I thought that I might have shocked or offended her due to her deeply conservative religious beliefs, but I sincerely wanted to know. She took a moment to contemplate this and then said decisively, "A ladybug — red with black spots. I think they're classy."

The next day, September 7, 2009, she died with dignity at age sixty-five.

Two days after that, I was about to perform my first wedding ceremony through my new business, Nonconformist Nuptials.

The wedding was being held at a golf course in Shakopee, Minnesota. I'd stepped into the clubhouse's ladies' room to freshen up and found the entire bridal party there, apparently hiding from the groomsmen and the groom. When I finished washing my hands, I reached into a paper-towel basket on the countertop beside the sink. My breath caught, and tears pooled in my eyes. When I turned back to face the bride and her friends, I extended my left hand, palm up, displaying a ladybug!

The girls all chorused, "Ooh, that's good luck!"

I said, "It's a heck of a lot more than just that, ladies…" and told them about Mavis. They all proceeded to yell at me for making them cry and messing up their make-up.

For the next hour, I ran around the place, showing the ladybug on my hand to anyone who would pay attention. I told them, "This is what my dead friend just sent me!" followed by the explanation of its poignancy. To their credit, the wedding guests all seemed appropriately awed, and several even murmured words about miracles.

The classy red bug with black spots sat contentedly on my palm and seemed to be preening itself. It didn't move from that spot for an entire hour! I realized it was going to be with me for the duration, and I resigned myself to delivering the ceremony with a ladybug on my hand.

After the ceremony was completed, I realized my forearm was cramping from holding my hand palm up for so long, so I said quite reasonably to the ladybug, "I have to shake out my hand. Why don't you climb up on my dress for a while?" I placed my hand next to my collarbone and watched, amazed, as the bug climbed from my hand to my dress and sat there like a tiny brooch!

The bridal party finished signing the marriage license, and I noticed the ladybug started climbing along my dress's neckline. I said to it, "I know, I know. You need to leave now." I replaced it on my palm and told it, "Just hang on a minute. I'll take you outside."

Once outside, I looked for an appropriate place to deposit my friend's otherworldly representative and decided on some lovely impatiens flowers near the waterfall in front of which we'd held the wedding ceremony.

I reached out to one of the purple-flowered plant's leaves, extending my index finger as a kind of bridge, and watched in reverence as the ladybug proceeded to walk down that digit to the patiently waiting impatiens.

Tears streamed down my face, and I looked heavenward. In a choked voice, I said, "Mavis, you ROCK!"

When I looked down again at the plant, the ladybug had vanished.

Hours later, as I was heading to my car to leave, I saw the bride running across the parking lot, calling out to me, "Tell your friend I said thank you for coming to my wedding!"

I have long believed that our spirits continue to exist, albeit in a new form, after we die. Even Albert Einstein said energy is neither created nor destroyed; it just changes form. I thank Mavis from the bottom of my heart for providing me the evidence that this is so. As the years have passed since this notable wedding, Mavis continues to send me red-and-black reminders that she is watching over me.

—Sid Korpi—

79

A Miraculous Recovery

*Never believe that a few caring people can't change the
world. For, indeed, that's all who ever have.*
~Margaret Mead

I turned in a slow 360-degree circle, eyes wide. Angels and
saints surrounded me. They were everywhere I looked.

"Please exit now," a voice called across the P.A. system in
English and several other languages. I let my gaze crawl up the
walls to the ceiling one last time and then followed the flow of tourists
toward the door, leaving the Sistine Chapel behind.

Despite the omnipresent cameras and tour books, I felt at peace in
this place. Behind gates and protected by guards, the Vatican retained
a feeling of holiness despite everything else in Rome that screamed
"tourist site." Knowing the Pope lived and walked on these grounds
and that prayers had been whispered over centuries in these halls
made me feel safe and secure.

Perhaps a little too safe.

After the chapel visit, I came across the Vatican post office and
thought I'd buy stamps and postcards. As I waited in line, I spotted
a young boy prowling around unattended, but I didn't pay him too
much attention. Thoughts of Michelangelo and his art drifted through
my mind. I still couldn't believe I was in Italy!

At the counter, as I stumbled through my Italian, I took my hands off my fanny pack for a moment. That's when it happened. When I reached for my wallet, it was gone.

Instantly, I realized who had taken it.

I spun around. "My wallet's gone! Did anyone see a little boy? My wallet was stolen!"

Immediately, a buzz of voices rose in the post office. The postal clerk started shouting, and two Vatican police officers ran up to me almost immediately. My heart pounded, but I explained the problem while the clerk gesticulated in rapid Italian.

My voice shook and limbs trembled. Hot tears welled in my eyes. More than the loss of my belongings, I felt violated by what had happened. Someone had come close enough to take my personal belongings off my body and I hadn't even noticed.

"It was a boy with a yellow shirt! And shorts down to here!" an American man called from the back of the line. The crowd parted, and the man swiped the space below his knee, indicating the length of the boy's shorts.

I nodded my thanks to the man. He'd seen what I hadn't.

One of the officers pushed the button on his walkie-talkie as I tried to stay calm. He spilled words into the device and then flew out of the Poste.

"What's going on?" I asked the people around me.

Another man in a suit stepped forward. In an authoritative voice, he said, "They've closed off all exits to the Vatican."

Silence swept through the room. And then, I heard whispering. Translations. "They've shut down the Vatican."

I pictured heavy, black gates coming down, clanging shut. I imagined armed officers positioning themselves in front of the gates, blocking the doors. Families and couples would whisper to one another, a little scared. They were trapped inside, all because of me.

Frozen in place and staring out the windows of the post office, I wondered what I should do. My driver's license, money and phone cards were in that wallet. How would I get home?

Nearby, a small, gray-haired woman leaned over the counter, writing a postcard. She stopped her pen, looked to me and said in a plain American accent, "Don't worry. You'll get it back." Then she went back to writing.

I stared at her. How could she know? Did this happen all the time? I couldn't speak, but I nodded. I hoped she was right. What would I do without that money? Without my ID?

Confused but appreciative of her sense of calm, I turned back to the window. A police officer rushed by and pushed through the door. He approached me and curled a finger inward. I followed him.

I hurried to keep up with the long-legged Vatican official. Two blue-uniformed guards joined us as we ducked some yellow ropes and dodged a procession of nuns. Finally, we reached another corridor that led to the public Vatican restrooms.

A young boy slouched against a wall.

I slowed to a stop and stared, my heart hammering in my chest. It had to be him.

Someone asked me, "Is this the boy?"

I shook my head. I didn't know. I barely had a look at him slinking through the Poste. It was so crowded, and my mind had been elsewhere.

"It's important for someone to identify the thief! Very important!" a guard shouted.

"A man at the post office said he wore a yellow shirt," I said, noticing the black shirt on this boy. A guard took off to find the American.

I turned back to the boy, who shoved his hands deep into his pockets. He wore long, baggy shorts and scruffy sneakers. He had bleached blond tips on his dark head and deeply tanned skin. A faint shadow of a mustache sat above his lip.

He neither trembled nor sighed even as I paced in front of him. It was as if he didn't see me.

Moments later, a guard emerged from the men's restroom with a dripping-wet wallet pinched between two fingers.

"That's it!" I said, going toward him. I unzipped the wallet but found it empty. When I let the police officers know, one of the men spoke quick, loud Italian words to the boy. The kid dug in his pocket and handed over the rest of my belongings—two hundred dollars, my credit card, driver's license, and phone card.

When the American man arrived, he nodded at the boy. "That's him. Probably stuffed the yellow shirt in a trash can."

"Thank you," I whispered, still shaking.

I spent the next hour filling out paperwork in a back room and speaking to more Vatican officials before I was set free.

If this had happened anywhere else in Italy, I doubt I would've gotten my wallet back. But on Vatican soil, I did, surrounded by angels who lifted and supported me. There's no other explanation.

Later that day, when I walked under the suspended gates of the Vatican and left the holy city behind, I took with me everything I'd brought inside and more: an experience I'll never forget.

I'd been surrounded by angels the entire visit. A full 360-degree circle around me. Everywhere.

And it was only afterward, looking back past the gates, that I realized how truly miraculous that was.

— Mary Jo Marcellus Wyse —

Divine
Coincidences

Perfect Timing

*We do not create our destiny; we participate in its
unfolding. Synchronicity works as a catalyst toward
the working out of that destiny.*
~David Richo, The Power of Coincidence

At the age of twenty-seven, I told people I was moving to New York City from Georgia to pursue acting, but it was really because a relationship had ended. I was heartbroken and wanted to get as far away as possible.

For the first three years I lived in New York City, I went to a total of one audition. My life was spent waiting on tables, dating an unavailable man, and cycling through emotional high and low periods. I had gone to acting school, and I knew I had talent, but I couldn't muster enough self-esteem to go to auditions.

In my early childhood, I had loved going to our small-town country church. I would look up to the sky and feel certain that someone called God knew I was here. My mother would often quote scripture about love and forgiveness when she thought someone was being mean.

My father, on the other hand, skipped church on Sundays. He worked hard at the paper mill, and he also drank hard, listened to country music, and played his guitar.

As his drinking escalated, so did my fearfulness. My parents divorced when I was nine. My mom, older sister and I moved around a lot. Things would feel stable for a while, only to be disrupted by another move. When I was fifteen, I ended up living with my dad again. His drinking was at its worst. I wasn't there long before going to live with two different grandmothers in two different states.

I moved in with my boyfriend when I was seventeen years old, because I needed some kind of stability. The feeling of connection to some divine energy that I had felt so deeply as a child diminished as I grew into adulthood. I still wanted to believe there was a presence that cared for me, who would help me, but for the most part I just felt scared and alone. My life would be good for a while, and then I would spiral into a dark hole. I smoked heavily as a way to cope.

But then one day, three years after I moved to New York, I was too depressed to even light up. I lay curled up in a ball, crying for hours. I was struggling to pay the rent. I was thirty and going nowhere. I barely had a high-school education. Most of my work experience was waiting tables.

I didn't see a way out. Life was too hard. I imagined taking pills and ending it, but where could I get the pills? I didn't really want to die. I just wanted out of the pain.

At some point, I needed to use the bathroom, and I pulled myself out of bed. I felt so tired and sad that I sunk to the floor. So I got on my knees and prayed. I cried and said out loud, "If there's anyone out there, please kill me or help me. I can't do this anymore." What I felt next was hunger. I managed to stand up and get dressed to go out and get food.

I walked to the neighborhood diner carrying my umbrella, but I never found the energy to open it even though it was raining. I sat at the counter, drenched, and ordered a grilled cheese. The sandwich arrived. I tried to take a bite and eat it, but my mouth was so dry that the bread and cheese felt like a rubber ball I was trying to chew and swallow. Finally, I spit it out in the napkin and paid the check.

I got up to leave, and as I was approaching the door, I noticed a tall man standing outside under the awning, obviously waiting for the rain to lighten. I opened the door and, to my surprise, I heard my own voice say, "If you're not going very far, I could share my umbrella with you."

He said, "That would be great. I'm going to 22nd and Park Avenue," which was a few blocks away. I handed him the umbrella. He opened it, and we walked quietly toward Park Avenue.

Shortly before arriving at his building, I asked, "What do you do?"

He said, "I'm a psychotherapist with a specialty in dysfunctional families and codependency." He suggested I come up to his office and get his card. He said the consultation would be free, and if it felt like we could work together, we could discuss the rate.

I took the card and put it in my nightstand drawer. A few months went by before I fell into another state of depression. Lying in bed, I opened the drawer to look for cigarettes and saw his business card. His name was almost glowing on the card. It was all I could see, like it was bigger in size than it actually was.

I made the call and saw him for a consultation. He asked how much I could afford to pay for sessions, and I said $40. Recently, I discovered that George's rate had been four times what I paid when I first started seeing him. I asked why he agreed to accept such a small payment. He said he could see the pain I was in, and he wanted to help as long as I showed up and did the work.

Soon after starting therapy with George, I lucked into an entry-level assistant job with a small, independent music-publicity firm. I carved out a career in music, and over two decades, I worked my way to Senior-Vice President of Publicity for Capitol Records. Instead of being embarrassed about my lack of formal education, I'm proud of all I've accomplished.

In 1999, George encouraged (pushed) me to give up my twenty-five-year, two-pack-a-day smoking addiction. It's the hardest thing I've ever done but now I'm celebrating twenty years of being smoke-free.

I don't want to imagine what my life would have been like (or if I would even still have a life) if I had never met George. Some might say it was a random series of coincidences that I would ask for help, end up at a diner on a rainy day and intersect with a therapist who happened to have no umbrella. I say it was a life-changing miracle, which I give thanks for every day.

— Janet Rich —

81

Hidden Messages

*When you live your life with an appreciation of
coincidences and their meanings, you connect with
the underlying field of infinite possibilities.*
~Deepak Chopra

My father had recently passed away after a long illness, so my spouse and I were helping my mother sort through his things and prepare the house for sale. Because my father had never trusted banks, she suspected that he had squirreled away a large cash reserve somewhere in the house or garage.

Like his father before him, my dad worked as a building contractor in his younger years. He became a part-time handyman during his retirement. He enjoyed continuing to ply his trade. He was also a packrat, saving lots of leftover building materials because he never knew when he might need them. Hiding away a big bundle of cash was just the kind of thing that he would do. It made sense to spend some time hunting for it.

The cleaning, packing and painting went on for months, with no sign of any big cash deposit. We found his wallet with some money in it and a bedside jar full of small change, but not the large nest egg we anticipated. We began to worry that even if it did actually exist, we would never find it. We didn't want to sell the house if it meant always wondering if we'd given away a small fortune along with it.

In addition to working on houses, my dad also built small boats in his spare time. He had always loved the sea, and making the crafts and taking them out on the water gave him great joy. So we had boats to sell off as well, and some friends who owned a hotel on a lake nearby asked us about purchasing them. One evening, we loaded one up to show to them, hoisting it onto the top of my father's trade van, which was equipped with a special roof rack for carrying it. We also threw a bunch of old life vests into the boat as a bonus gift to sweeten the deal, since the hotel owners would need them for their guests if they made the acquisition.

We drove to the hotel and parked right in front of the large restaurant terrace. We planned to have a nice dinner and drinks with our friends while discussing the boat deal. The evening was perfect, and the hoteliers were leaning heavily toward making the purchase.

Suddenly, we heard a bloodcurdling scream, and then a resounding boom as the boat seemed to explode right before our eyes. The van was rocking from the impact, and a cloud of dust billowed out of the boat. Drinks were spilled and plates were shattered by startled dining patrons. Directly behind us, more screaming ensued as a man came running out of the hotel onto the terrace, gesturing wildly in what seemed to be a crazed panic.

The man stammered that he'd been taking photos of his wife on their room's balcony, a floor above, when she leaned over too far and fell right off. Down she went, tumbling directly into our boat. Hearing that, we raced off the deck toward the van. Standing on our tiptoes, we managed to peer through the dust cloud into the boat. The unfortunate woman was lying there in a heap, moaning in agony. But she was alive! The old, dusty life vests in the bottom of the boat had cushioned her fall.

An ambulance was called, which soon whisked her to the nearest hospital, leaving her fretful husband to explain things to the police. Before we closed out the shocking evening with our friends, we were informed that she was badly shaken and bruised, but otherwise in remarkably good shape. By some great miracle, my father's boat padded with old life preservers had saved her.

Finally calling it a night, we were driving home when my spouse noticed that the interior headliner on the van had been partly separated in one corner by the impact. Something was sticking out of the opening. Carefully shoving her hand up into the gap as I drove, she pulled out a handful of banknotes. Eureka! Perhaps we had inadvertently found the financial hoard we'd been hunting for so long.

Once home, we excitedly pried open the tear in the van ceiling wide enough to gape inside and find the huge stash of cash we had been looking for. It was turning into a night of miracles. We also found a well worn notebook bundled along with it, which surprisingly turned out to be a diary.

My father had always been the strong, silent type, showing that he loved us through his actions rather than with words. However, during his last year of life, it seemed he had kept this secret diary. In it were proclamations of love to my mother and touching messages for the rest of the family. We were stunned. This was a real miracle, indeed. It was a written jewel that all of us, especially my mother, would treasure for the rest of our lives.

And so ended our night of miracles, both big and small.

The woman whose life was saved by our boat wrote us on the first anniversary of her miraculous survival. She mentioned that after her husband was cleared of foul play, they went boating to celebrate their good luck. Now she cherishes life even more and appreciates the moments she used to take for granted.

My mother made enough from the sale of the house and the treasure trove we discovered to live comfortably. She's become a packrat herself in her old age. Hopefully, she'll leave us a map to any hidden valuables.

In unending gratitude for having our boat in the right place at the right time, the hoteliers regularly take us out for nostalgic spins in one of the boats they purchased from us. Our friendship has grown immensely over the whole experience.

And our entire family continues to enjoy the delightful diary of love messages that my quiet yet thoughtful father miraculously left us, bonding us forever.

— Sergio Del Bianco —

82

A Tap on the Shoulder

*Sometimes, reaching out and taking someone's hand is
the beginning of a journey. At other times,
it is allowing another to take yours.*
~Vera Nazarian,
The Perpetual Calendar of Inspiration

One morning, I received the call I'd been waiting for. "Mom, I got in!"

My daughter had been accepted into graduate school. After months of praying for her as she completed applications, travel, and interviews, I felt relieved and full of gratitude. And with that came a compulsion to give back, to do something special in thanks that my prayers had been answered.

I decided to complete a daily devotional. I found a book that included a reflection each day followed by a suggested daily assignment. I liked this book for two reasons. One, it contained only seven entries. And two, the assignments would allow me to, in the words of Mahatma Gandhi, "Be the change that you wish to see in the world."

I dove right in.

Day One's assignment read: "Start a conversation with an elderly person." Simple. I called Aunt Elizabeth, who answered on the first ring. We chatted about the injection she had received in her bad knee. We discussed the details of my daughter's wedding invitation, and how Uncle Thomas would need to have his sauce on the side.

Day One's task had been conquered successfully.

On Day Two, the instructions read: "Help someone you don't know." Hmm. I could assist a person crossing the street. Would that count? Or I could carry someone's groceries to the car. First, I had to meet a stranger, and then help him or her. Day Two's task might not be so easy.

I went off to the grocery store. After a few minutes of browsing the shelves, I saw a young mom rounding the corner pushing a shopping cart with a strapped-in toddler and a slightly larger boy perched in the back on a pack of diapers. As they passed through the cereal aisle, the boy stood and reached for a box of Honey Nut Cheerios. He knocked over the whole display.

"Jake!" The mom pulled the boy to safety.

"This is it," I said. I probably shouldn't have said it aloud. While I felt relieved the boy hadn't been hurt, I was ecstatic that I could now help a stranger.

I bent next to the frazzled, young mom. "I'll clean this up. You take care of the kids."

"I can get it," she said. Then, "Jake, sit down."

"I don't mind, really." I took a dented box from her grasp and did my best to un-crinkle it.

She stood and popped a pacifier into the toddler's mouth. "Thank you," she said, and then took off with her kids, undoubtedly trying to get out of the store quickly without any more mishaps.

As I straightened the boxes, I thought about how great it had felt to catch up with Aunt Elizabeth, a task that had been on my list for weeks. And now, helping this stranger took no effort at all. My thank-you-for-the-answered-prayers devotional was going far better than I had anticipated.

The tasks assigned for Days Three through Six were equally doable. I purchased toys for the playroom at the children's hospital. I delivered most of our coat closet's contents to the donation center. I stocked the car with cases of canned soup and drove to the local food bank drop-off. Finally, after clearing my bookshelf, I donated boxes of books to the senior center in the heart of town.

This process was turning out to be both purging and therapeutic.

I couldn't wait to read the next day's task.

Then it came. Day Seven. The final day of my gratitude week. My thank-you mission was almost accomplished. After I read my passage and daily assignment, I needed to come up with a plan. How would I reach out to a homeless person? I had a meeting at 9:00 a.m., a doctor's appointment at 11:30, and a haircut at 2:00. Then I needed to be in the school parking lot to pick up my son from practice by 4:45.

There was one possible solution. Nearly every day on my way to the field, I drove past a homeless man who stood on a tiny stretch of concrete in a complicated intersection holding a cardboard sign and a plastic drink cup. I decided to give him a few bills and be done with my task.

I raced from meeting to appointment and jumped out of the salon chair around 3:15. I had plenty of time to stop at the intersection, carry out my goodwill activity, and be at the practice field on time. My day was proceeding according to plan.

Heading toward the intersection, I focused on the spot where the man usually stood. Usually. But where was he today?

In that moment, my simple task became a stressful challenge. I looked around. I just had to find someone. And so I detoured.

I drove up and down streets I had never traversed, hoping to spot a person in need. After a while without success, I decided to give up and head to the coffee shop. I had thirty minutes before practice ended. On the way home, I'd stop at a church and drop the money into a donation box. It wasn't completing the task as assigned, but it was better than doing nothing at all.

Sort of.

Admittedly, my week of fulfillment had come crashing to a disappointing end.

After ordering my coffee, I settled into a booth, opened my laptop, and lost track of the time.

And then it came, startling and intrusive. A *rap-tap-tap* on my left shoulder.

"Excuse me, ma'am."

I flinched and nearly spilled what remained of my coffee.

The stranger bent and whispered in my ear. "Didn't mean to scare you."

He was so close I couldn't look him in the eye, but I could feel his presence. His heavy layers of coats. Torn pants. Worn shoes. Unshaven face and unkempt hair. I didn't flinch again, nor pull away.

This was it. This was my moment.

"Can you spare some change for a bowl of soup?"

Speechless, I rummaged through my purse. In all the day's haste, I had forgotten to make sure my wallet contained cash.

The man stayed bent beside me as I hunted and dug. And then, in the deepest pocket with the partially jammed zipper, I found a bill I kept stashed for emergencies.

This was an emergency of a very special kind.

The bill's newness crinkled as I pulled it out and placed it into the man's gloved hands.

"Thank you, ma'am." He bowed low without looking at the bill. "Bless you," he said.

I smiled wide. "Bless you."

But he had already found his place in line at the counter.

When I had given up on the task I had planned, the solution had surfaced. It came as a gift. This man was a gift.

I had never seen a homeless person in that coffee shop before, and I haven't seen one since. That mysterious encounter happened only once in a single moment, when a man took a chance and tapped me on the shoulder.

During my week of gratitude, I had set out to make my own little difference in the world. Instead, an unexpected stranger made a grand difference in mine.

—Judith Burnett Schneider—

83

Synchronicity on the Ski Trail

Synchronicity: A meaningful coincidence of two or more events where something other than the probability of chance is involved.
~Carl Jung

"Yippee!" I cried, practically hopping with excitement when I saw Tori's car pull into my driveway. I was home for the holidays, and I hadn't seen my friend in several months. We had decided to catch up over one of our favorite activities: cross-country skiing. The sun was shining, the air was crisp, and the snow sparkled. It was the perfect winter day in snowy Sault Ste. Marie, Ontario.

Adding to the excitement, it was the day before Christmas, and there'd just been a fresh snowfall. The winter gods must have known I was traveling home for the holidays, all the way from London, England, where I was currently living and working.

Just like the snow, Tori's eyes sparkled. "How are you? I want to hear everything!" she said. Tori was also home for the holidays and excited to go cross-country skiing. We both did a little dance in the car, reveling in the beauty of the day and our hometown.

It was challenging to plan our get-togethers; we were both juggling a range of commitments over our never-long-enough holidays. After tossing several dates and times back and forth, we decided to meet on December 24th at 11:00 a.m., which would leave us both plenty of time to get ready for our respective Christmas Eve celebrations with our families.

I had already been out earlier that morning preparing for one of my family's traditions. Uncle Gary and I had gone to the cemetery to shovel a path through the fresh snow so my extended family could gather at my dad's grave in the evening. My dad had passed away in a tragic accident when I was a teenager, and every year since my family followed a Finnish custom of placing a special candle on his tombstone on Christmas Eve, an important tradition given that my dad's side are all Finnish.

Having been a keen cross-country skier himself, my dad had introduced me to the sport at a young age, and I still felt a special connection to him each time I went out skiing. Plus, the fresh air, beautiful snow-covered trees, and sun glistening on the tracks always made me feel unbelievably alive and rejuvenated.

"Should we go into the store and get passes or just head to the trails and pay later?" I asked Tori. We couldn't wait to get skiing, but we decided to go in and get the passes first anyway.

Finally, we were off, snapping our boots into our skis and heading out for our first ski of the season. There was something magical about the ski resort, Hiawatha Highlands. Its towering trees and ancient rocks had an eternal quality. Something about this place resonated with me.

"Should we take the Mockingbird Hill Extension?" asked Tori. We had opted to do a four-kilometer trail called "The Pinder," which had a couple of optional extensions.

"Sure, why not?" I replied eagerly, wanting to prolong my time in this winter wonderland.

Ahead of us on the extension trail were two men. One looked to be in his early fifties and the other potentially his father. The younger man skied with strength, grace and skill. I admired the way he made the sport look so effortless. As we got closer, I could tell he was speaking a unique language, one that was distantly familiar to me.

"*Joo*," said the man, which I recognized instantly as a common word for "yes" in Finnish.

As we were about to ski past, I asked the man, "Is that Finn you're speaking?"

"Yes, it is," the man replied. "Do you speak Finn?"

"Well, no, but my last name is Kovala — I have Finnish relatives."

I wasn't sure if the man heard me correctly or maybe had trouble understanding English because his face went blank. To my surprise, he said, "Kovala. Like John Kovala."

"Yes!" I was astonished. "That was my father!"

The man's face said it all. "I can't believe it," he replied. "My name is Timo Tikka, and I skied with your father on the Northern Ontario biathlon team in the 1980s. We won gold at the Canadian Championships, and then we skied as members of Canada's National Biathlon Team!"

That nearly knocked me off my skis. After all the decisions that went into getting me on that particular trail on that particular day at that particular time, there I was next to one of my dad's old teammates. Timo joined us for part of the Mockingbird trail, and he went on to recall stories of their ski days.

"Did we ever rake in the medals that year!" he reminisced. I had seen a photo or two and heard the odd snippet, but hearing the stories from Timo brought them to life. Timo explained he was now a structural engineer working in mining, and he lived out west in Victoria, Canada, with his wife. Like Tori and me, he was just visiting for the holidays.

Eventually, Tori and I skied on; this time my eyes were sparkling. "Tori, if I didn't know better, I would wonder if that really happened. What a coincidence." By this point, there was no longer any sign of Timo on the trail and meeting him felt so surreal. I wondered if, in the same way I felt connected to my father when I was out skiing, my father felt connected to me, too.

It struck me that maybe meeting Timo wasn't a coincidence. Maybe there was a greater force at play, one that made the day seem to sparkle. The one thing I knew for sure was that a certain spirit was in the air that made the day very special.

Later that evening, as my family huddled around the tombstone under a clear starry sky, I took a deep breath of the fresh, crisp air and said: "You will never guess who I met on the ski trail today...."

—Stephanie Kovala—

84

Humpback's Song

There are some people who live in a dream world,
and there are some who face reality; and then there
are those who turn one into the other.
~Douglas H. Everett

I stood in the morning light facing Waiulua Bay on the "Big Island" of Hawaii. My daughter Abigail had suggested this trip so we could spend time together before she deployed with the United States Army to God-knows-where in a couple of months.

Abigail had spent three weeks exploring the big island as part of her geological studies at Virginia's Washington and Lee University. She wanted some special time with me before deployment to share what she had loved and learned about the island. Despite mounting tuition bills for her three younger siblings, we both knew I would say yes.

It was my first venture off the U.S. mainland and across the ocean. From the time I was a little girl, oceans had captured my imagination. I marveled at their untamable vastness, great diversity of creatures, and haunting depths. I loved my family's infrequent visits to the shore. I hungered for every new episode of *The Undersea World of Jacques Cousteau*. I begged for a subscription to *National Geographic* with the expectation that one day a whale would grace its cover. The January 1979 edition proved me more than right. It also included a black vinyl recording of humpback songs. I cut out the floppy disk and played it again and again.

Some people love dogs or cats. I loved whales and hoped to see some on this trip. "The migration ended a few weeks ago," the woman at the gift shop informed me, deflating my hopes only a few hours after our arrival.

"Well, you never know," my daughter countered encouragingly, dismissing the attendant with a look.

Abigail and I spent our first days on the island retracing the route of her Washington and Lee studies. We experienced the stunning views of the Pololū and the Waipi'o Valleys, and the lava flows of Kīlauea. Abigail meticulously added other sites, each chosen for its geological wonder, biological diversity, and historical value. The hours were filled with snorkeling encounters with sea turtles and jellyfish, motor-tours through rainbow-covered roadways, and hikes along rocky beaches and glowing lava flows. Still, whenever the ocean came into view, I could not help myself. I scanned the vast waters. Hoping.

As we passed one late-week afternoon relaxing in the seaside sun, tourist ships glided along the coast. We saw glass-bottom boats and whale-sighting vessels.

"We could try to get tickets," Abigail said, without my asking.

She was right, of course. We could try. But this trip had a more singular purpose: to taste and touch, to hear, to see, to share something of what she loved. And then to sear the memory forever in my heart — insurance against the unspeakable.

We had done what we came for. Mission accomplished.

So from a high vantage point on the island that last morning, I stood facing the bay, filling my lungs with its salty air and treasuring the last moments in this worldly paradise.

"I'll see you back at the room," Abigail said, before setting off on her morning run. I nodded.

For some time, I watched her, wondering where the time had gone and how she had grown so fast. Would the woman jogging away from me now be the same one returning to me after the war? Pinning back the strands of wind-tossed hair blowing across my face, I scanned the immense expanse of blue. Hoping. One last time.

"Beautiful view," a man said, walking past.

"I'm hoping for a humpback," I blurted out to this total stranger. Surprising myself with my public admission, I felt the flush in my cheeks. "I've been told it's unlikely," I added, trying not to sound stupid or, worse, desperate. And I most certainly didn't wish to sound ungrateful.

He looked intently to the sea. "Well, I wouldn't give up," he said confidently.

My heart leapt at the encouragement. I followed his gaze.

Only a moment or two passed before a mother and calf breached the waters — soaring, then twisting and splashing down in that wonderful, peculiar way humpbacks play.

Again.

And again.

And again.

Right before my eyes.

Right where he had shown me.

I turned toward the path that ran in front of the lounge chairs.

I glanced back at the hotel.

I scanned the grounds all around as far as I could.

But the man had vanished.

For twenty minutes, I watched mother and calf. For twenty minutes, I felt the childlike joy of experiencing something wonderful and miraculous, something long awaited and yet unexpected.

A gift.

Like the words of a stranger.

And even more — like a daughter grown into womanhood.

— M. Elizabeth Gage —

85

A Second Chance

Be an angel to someone else whenever you can,
as a way of thanking God for the help
your angel has given you.
~Eileen Elias Freeman,
The Angels' Little Instruction Book

As I glanced at the balance in my checkbook, I wondered. What had made me think I could do this?

That morning, when Pastor Tipton spoke about the Christmas Connection program, I'd felt a tug on my heart. He painted such a heartrending portrait of needy children in our community — children who had little hope of a happy Christmas if not for the generosity of others — that I knew I had to help. When he first mentioned the program the week before, many in our congregation stepped up gladly, but there were still three names left in the basket. Although I was barely getting by on my teacher's aide salary, I was sure I felt God's urging. The suggested gift amount was twenty-five dollars, which I really couldn't spare, but wasn't sacrificial love what Christmas was all about?

When the service ended, I pulled an envelope from the basket, envisioning a little girl I would provide with a doll, book, or warm, cozy blanket. Opening the envelope, I discovered that my child was a thirteen-year-old boy. His wish list included only one item: a pair of name brand, high-top sneakers, black, size 9.

Now, sitting with my after-church coffee and my checkbook open in front of me, I was rethinking my decision. Those sneakers were going to cost twice the suggested amount. After I paid my bills, put gas in the car, and bought groceries, I would have approximately thirty dollars left. No way was I going to find name-brand sneakers for that price. But how could I let down that boy?

"God," I whispered, "please show me."

I put away my checkbook and went about my day, with thoughts of high-top sneakers following me like size-nine black shadows. The situation brought back a painful memory of another boy, another Christmas, many years before.

As much as we try not to, we educators have our favorites. My first year on the job, I fell in love with Cameron, a rough-and-tumble first-grader with big, blue eyes. His father was often unemployed, and in the four months since the school year began, Cameron's family had already moved twice. But it wasn't only that I felt sorry for him. Despite his rough upbringing, Cameron had a sunny disposition and a smile that could melt a snowman's heart. He wanted a scooter for Christmas, and I was determined to see that he got one.

Our school had a program where donated gifts were given to the parents of needy students to be opened on Christmas morning. Without a second thought, I took my entire Christmas bonus, purchased the scooter, and parked it in the school office with the other donations.

I could hardly wait for the end of the holiday break. As the morning bell rang, I helped Cameron out of his coat and boots.

"What did Santa bring you for Christmas?" I asked.

"A coloring book and crayons. And some socks."

Unable to believe my ears, I asked, "Anything else?"

"No."

"You… didn't get your scooter?"

He shook his head.

After school, I paid a visit to the principal.

"Cameron said he didn't get the scooter I bought. I don't know quite what to think."

"You didn't by any chance leave the price tag on it, did you?"

"Yes, I even included the receipt, in case there was anything wrong with it. Shouldn't I have?"

Then Marybeth told me something shocking. It was possible Cameron's parents returned the scooter to the store and pocketed the money.

I stared at her, feeling sick.

"It's an unfortunate reflection of the society we live in. But remember, no act of love is ever wasted. We can't get discouraged. We can't stop trying."

I'm ashamed to say that I did stop trying. My entire Christmas bonus had been blown on Lord knew what. That was the last time I bought a gift for a needy child. Until now.

The next day, after work I stopped at a shoe store. As I perused the aisles, I got a sinking feeling in my stomach again. The high-top sneakers ranged in price from $59.99 to $129.99. Checking the price tags, I wanted to cry.

"God, I really want to do this for this boy. Please… help me find a way."

After another pass down the aisle in the hope I'd somehow missed something, I decided to give up. Maybe I could find something similar at a discount store.

"They're all so expensive," I murmured.

"Ma'am, try the bargain aisle."

I hadn't seen the man approach. Startled, I said, "Excuse me?"

"There's a clearance rack in the back. You might find what you're looking for there."

He was an ordinary-looking man, but somehow his presence was calming. His voice, like honey, soothed my frayed nerves.

I thanked him and headed for the clearance aisle, knowing I would not find these particular sneakers there. Dutifully, I checked each shelf. To my utter amazement, in the bottom row, stuffed behind a pair of work boots, was a large, beat-up box bearing the name-brand logo I was searching for. With trembling hands, I lifted the lid. Nestled inside, I discovered a pair of black, high-top sneakers, size 9. The price tag said $24.99.

I almost fell to my knees right there in the clearance aisle.

Cheerfully, the clerk rang up my purchase. "Find everything you need?"

"I sure did," I said, smiling widely. "I don't know if your salespeople work on commission, but there was a gentleman who pointed me in the right direction. I didn't get his name, but he was tall with reddish hair."

"I don't know who that could have been," the girl said. "There aren't any male sales associates working today."

I glanced around the empty store. "Maybe it was a customer then."

The girl gave me a quizzical glance. "Ma'am, you're the only customer who's been in for the last hour."

How strange, I thought.

At home, I wrapped the sneakers in bright red paper, adding a candy cane and a heartfelt prayer that the boy would receive and enjoy the gift.

It wasn't until that evening, when I thought about my strange experience in the shoe store, that I remembered a Bible verse about entertaining angels unaware. All at once, I was chilled with goose bumps. Surely God wouldn't dispatch an angel for something so trivial... Would he?

The answer whispered across my heart in Marybeth's long-ago words: No act of kindness is ever wasted. Who knew what long-reaching impact a simple pair of sneakers might have on a needy young boy?

Weeks later, a thank-you card arrived at our church. Tucked inside was a photo of a boy proudly wearing a pair of black high-top sneakers — a boy with big, blue eyes and a smile as wide as the sky.

— M. Jean Pike —

86

Looking for the Sale Sign

The most incredible thing about miracles
is that they happen.
~G.K. Chesterton

As the executor of the estate, it was my job to sell Mom's car. I had hoped it would be an easy transaction. The car, a 2015 Ford Edge, had low mileage and was in excellent condition. Mom had only driven it to do errands, and the car had barely left the county.

Dad bought the car for Mom shortly after he was diagnosed with a recurrence of breast cancer. He must have known his health would deteriorate quickly. It gave him comfort to know she'd have a reliable vehicle once he was gone. He passed away a few months after the purchase.

Five months after Dad died, I was devastated when Mom was diagnosed with terminal cancer. She chose to remain in her home for as long as possible with the help of hospice.

As Mom lay in her hospice room during her final weeks, she thought about ways to make my life easier. "When it's time to sell the car, just take it to the dealership where Dad bought it," she said. I was happy to fulfill her wishes.

After Mom had been gone a month, I called the dealership and explained the situation. The man who answered the phone stated rudely that he didn't have a need for the vehicle and hung up before I had a chance to say more.

Clearly, Mom's best-laid plans didn't work. I needed a Plan B.

"Please give me a sign," I said aloud. "I need to know where to sell your car."

The next day, I drove to a dealership forty-five minutes away that was known for its good reputation. I was greeted warmly by a manager who spent about thirty minutes examining the car while I sat comfortably in the waiting room until he returned with an offer. He said it was a generous offer, which was true, but it didn't feel right for some reason. I tend to rely on intuition when making decisions. I told the manager I wasn't ready to sell the car. Instead, I was going to get a few more offers. He said the offer was good for a week or two, and he hoped I'd return.

On the way home, I stopped at another dealership. I was told to wait for a salesperson, but after thirty minutes of being ignored, I left. I wasn't feeling it at that location, either.

I was starting to feel defeated. I called my brother who lived out of state and asked for his opinion.

"You might want to take it to CarMax," he said. "I've had good luck with them over the years."

I called the nearest CarMax — two hours away — and chatted with a salesperson who told me the offer I had received from the dealership would be hard to beat. "Run with it!" he said. "I wouldn't be able to give you that amount." I thanked him for his honesty and hung up.

The next afternoon, I Googled Ford dealerships near me. A result popped up that I hadn't previously considered. I called and spoke with a manager who said he'd like to see the vehicle. He suggested I arrive the following morning at 10:00 a.m.

It was raining as I drove to the dealership that morning. "Please show me a sign. I'd like to sell this car today," I said aloud.

When I drove into the lot, I was greeted by a friendly man who asked how he could help me. He guided me to his desk, pulled out his business card, and brought me a cup of coffee. The manager I had expected to meet was busy with other customers, but this gentleman said he'd help me as much as he could.

"Shelton is your last name?" I asked. It was the first thing I noticed when I sat down and looked at his business card. "My maiden name is Sheldon. It's spelled D-O-N instead of T-O-N."

"People often misspell my last name," he said, smiling. We talked a bit about why I was there. He said he was sorry for the loss of my mom, which I appreciated. He admitted he hadn't been in the car business long, but he could gather preliminary information to get started.

"Does the car have a backup camera? Heated seats? Dual-zone automatic climate control?"

I answered the questions the best I could — after all, it had never been my car — and he excused himself and walked outside to finish his checklist of items.

When he returned and began typing on his computer keyboard, he asked if I had the car title with me.

"I'll need the name that appears on the title," he said. "First and last name."

"Carol," I said. "C-A-R-O-L. The last name is Sheldon, S-H-E-L-D-O-N."

"Huh, that's funny. My mom's name is Carol, too," he said. "What are the chances?" He stopped typing for a moment.

I couldn't believe it. Our moms had the same first name and similar last names. "If you don't mind me asking, what's your mom's middle name?" I asked.

"Mae," he said, shuffling some papers around.

"Is that spelled M-A-E?" I asked.

"It sure is," he said. He stopped what he was doing and looked in my direction.

I was grinning from ear to ear.

"Is that your mom's middle name, too?" he asked. By this time, his eyes had grown wide.

"No," I said, laughing. "It's Rae. It's spelled R-A-E."

I couldn't stop smiling.

The manager walked over and apologized for keeping me waiting. I stood up to introduce myself.

"I'm selling this car today, either to you or to the dealership that gave me this solid offer," I said, handing the offer to the manager.

"Is there a number you're looking for?" he asked, walking toward his office.

"I need you to match this offer," I said. "Or give me a better one." I smiled.

Several minutes later, the manager emerged from his office. "I believe we have a deal here," he said, shaking my hand. "The car is like new. Typically, I wouldn't make such a good offer, but as long as you drove all the way out here, I matched it."

"Thank you. I appreciate it," I said. "I have to tell you, Mr. Shelton is the reason I'm selling the car to you today."

The manager looked a bit confused.

"As I mentioned, this is my mom's car. She died earlier this year. My mom's name is Carol Rae Sheldon. You can see it printed on the title. His mom's name is Carol Mae Shelton. The names are identical except for two letters."

"Wow, that's quite a coincidence," the manager said, shrugging his shoulders. He didn't seem to know what to say as I stood there beaming. He congratulated me on selling the car and was on his way.

I asked for a sign, and it appeared. I felt like I was on top of the world.

While I finished up the paperwork needed to finalize the sale of the car, I told the story to any employee who would listen.

I knew I was exactly where I was supposed to be.

— Tyann Sheldon Rouw —

A Warm Night in Vermont

We can only be said to be alive in those moments when
our hearts are conscious of our treasures.
~Thornton Wilder

Within moments of stepping through the front door of the stately Victorian mansion, I felt a strange surge of kinetic energy running through my entire body. It was so strong that it startled me, and I struggled not to react, worried that I might lose control. The home was part of the Marsh-Billings-Rockefeller National Historical Park in Woodstock, Vermont. Built in the 1800s, it had last been inhabited by Mary French Rockefeller and her husband, Laurance Rockefeller.

After the strange feeling passed, I continued touring the house without drawing attention to myself or mentioning it to my husband. We entered a cozy study filled with leather-bound books and traditional furniture.

It was easy to imagine the family, whose photographs graced the room, reading and enjoying afternoon tea. Gazing toward the mantel, I was overcome with emotion and a feeling of wellbeing. Suddenly, out of nowhere, it felt as if someone very loving wrapped his or her arms around me. Instinctively, I looked over my shoulder for my husband, but he was across the room. It was odd, but whatever the presence was, it felt benevolent.

Afterward, I considered the possibility of some sort of supernatural encounter. I have sometimes felt an almost claustrophobic energy in old houses, but never anything like what I felt that morning. Even my very down-to-earth husband agreed there was strong energy in the house when I told him what had happened.

The following day was our last full day to explore Vermont before returning to Los Angeles. It was dark and starting to rain when we left our final stop. We figured that if we took the freeway, we would be back to our hotel in an hour. After losing cell service and not sure of the directions, we got off the freeway and headed west toward our hotel.

Quickly, we realized that we had exited too soon. Rather than go back to the freeway, we decided to take the scenic byway that we had taken that morning. To our surprise, after a short time traveling on the dark, nearly deserted road, the rain turned into snow.

Soon, giant snowflakes were coming down forcefully and pelting our windshield. My husband, not used to winter driving, struggled to stay on the road in our rented Mustang. Both of us were becoming uneasy as the landscape turned steadily white.

As we inched our way anxiously toward our hotel, I thought about my experience at the mansion the previous day. I began to wonder if my strange encounter was a premonition of impending doom; I struggled not to think the worst. At the same time, I wanted to believe that benevolent spirits, like the one that had wrapped its arms around me at the mansion, were protecting us on this cold, dark night.

Each mile seemed to be an eternity as my husband and I tried to gauge how far we were from our hotel. Feeling helpless as the snow on the road grew thicker, we finally came to what looked like a familiar junction with a dimly lit gas station.

We pulled in, and a woman, obviously in a hurry to leave, informed us that everything was closed due to the surprise snowstorm. Discussing our lack of snow tires, she advised us to take an alternate side road to our hotel.

"Otherwise, you're going to run into a big hill, and people have been killed sliding off the highway there," she told us.

I was flabbergasted, but she assured us that if we took the side road, which was straight and flat, we would be okay.

The "side road" was dark and desolate. After several minutes, it became extremely icy. Despite barely moving, the car was slipping and sliding. Our visibility was nonexistent, as if we were trapped in a snow globe. Suddenly, we hit a dip in the road and swerved into a ditch banked by a wall of snow.

We were stuck. Both of us started shivering in our light jackets when my husband turned off the ignition. I felt my adrenaline pumping, and my husband's face was white with fear.

"We can't stay here," I uttered. My throat was so dry that I could barely speak.

We got out of the car and started walking back toward the junction. For a second or two, it seemed like the snow was abating, and darkness surrounded us. Then, away from the road, I thought I saw a glimmer of light.

My husband seemed incredulous, but he followed me as we trudged through the snow, shivering. As my eyes adjusted, I could see a few buildings and lots of trees. Through the trees, it looked like someone was holding a lantern, but who would be out on a night like this?

I kept walking toward the light, and my husband, unable to protest, followed behind me. I realized I was on someone's property, and the sliver of light was coming through a window. Without hesitation, I knocked on the door. *This has all the makings of a good horror movie,* I thought. I prayed that someone friendly would answer.

The door was opened by an elderly man. A woman stood behind him. Without hesitation, they ushered us inside, and we explained our situation. They couldn't have been kinder as they poured glasses of wine and offered to share their dinner.

"This snowstorm has caught everybody off guard," said the man. "I don't have my snow tires on yet, and I won't be able to make my doctor's appointment tomorrow."

We used their phone to call the auto club, but it turned out they were swamped and wouldn't be able to help us for at least a couple of hours.

So, we accepted the offer of our gracious hosts and sat down for a dinner of shrimp scampi. It turned out that we were by a lake, and the area was considered vacation property, mostly occupied only in the summer. But our lovely hosts, who were in their eighties, had lived here all their lives and owned the local newspaper.

As we waited for the auto club, we chatted and were made to feel as if we were invited dinner guests. The conversation was so warm and friendly that it was almost as if we were visiting family.

As the evening wore on, we touched on the subject of where we had visited the last few days. We told them how much we loved the Rockefeller House, but I made no mention of my strange experience.

"It's an amazing place," agreed our host. "I used to mow the lawn and picnic with the family every summer when I was a kid. Later on, I worked for Laurance Rockefeller."

Then he added, "I'm the only person in town still alive with a connection to the property before it became a National Park."

I nearly fell off my chair.

— Jean S. Anker —

88

A Watchful Eye

For thousands of years, father and son have stretched
wistful hands across the canyon of time.
~Author Unknown

I was in the kitchen making a special dinner for my husband, one of his favorite meals growing up. I had just gotten the bierock recipe from his mother. He hadn't had them in ages, and I wanted to surprise him. The oven beeped, indicating it had finally pre-heated to the correct temperature. Just as I opened the oven door, I heard the telephone ring.

The Caller ID indicated I was receiving a call from a local hospital. My husband's cousin was an ER nurse, so I naturally assumed it was him and answered casually. But it was not his voice on the other end.

"Mrs. Cooper?" the male voice inquired.

"Um, yes. This is she," I responded hesitantly.

"Your husband has been in a car accident…" Beyond that, I didn't hear much more. The world closed in on me, and I dropped the phone after I finished what was a lousy attempt at conversation with the man from the hospital. With hands shaking from the adrenaline coursing throughout my body, I attempted to refrain from being hysterical and reached out to family members via text message since I was incapable of making phone calls.

My husband's cousin, who called me immediately after the text message went out, gave me directions to the hospital, but God bless my parents for picking me up at that late hour to drive me. Without their assistance, I am pretty sure I would have driven aimlessly for hours, having lost all ability to function after receiving the news. The whole experience felt like a surreal nightmare.

Once we got to the hospital, we received more information about the accident. It turns out my husband had had a seizure. Luckily, no one else was involved, but he ended up knocking down a telephone pole and a fence, and was ultimately stopped by a tree. He had to be cut out of his mangled car. They had taken him for X-rays and tests.

While I waited to learn more, I thought about how I had been so carefree, happily making his special dinner while all of this chaos ensued a mere mile and a half from our house. After what seemed like an eternity, we learned that he had been moved to the ICU. Unbelievably, he had no broken bones, but he did have some worrisome head trauma involving a spot on his brain that was bleeding internally. By that time, everyone else had left and I made my way up to the ICU on my own.

"Hi, there. Who can I help you find?" a sweet nurse asked with a friendly smile.

"I am here to see my husband. The last name is Cooper," I replied.

"Oh, we have two Mr. Coopers here. Is it Jack Cooper or Hollis Cooper?" she inquired.

"Um, my husband is Jack Hollis Cooper," I said with a confused look on my face. The nurse seemed just as puzzled.

"They are actually right across from one another," she mused, looking at her computer screen. "Let me bring you over." She led me back to the row of beds. As she tentatively pulled back the curtain, I saw a very puffy, black-and-blue version of my husband. My heart hurt like I never imagined it could, but warmed a bit once I saw him smile at me.

The nurse seemed relieved that she had brought me over to the correct "Mr. Cooper," as we began to hear the other Mr. Cooper yelling belligerently across the way and threatening to yank his catheter out on his own. The expression on the nurse's face said it all, and she was as attentive as could be with my husband to avoid having to go near that other patient.

"He came in the same time as your husband," she explained. "Your husband is very lucky to still be with us. We just want to keep an eye on the bleeding in his brain before we can release him."

The pugnaciousness across the way continued over the next two days. The man would have conversations with people who were not there. He was combative with the nurses and staff, and his moods changed in an instant.

By the third evening, my husband's scans were looking much better and they were ready to release him in the morning as long as the night went well. As soon as we got the good news, we noticed that the other Mr. Cooper had quieted down. And then he was moved.

"Well, it sure is nice to have that racket gone," I noted, "but I am also glad he is gone so they won't keep mixing the two of you up." Throughout our time in the ICU, the fact that the man across the way had the same last name, along with a first name matching my husband's middle name, often confused the nursing staff with each shift change.

My husband smiled up at me and commented, "But he had to stay here until he knew I had a clean bill of health. And, of course he would show up in such an unstable package." He laughed boisterously in a way that I loved so much about him. My face wrinkled up inquisitively, but then it clicked.

"No," I whispered breathlessly. "Hollis Cooper." I said his father's name aloud. My brain had been so clouded through the entire chain of events that I wasn't functioning anywhere near 100 percent. But with that one comment, I had a moment of clarity that caused my mouth to gape.

My husband's middle name was his father's first name. His father, Hollis Cooper, had been gone for ten years. He had been a brilliant man, with a master's degree in psychology. As he was a social worker, he spent a great deal of time working with severely mentally ill patients over the years. He knew how to act like one, and he knew how to make his son aware of his presence in the bed across the way, where he stayed, watching over him until he was sure that his boy was okay.

— Gwen Cooper —

89

The Dragon-Wagon

Make yourself familiar with the angels, and behold
them frequently in spirit; for, without being seen,
they are present with you.
~St. Francis de Sales

When I first met my husband, it was clear that he wanted children. He is seven years older than me, so he wanted to start a family right away. He welcomed my daughter from a previous marriage straight into his heart. He adopted her and gave her his last name, which spoke volumes to the kind of heart and character he had.

Deep down, I knew my husband would've loved to have a son. My husband's brother was blessed with all daughters, so the pressure was on for my husband to have a boy. There wasn't another in the family to carry on the last name. Nobody actually put this pressure on him, but we all knew of his desire for a son deep in his heart.

It wasn't long before I was expecting a baby, and it was time for a sonogram. The test revealed what we'd hope for: We were having a boy! Everyone was ecstatic, but bad news was right around the corner.

In one phone call, my husband was dealt a devastating blow. His grandfather's health was failing, and we needed to get to the hospital right away to say goodbye. I hadn't had the privilege of meeting his grandfather before the call came in, but it was evident when I walked into that hospital room for my first and last conversation with the man that he was loved dearly by many. I shared with him the gender of the baby I was carrying.

He looked at me skeptically and asked, "Well, how do you know it's a boy?"

I explained we had a test that determined the baby's gender, and we wanted to use his name as our son's middle name. He smiled and seemed contented with the news, but I could tell he was exhausted. Our conversation was brief, but I was glad I was able to share that his name would continue with our future son. He passed not long after our hospital visit.

When our son was born, we bought a new trailer and set it up in a rural area. Shopping, work, visiting a doctor, or spending time with friends and family required at least forty-five minutes behind the wheel of a vehicle. We didn't have much money, so we could only afford one car. My in-laws did not like the idea of us being so isolated in an area that was also referred to as the "snow belt of the county."

One day, my in-laws surprised us with a car. It was a bright, white station wagon with wood paneling trim down the sides and a blue velour interior. It wasn't exactly what I would've chosen for myself at a car lot, but I was grateful because it was stable, safe, and big enough to haul our family around. It also belonged to my husband's late grandfather. We named the car the "Dragon-Wagon" because of the sheer size of it.

Like many young couples, we struggled to make ends meet. I was a stay-at-home mom, and my husband worked swing shifts. There came a time when we were close to having our electricity turned off. I got our daughter off to school one day, and I was going to drive with our son, then two years old, to the post office and electric company. I needed to drop off a payment in the company drop-box so we didn't lose our electric services.

My son was an early walker, but a late talker. He barely verbalized. It used to concern me that he hollered and pointed to express himself, but I assumed that was mainly due to his sister always speaking for him and that he'd catch up in time.

I got him ready to leave that morning. We headed out to the Dragon-Wagon, and when we approached the car, my son proceeded to scream at the top of his lungs. I opened the door and tried putting him in his car seat, but he fought me with a strength that was otherworldly for such a small child.

He hit me, kicked me, and pulled my hair every time I tried to put him in the vehicle, shrieking loud enough to make our neighbors stare. I checked him over to see if his clothes might be pinching him or if his shoes were on wrong, but there was nothing visibly out of the ordinary. I tried putting him in the seat again, but he kept freaking out. He just continued to point at the other side of the back seat.

Exasperated, I asked him to please talk and tell me what he wanted. I explained that I couldn't fix what was wrong unless he let me in on the problem. Again, he cried and pointed to the other side of the car.

"There's nothing there," I insisted and tried to place him in his car seat, but it was to no avail.

After a good five minutes of this, my tiny two-year-old screamed with all his might in my face and shouted, "SIT!" He pointed to the other side of the car.

Admittedly, I was mad at him. I asked, "So, you want me to move your car seat to the other side?" He just sobbed and nodded his head.

I said sarcastically, "Your mommy is trying to keep the lights on, but if you're going to insist, I guess I'll just have to move you. This isn't at all convenient. No worries, buddy. I have plenty of time for this." I'm not proud of my response, but I think most parents can admit to being upset over their children's behavior.

I went ahead and gave in to his fit. I moved his car seat. He seemed quite pleased with himself and calmed down immediately. Finally, we set off for our daily errands. I was still grumpy about it when we stopped off at the post office to purchase stamps. I took my son inside, and I recall the woman behind the desk being so kind. She gave him a lollipop and told me what a beautiful boy he was.

The lady in the post office was so nice that I left smiling despite the morning's tantrum. I loaded my son back in the Dragon-Wagon, and this time there were no issues. He was happy with his new seating arrangement, and I felt it best not to question it.

When I went to pull out of the small parking lot of the post office and head left toward our electric company, I looked both left and right.

To my left, there was a small hill. To my right, on my son's new side of the car, was a flat stretch of road. The speed limit was just thirty-five miles per hour in that small section due to the hill, the homes, and the post office. I looked again to my left. Nothing was coming, so I pulled out. Just then, a car came barreling over the hill right toward us. I was already out on the road. There wasn't time to throw the car in reverse. I decided to hit the gas instead to try to get out of the way before catastrophe struck, but I wasn't quick enough. The speeding car slammed into the side of my car at full speed. It hit the driver's side back seat with such force that it spun the Dragon-Wagon around in a circle, and the front of my car was imbedded into the hillside. Glass shattered all over my child and me. When we finally stopped spinning and I was certain it was over, I looked in the back seat. There was my son, looking wide-eyed but otherwise perfectly fine.

I don't remember much after that. I recall the police coming. Some very nice local people took my son to safety inside their home while both the speeding driver and I were questioned by the police.

I ended up with whiplash after the accident, something that didn't show itself until hours later due to the adrenaline rush I must've been experiencing. The thing that stands out the most from that day was staring at my car in horror. The side of the vehicle that my son would've normally been sitting on was completely caved in from the impact. I shook with the realization of what could have been. If my son had been sitting there, he wouldn't be with me today.

He's now nineteen and perfectly healthy. I've always felt that my son knew somehow that something was going to happen, that someone or something told him that he needed to urgently convey his wishes to me. Since he couldn't talk, he used a temper tantrum. Maybe his grandfather and namesake, the original owner of the Dragon-Wagon, had protected him. Maybe he is my son's guardian angel. Whatever the reason, it was a divine intervention that we'll never forget.

— Mandi Raybuck —

90

Secret Garden Angel

*Miracles are instantaneous. They cannot be summoned,
but come of themselves, usually at unlikely moments
and to those who least expect them.*
~Katherine Porter

My friend was producing a performance of *The Secret Garden* at the Confederation Centre of the Arts in Charlottetown, Prince Edward Island. At the last minute, I decided to attend. I had tried unsuccessfully to find a friend to go with me, so I hopped in the car and went alone.

I was recovering from a mastectomy and felt that I needed an evening of enjoyment. Breast cancer was not going to keep me down!

I had a casual conversation with the lady seated next to me before the curtain went up. We enjoyed Act I, and then it was intermission. A friend came over to say hello and asked how I was feeling. After she left, the lady next to me said, "You have been ill."

I said, "Yes, I am recovering from breast-cancer surgery, and things are going well."

I told her that my mother had died of breast cancer in 1967, and I was only seventeen at the time. Somehow during the conversation, I mentioned my maiden name, Carmichael. She said, "Are you Marlene, and did you live in Sherwood? Was your mother Ruth?" I was taken aback by her response, as I had never met this lady before.

She said, "I was your mother's private-duty nurse at her home. I was on vacation when she died. I was so sorry to hear that she passed knowing that she was leaving behind a husband and four young children."

This lady told me that she loved looking after my mother, who was only forty at the time. She went on to say that I had paid her a visit after Mom had died. I asked, "Are you sure it was me?" She assured me that I was the only one of the children with a driver's license, and she remembered my visit.

This whole event sent goose bumps up my arms. What were the chances of sitting next to this lady in the large Confederation Centre? What were the odds that I would mention my maiden name? Why was I meeting this lady thirty-one years after my mother's death? Why was I meeting her now after my own breast surgery?

I sat amazed and awestruck that this lady had been my mother's nurse. I remember a sense of peace and calm coming over me as if my mom was telling me that everything was going to be okay and not to worry.

It has been twenty years since my first bout with cancer. The cancer came back in 2001, requiring more surgery, chemotherapy and radiation, but I am thankful that God has given me all these years to enjoy my family, grandchildren and friends.

I never did cross paths with that lady again. Although I think of her occasionally, I still marvel at this mystery. I am so grateful to have met her right when I needed a connection to my mother. I've always wondered if my mother somehow had a hand in putting us together that day.

— Marlene Bryenton —

91

More than a Souvenir

Coincidences mean you're on the right path.
~Simon Van Booy,
Love Begins in Winter: Five Stories

 small wicker basket sat next to the cash register in a gift shop on the Blue Ridge Parkway. "POCKET ANGELS" the sign beside it said. "ONE DOLLAR EACH." I reached into the basket and removed a nickel-sized pewter disk. On it was a three-dimensional figure of an angel, wings aflutter and hands folded in prayer.

"Cute souvenir," I said to the lady behind the counter.

"It's more than a souvenir," she said, nodding her head in a knowing kind of way. "Keep one in your pocket, and she'll protect you in your travels."

Hmmm. When it came to angels, I was something of a skeptic. But as an inexperienced and insecure motorcycle rider, I figured I needed all the help I could get on this first-ever motorcycle trip. I handed the lady a dollar and dropped the angel into my pocket.

My husband George and our friends had gone on to the adjoining restaurant while I shopped. They looked a little forlorn as I joined them. "The griddle's out of order," George told me. "They've got a guy working on it, but if we want burgers it will be at least half an hour. Otherwise, it's cold sandwiches."

"Let's wait," I said. "My mouth's been watering for a cheeseburger all day." Everyone nodded in agreement.

As we sat gazing out the big picture window, storm clouds began to gather. The sky quickly changed from blue to almost black, and the trees that covered the mountainside swayed violently in the wind. Lightning cracked, and thunder boomed. Rain came down in sheets. But the electricity in the restaurant didn't go out. The repairman finally fixed the griddle. And by the time we finished our delicious cheeseburgers, the storm had passed, and the sky was turning blue again. I stood with George at the cash register as he paid for our lunch. The lady who'd sold me the pocket angel was still working the cash register. She smiled at me and mouthed the words, "Told you."

A shiver ran up my spine as I reached into my pocket and touched the little pewter disk.

We made it through the rest of the day without incident and arrived at our motel just before the sun went down. "Thank you, angel," I whispered, wondering how she knew I was terrified of riding after dark.

After a good night's sleep and a hearty breakfast, my traveling companions and I gathered in the parking lot to warm up our bikes while we suited up. But our friend Tim couldn't find his motorcycle key. "I'm sure it was right here," he said, fumbling around for the umpteenth time through the zippered chest pocket of his leather jacket. But the key wasn't there. Nor was it in any of his other pockets.

While everyone else searched the parking lot, I went inside to the registration desk. "Has anyone turned in a motorcycle key?" I asked. The desk clerk shook his head. The whole gang went to the room where Tim had slept and turned it practically upside down looking for the key. Nothing. We scoured the parking lot again. Still no key. What were we going to do? We had a two-hundred-mile day ahead of us and were already an hour late departing.

A lady with a fluffy dog on a sparkly pink leash walked over. "Are you by chance looking for this?" She held Tim's key in her hand. "Princess was sniffing around and found it." She pointed to the bench where Tim had sat drinking his coffee earlier that morning. He thanked her, patted Princess, and we were off. But we hadn't ridden more than a couple of miles when we came upon flashing blue lights. A half-dozen park rangers had the road blocked.

George got off his bike and approached the nearest ranger. "What's going on?"

"Rock slide. A big one, about an hour ago. As far as we can tell, no one was hurt. But if you'd been there on your motorcycles when it happened…" The man's voice trailed off. Again, I felt a shiver run up my spine as I reached into my pocket and touched the angel.

We had to detour off the parkway to an awful highway. We drove through never-ending traffic, including eighteen-wheelers that made my motorcycle and my nerves tremble every time they blew past. Potholes. Sharp turns and steep drop-offs with no guardrails. But whenever I'd find my heart beating too hard, my breath coming too shallow, and my hands gripping the handlebars too tightly, I'd remind myself of the angel in my pocket, protecting me in my travels.

We all arrived safely at our destination.

Many years have passed since I stopped at that gift shop on the Blue Ridge Parkway. I've traveled countless accident-free miles on my motorcycle since then, always with my angel in my pocket. But one day not long ago, after a near miss at a traffic light left me sitting in my car shaken and sobbing, I realized I need my angel for more than motorcycle trips. So I had a hole drilled into the little pewter disk and a pretty chain run through it. Now my angel hangs around my neck and travels with me everywhere I go — whether by foot, bicycle, horseback or car. Or motorcycle, of course.

The lady behind the cash register that long-ago day was right. A pocket angel is more than a one-dollar souvenir. She's priceless.

— Jennie Ivey —

Chapter
10

Messages from
Heaven

Photographs from Mom

God could not be everywhere, so he created mothers.
~Jewish Proverb

I sat at the kitchen table, coffee in hand, looking at job ads on my computer. I had recently been a victim of downsizing at the veterinarian's office where I had worked for the past two years as a tech assistant.

"Mom, please send me the perfect job," I said to the empty room. My mother had passed a few years prior, but I still talked to her often. I just knew she could still hear me.

Just then, I saw an ad from a school that was looking for an Early Childhood teacher. Since I had a degree in Education and had taught previously, I thought this might be a potential match. I e-mailed my résumé and inquiry letter and hoped for the best. After that was done, I decided to take a break and do some household chores.

I opened the door that led to the basement stairs. As I turned to go down, something caught my eye. A photograph lay on the floor at the top of the stairs. The picture was of me, around age six I guessed, on a family vacation. I was sitting on a chair by a lake with a black Labrador Retriever by my side. It wasn't our dog, but I always managed to find a dog to hang out with on every vacation because I loved them so much. I smiled as I picked it up. Shelves at the top of the stairs held a hodgepodge of items, including photo albums and picture boxes.

It must have fallen out somehow. I tucked the photo into one of the boxes and went on with my day.

The next day started the same way—at the kitchen table with my computer. I was pleased to see I had gotten a response from the teaching inquiry I had sent the day before.

"Thanks, Mom," I said as I responded to their e-mail, accepting one of the times offered for an interview. The buzzer of the dryer startled me. I put aside my computer and went to go change loads. As I opened the basement door, I was surprised to see yet another picture on the floor. In this one, I was about eleven years old and was preparing to race at a swim meet. I was wearing my burgundy and yellow Speedo, along with a yellow bathing cap. How I loved to swim when I was younger! We had a pool in our yard, and I was on the town swim team in the summer and a traveling team during the winter. In high school, I was the captain of the swim team. I picked up the photo and put it in an album.

Later that day, I needed something from one of the basement shelves. I opened the door. "How strange," I said as I encountered yet another picture! This one was of my childhood friend and me. We must have been about twelve years old. We still kept in touch, and when I saw the photo I realized I hadn't talked to her in a while. I decided to give her a call.

"Hi, Kim," I said when she answered. "I came across a picture of us, and I thought I would call and see how you are." We visited for a bit, catching up on life events. I told her that I was job searching, and then I asked her about her dog.

"Koda is recovering from an injury to his knee," Kim said. "He has been doing hydrotherapy twice a week. It really seems to be help-ing." We chatted about the benefits of swimming for rehab of many different ailments.

"Amy," Kim said suddenly. "Why don't you apply for a job at the hydrotherapy center? I will put in a good word for you with the owner."

I thought, *Why not?* This combined my love of swimming with my experience at the vet's office. No sooner had I sent out an e-mail than I got one back from the owner. She had a position opening up in a month because someone was getting married and leaving. Because of my experience with dogs and a glowing recommendation from Kim, she thought I would be perfect for the job and asked me to come in as soon as I could for a meeting.

Suddenly, it occurred to me that my mom had led me to this job! She must have put the pictures in my path at the top of the stairs. The first photo had a dog in it, and the second reminded me how I used to swim. The third prompted me to call my friend, who suggested the position.

I cancelled my interview at the school and enthusiastically accepted the position at the canine hydrotherapy center, assisting dogs swimming for rehabilitation.

"Thanks, Mom," I said. "You truly sent me the perfect job."

— Amy Rovtar Payne —

93

Hummingbird Angel

*Quick as a hummingbird is my love, dipping into
the hearts of flowers — she darts so eagerly, swiftly,
sweetly dipping into the flowers of my heart.*
~James Oppenheim

My mom loved watching hummingbirds. She had my dad strategically place hummingbird feeders around our house so that, no matter which window we looked out, a feeder was in sight. People began sending her hummingbird cards, little glass hummingbirds and hummingbird pictures as gifts. In her later years, she would talk about her hummingbirds and fuss at them. She would tell me about the ruby-throated one that was bossy and would chase all the others away from the feeders, or the emerald-capped one that would only eat from one feeder. I found myself looking forward to the latest hummingbird drama whenever I'd call for a chat.

Mom passed away in 2000 at the age of seventy-two — too early, as far as I was concerned. As she had requested, Dad had her cremated. Although my two sisters and I had offered to go with him to spread her ashes, he insisted on doing it alone. He said that they had discussed where she wanted to be sprinkled.

Dad died four years later. His wish was to be cremated and sprinkled where he had taken Mom's ashes. He left us written directions. We knew the place well. It was where he and Mom had honeymooned in 1953 and where we had gone on vacation every summer while growing up. So, when Dad's ashes arrived, my sisters and my dad's two brothers all piled in the van, with the urn containing Dad's ashes packed carefully in the back for the road trip to join him with Mom.

Arriving at the spot, we got out of the van and walked to the edge of the river where, as children, we would play and float in the beautiful, clear water every summer. Later, we brought our own children there. We spent countless nights around the campfire, all freshly showered and smelling like Ivory soap, except for Dad, who was a Dial man. Days were spent hiking, canoeing, swimming and floating in the river. Nights were spent singing, making s'mores and telling stories. It was a special place that held so many wonderful, happy memories. Surely, this was where Dad wanted us to come. A canoe glided by as we all enjoyed the sights, sounds and smells of our favorite vacation spot. One of the inhabitants of the canoe raised his paddle in greeting.

We all took turns saying our last goodbyes to Dad. Glancing at my sisters, I slowly took the lid off of the tin container that contained Dad's ashes. I know that we were all thinking the same thing, hoping this was the right place.

"Well, Dad," I said. "During your short time on Earth, this was your little piece of Heaven." Just as I was about to scoop out some ashes, a hummingbird with a bright yellow belly appeared right in front of my face. I was shocked! It looked me right in the eyes for several seconds before flying to each of my sisters and doing the same. Then, just as suddenly as it had appeared, it was gone. My sisters and I began laughing, and then the tears came. Tears of joy!

Now we were sure that we had come to the right spot. Mom had just confirmed it.

— Donna Adams Stare —

94

The Weathervane

Where we love is home, home that our feet may leave,
but not our hearts.
~Oliver Wendell Holmes

It had been almost a year since my husband Mike had died after being diagnosed with Stage IV lung cancer. It was only six months from his diagnosis to his death, leaving me no real time to prepare for what lie ahead. He was forty-nine, and our son Jake was just fourteen. I was still in a state of survival shock and emotional grief. We had been married almost twenty years, and life as a widow looked very different and uncertain.

The house we had been renting was starting to fall apart, and the landlord had no intention of fixing anything more than the bare necessities. The day I found a mouse and told him about it, he thought we had gotten a pet and asked me what we had named it!

So when the life-insurance money finally came in, I decided to buy a house. I wanted a place where Jake could have his friends over to play video games and hang out on the weekends. A place that was safe. A place that I prayed wouldn't have mice!

I started my search looking at older homes in established areas, but none seemed right. The bedrooms were too small, or the kitchen needed repairs. Plus, I couldn't find one house that fit our furniture. Mike and I had purchased the furniture together during the time we were married, and I had no intention of getting rid of it. Adding to the mix was the fact that we had also rescued a dog that needed a back yard. We looked at dozens of homes with four different real estate agents, but we still could not find one that was worth buying.

My stepfather suggested that I look at some newer subdivisions and build a home. I thought he was crazy! Mike was a bricklayer by trade and was the builder, not me. Sure, that had been our plan when Mike was alive, but what did I know about building a house without him? And who could I trust? After all, my mom and stepfather lived out of state, and the life-insurance money was all we had. Plus, I was saving a large portion of it so Jake could go to college.

My dream to own a home was quickly becoming unrealistic. But every weekend, I'd search anyway. And then, every night, I would cry myself to sleep, wondering what Mike would have done and praying I was making the right move.

One agent I was working with kept telling me to check out a new subdivision that was just getting started on the edge of town. I drove over there three times and saw nothing but an empty road. It paralleled exactly how my life was sadly starting to feel. I was beginning to think she was nuts! Three times, I started down that road. And three times I turned around because I thought nothing was there.

Luckily, I can be pretty stubborn because the fourth time I drove in a little farther and saw the start of a few houses. I thought to myself, *What a waste of time this was,* and almost turned around again, but I didn't. Call it divine intervention, but this time I found the builder's office and went in to see what this subdivision was all about. Boy, was I surprised!

As I searched through the possible floor plans, I found one that I knew would be perfect! My heart was racing because it was more money than I really wanted to spend. I vaguely remember Mike telling me that he thought this builder was one of the better ones and could be trusted. But did I dare build a house without his approval or help? Where would I find the strength and courage?

Now that I had picked out a plan, I was told there was only one available lot left in the section that could fit that house. It was on a street called Weathervane Drive. I was so nervous about making a financial move like this that I called my mom and stepdad for advice.

I was told that I could put a small amount of earnest money on the lot to hold it and take a few days to decide. My stepdad recommended doing that, so I did.

Now, not only was my heart racing, but so was my mind! Jake was definitely all in and so excited at the possibility of building a new house. But all I could think about was what Mike would think or say.

Letting my fears get the best of me, I was ready to back out of the deal and risk losing the earnest money. In an attempt to burn off some nervous energy, I decided to clean out the garage. It was a mess — an emotional mess like me — since it was filled with Mike's tools and various odds and ends we had collected over the years.

Feeling pretty much drained and defeated sorting through clutter, I decided to tackle one last corner and call it a day. Hidden behind some boxes was the answer I was looking for. It was an old, metal weathervane, the kind that stands proudly on the roof against all types of wind and rain. It looked like it had seen its share of storms, as the yellow paint had begun to peel, and gray metal was showing through. Mike loved to go antiquing and to garage sales, and he must have bought it without me knowing because I had never seen it before.

Holding that precious weathervane in my hands, I burst into tears. I knew it was Mike's way of telling me to build that house on Weathervane Drive. He was with me.

So I built that house for Jake and me on Weathervane Drive, and we moved in six months later, bringing all of Mike's love and memories — and his weathervane — with us.

— Debra Zemke —

95

Marco

Pay attention to your dreams — God's angels often
speak directly to our hearts when we are asleep.
~Eileen Elias Freeman,
The Angels' Little Instruction Book

I felt a nudge in my ribs. "Have you checked out the new guy?" Jessie whispered. We were on a college trip to Italy and were supposed to be listening to the tour guide enthuse about the frescoes and the architecture, but we'd started chatting instead.

I put a finger to my lips and stifled a giggle. "Shhhh! Everyone's listening!" I whispered, nodding my head toward the tour guide, who was now looking sternly in our direction.

"Okay... then write your answer on my notepad if you're not going to say it out loud." Jessie rolled her eyes at me in exasperation.

I hesitated. I had noticed Marco, and I was intrigued. He'd joined our group in Milan. We'd been on the same tours and had stolen a few glances across the bustling piazzas. There was something about him that I felt oddly drawn to. I couldn't explain it myself, but I put it in language I thought Jessie would understand.

YES, HE IS CUTE, I wrote on the notepad and pushed it back to Jessie.

"I knew it," she mouthed at me. Jessie scribbled something on the notepad and held it up for me to read: LET'S GET OUT OF HERE — COFFEE?

I nodded. We snuck away from the group as inconspicuously as we could, blinking as our eyes and ears made the transition from the gloomy interior of the quiet church to the dazzling sunlight of the noisy piazza.

The aroma of fresh cappuccino hit me as we walked into Caffe Vergnano. An exquisitely dressed Italian woman with bright red lips was arguing intensely with a companion. All at once, they stopped, embraced, and then carried on their heated conversation like nothing had happened. I had never felt more aware of my teenage awkwardness. Everything in Italy was sublime, from the language, to the people, to the places. I was on sensory overload.

After finding a table, we carried on our conversation.

"So, have you spoken to Marco yet?"

"Not really, but he keeps looking at me… not in a creepy way. I can't explain it… the way he looks at me." I dropped my voice. "It's like he's looking into my soul."

"Well, if that doesn't sound creepy, I don't know what does!" Jessie laughed.

"Ha ha," I said sarcastically. Inwardly, I resolved to get to know Marco. Something about him made me desperate to know more.

It took me a few days to summon the courage to start a conversation. When I finally did, under the watchful eyes of the stone angels that guarded the piazza, the air was electric with promise.

"Aaaah, Carrie, you are very beautiful. Bellissimo. But we can only be friends. Surely, you know this?" He looked at me intently with big, brown eyes, a lock of his curly hair falling over his face. I held my breath and then let it out slowly.

"I understand. It's because it could never work, isn't it? You're here, and I'm there." I pointed vaguely in what I thought was the direction of the UK. It felt a million miles from the frescoes and fountains of Italy.

"But you'll always be here…." He touched his head and then his chest. "And here."

I looked at the floor. He was right, of course. It was a vacation crush, and I was a fool to think it was anything more.

"Shall we walk back?" We linked arms, like friends do, and headed off into the balmy evening.

Over the next few weeks, we spoke more times, and with every conversation we edged that bit closer to the precipice. I had already fallen; I just needed him to be at the bottom to catch me. Every small touch or look was loaded with everything we wanted to say but couldn't. The words I needed him to say bubbled under the surface but remained unspoken.

On Marco's last night, we made a pact to see each other again no matter what. We were on the cusp of something tangible and real. We still hadn't shared a kiss, but I was glad because it gave us both a reason to keep our feelings alive. With a heavy heart, I helped him pack his things as he prepared to leave.

"You won't forget me, will you?" I asked.

"You, Carrie? No… not in a million years. I cannot go through life without seeing you again. That is my solemn promise." He put his hand on his chest to show he meant it. We embraced as friends, and he left my life as suddenly as he had walked into it.

That night, I had what I can only describe as the most vivid dream I have ever experienced. It is as real to me now as it was to my eighteen-year-old self.

I was floating in an ethereal sky when I was joined suddenly by Marco, who was dressed in a white robe. He had no hair, but I wasn't scared. I was just pleased to see him. He took my hand and led me to two archways. I looked inside the first one to see what I recognised as a waiting area. Chairs were lined up around the sides, although the room was empty. The second archway was much less discernible but was emanating mist and seemed to hold secrets that my mind couldn't interpret.

When Marco spoke, I could sense some sort of battle he was fighting with something unseen.

"Carrie, kiss me. You have to kiss me now," he said urgently.

"Why?"

"There isn't time. Please, I want to kiss you so much."

I didn't need him to ask me again. It was a bittersweet moment that was over too quickly.

"Goodbye, Carrie," Marco whispered as he stepped away from

me toward the second arch.

"Wait! Marco! What's the hurry? Come back!"

And with that, he was gone.

I awoke the next morning feeling completely disoriented. I hadn't forgotten my strange dream, but what did it mean?

I didn't have to wait long to find out.

"Carrie… CARRIE!" I heard Jessie shouting outside my room. I opened the door, and she practically fell on the floor. "It's all over the news, Carrie. There's been a plane crash at Milan airport…."

I didn't need to hear anything else. In any case, I had stopped listening.

Marco had been on that plane. His visit to me in my dream was an attempt to resolve everything that had been left undone before he passed over.

— Carrie Roope —

96

A Fragrant Reminder

Because I feel that, in the Heavens above, the angels,
whispering to one another, can find, among their
burning terms of love, none so devotional
as that of "Mother."
~Edgar Allen Poe

It had been a heartbreaking, mind-numbing month, and it was about to get worse. It began in the doctor's office when my doctor handed me a sealed envelope to give to the surgeon who would be removing my left ovary. He explained that the test results revealed it was important that it be removed.

Of course, the minute I got in the car, I ripped open the envelope, and the words "possible malignancy" reached out from the paper and rendered me speechless. My hands shook as I came to terms with this unexpected news that had the power to possibly change my life forever. I thought of the people who needed me. My daughters were ten and twelve years of age. What would they do without their mother? How would my husband raise them alone if something were to happen to me?

And my own mom had recently been diagnosed with cancer. I had always been there for her. How could I be absent now when she needed me most? These thoughts were heavy on my mind the day I met the surgeon. She scheduled my surgery for the first Thursday in April, which was only a few weeks away. She told me to hope for the best and have a positive attitude. Easier said than done.

My mom succumbed unexpectedly to her cancer only eight weeks after being diagnosed. We buried her five days before my surgery.

My husband and I arrived at the hospital bright and early on that warm and cloudy April morning. I was a bundle of nerves, and when they placed me on the gurney and started to prep me, it only got scarier.

My heart-rhythm problem, which had previously been controlled with medication, was now beating out of control.

I lay there staring at the ceiling while they called my primary physician. My heart was racing faster than the worry running through my veins. I began to focus on Mom and all that she had gone through these past few months.

It seemed like mere minutes when I heard someone calling my name. I was sure they were going to tell me that the surgery had to be postponed.

Being in a semi-groggy state, I also began to recognize a familiar flowery aroma filling the room. From the second I inhaled it, I was instantly transported to a warm and comfortable state of wellbeing. I knew right away that this was the White Shoulders perfume my mom wore for as long as I could remember.

I had surprised her with a bottle for her birthday that year. I had lightly spritzed her body from that same bottle just before her wake.

I lay there in the stark recovery room soaking up the serenity of this visit from beyond when someone wearing scrubs leaned over the bed rail to tell me that everything looked good. The words "NO CANCER" rang out loud and clear. The soothing scent surrounding me was a sign that my mom was there to hear the good news, too.

I would come to feel my mom's presence, through her favorite fragrance, a few more times in the years to follow. She was there four years later when I needed a hysterectomy at age thirty-seven and again a few years after that when I needed emergency bowel surgery. That signature scent was the reassurance I needed that my mother was still there for me.

— Kathy Whirity —

Get Up!

Don't give up before the miracle happens.
~Fannie Flagg

He never missed a day of school until the second month of the term, when he was gone for three days straight. I just assumed he had a cold until two of his friends approached me after class.

"Mr. Schultz, we need to tell you something that only a few people know. Griffin has cancer. The chemo has messed up his liver, and he's in the hospital. We don't know if he's going to make it."

I thought they had the wrong name. Griffin was a top athlete who played football, soccer, and volleyball. I had just seen him a few days earlier, smiling and looking as healthy as anyone else. I couldn't fathom him having cancer, let alone dying.

Griffin's friends looked so scared. They just wanted someone to heal their friend. All alone in the classroom, I sat at Griffin's desk looking for answers. I prayed for him.

Two days later, Griffin walked through the classroom door and sat at his desk. I had to hide my smile. I said, "How are you?"

He responded, "Good," with a perplexed tone as if he were thinking, *Why wouldn't I be okay?* He didn't know that I knew. So I wrote him a letter and offered to open up a dialogue if he wanted it. We started meeting during lunch, and his story had so many more layers to it.

Griffin was adopted. He had never known his biological parents, but the mom who raised him died in August 2011 of cancer. Two

Messages from Heaven | 309

weeks later, without any time to grieve, Griffin was diagnosed with testicular cancer.

He told me, "I just spent a year watching the closest person in my life deteriorate, become bedridden because of the chemo treatments, and die. Then, just days after burying my mother, I'm sitting alone in a doctor's office, and he tells me I have cancer. I have to start chemo right away."

On August 24, 2011, a week before he would begin his sophomore year of high school, Griffin began his first cycle of chemo. "During chemo," Griffin said, "everything hurts. You're always so tired. You get no reprieve. The last day or two on a cycle, you start to feel somewhat normal again, and then they start another chemo treatment. Each session is worse than the last."

I couldn't believe it. This young man had been undergoing chemo treatments, attending school and, most startling of all, attending football practice every day. I asked him what his football coaches said to him about his cancer. He said, "They don't know I have it. No one knows. Only a few close friends. I don't want people treating me differently or looking at me as the cancer kid."

Then Griffin missed school again. I went and met him for lunch. He told me he just wanted to reach his sixteenth birthday, but it wasn't going to happen anymore because he'd decided to stop the chemo. It was just too painful. I remember hugging him as we left lunch, not wanting to let go, as I did not know if I would see him again.

Two days later, to my surprise, Griffin was at his desk. He asked if we could talk after school. When the final bell of the afternoon rang, the door opened and Griffin walked in with a smile on his face.

"Yesterday morning, I woke up in so much pain that I couldn't get out of bed," he said. "I just wanted to die, to be with my mother again. But then I saw her in the room with me. She looked like an angel. I heard her shout, 'Get up! Get up!' I knew she wanted me to keep going. I got out of bed and decided to start treatment again. My mom wasn't ready for me just yet."

Griffin and I made a pact that day. Not only would he reach his sixteenth birthday but he would graduate, and I would be there for both.

On Griffin's graduation day, I could not sit in the audience because I was on stage. I had to give a speech to accept the Teacher of the Year award. I asked Griffin if I could talk about him, and he agreed as long as I didn't mention his name because he still didn't want to be known as a cancer kid.

As I stood on the podium and looked out at all those kids in their caps and gowns, with their adoring parents looking on, I made eye contact with Griffin. A tear fell from my face as I looked at a kid who wasn't sure if he would reach his sixteenth birthday. Now he was eighteen and graduating. I spoke to the audience about love and how it allows us to "Get up!" when life's pains pin us to the ground. I said that life is shorter than we think, and our parents aren't here forever. I spoke about another student who died and didn't reach graduation, and the need for parents to hug their children more often and be affectionate. I advised the students not to focus on getting first place in life, but on leading their lives where they place love first. I told them about a student whom we almost lost but was still here. And I let them know that angels are real.

Many in the audience were crying, but Griffin was smiling.

It's been some years since then, and Griffin and I still meet up. When he gave me permission to share his story in this book, using his name, I asked what it would mean to him if someone read this and wrote to tell him that his story had helped them get up and keep going. Griffin said simply, "It would mean all the pain I endured was worth it."

— Steve Schultz —

98

Time for Mass

*Our angel friends watch over us when we're asleep at
night and guard us with their gentle wings
until the morning light.*
~Author Unknown

I met Jeannie when I was nine, and she was twelve. She lived behind my cousin's house in a second-floor apartment. My cousin and I were the same age and spent a lot of time together until I met Jeannie. Then I started spending time alone with Jeannie and my cousin didn't understand why. But it was because Jeannie and I did something that my cousin wouldn't have liked; we pretended to be at religious school.

Although I was born a Catholic and had received my First Holy Communion, my family attended church on Easter and Christmas only. Jeannie, on the other hand, attended Catholic school and wore a gray plaid uniform. She would go over all her papers from school with me. I learned as much from Jeannie about God, the church and its sacraments as I did in a year of faith classes.

Her love of faith included coming to my house at 8:00 a.m. every Sunday morning to take me to the 9:00 a.m. children's mass. I was always asleep, and my mom would yell, "Jeannie's here for church." I always went. We walked there together every Sunday where I learned about being in God's House for the Sabbath.

We moved when I was twelve, and I didn't get to see Jeannie after that.

Years later, I attended a faith-sharing class, and we were asked to name a person who was our foundation in faith. Immediately, I thought of Jeannie. I thought about her all that day and tried to reach her through her brother, who was still listed locally. He remembered me and told me the sad news that she had recently passed from a weak heart that she'd had since childhood. I never knew of her condition. We both cried. I told him I would have a mass said for her on her birth date.

The only opening my church had on that date for her mass was in the Catholic school where masses are said one day a week. It would be at 8:00 a.m.

But on that date several months later, I forgot to set the alarm. And to make that mass I would have to get up much earlier than usual.

Early that morning in the still darkness, I woke suddenly. Next to my bed, a brightly shining figure stood next to me. I was stunned but not afraid. It looked like an angel, and I had never had any visions or hallucinations my entire life. Or was it a dream? Then I saw Jeannie's distinctive red hair and was reminded of the mass.

I jumped out of bed, waking my husband. We scurried to get dressed and leave on time for the school mass.

At the school, I felt Jeannie's presence. The schoolchildren even wore the same uniform I remembered from her schooldays.

Do I believe that Jeannie woke me up for her mass? Yes, I do. How fitting that my dear, sweet friend would come again to my house to take me to a Catholic school children's mass.

— Fran Signorino —

99

The Pull of the Magnet

*The love of a mother is the veil of a softer light between
the heart and the heavenly Father.*
~Samuel Taylor Coleridge

When my mother was dying I told her, "Mom, you have to give me a sign. Let me know you made it, okay?" She smiled and nodded. Her mouth was too dry to speak. She'd been in hospice for weeks and was reaching the end. She was more than ready.

After she passed away, I was at her house preparing for an estate sale. Family and friends had taken keepsakes, mementos, and the cherished family heirlooms they wanted. Only the stuff of life was left — pots and pans, pillows and blankets, jigsaw puzzles and books. And a large collection of magnets Mom had collected on her travels and had gotten from family and friends.

Nearly two hundred magnets covered the white refrigerator — not that anyone could see the underlying color. I managed to make room for a sign that said "2 for 25 cents."

My sisters helped with the estate sale the next day. It was a big success because it was an unseasonably warm January day. One young man was thrilled to get Dad's claw-foot hammer and box of finishing nails for $2.00. On his way to pay, he lingered at the refrigerator, carefully selecting a single magnet — the Portuguese rooster Mom had bought in Lisbon.

He gave my sister $2.25. "The magnets are two for 25 cents," she said.

"One's good," he said. "Thank you."

Two months later, I was finishing an exhaustive search for a new house and I was touring a beautifully renovated home. It was so pretty it looked like it had been staged. It was bright and inviting with an open floor plan. It was just the right size and right price. Everything was perfectly arranged, right down to the throw pillows. Even though it was somewhat impersonal, without a sense of who had lived in this house and who had carefully restored it, I felt a pull of some kind. Maybe this was the right house.

Once I entered the kitchen, I knew. On the refrigerator was a single magnet — my mom's Portuguese rooster. She had sent me a sign. We were both home.

— Teresa Otto —

100

The Mansion of Many Rooms

*One flesh. Or if you prefer, one ship. The starboard
engine has gone. I, the port engine, must chug along
somehow till we make harbour. Or rather,
till the journey ends.*
~C.S. Lewis

My wife Betsy was a two-time breast-cancer survivor when the disease returned in May 2016, this time in her liver. We'd been friends since 1980, a couple since 1983, and married since 1987, and the thought of losing her was terrifying. Still, I thought, we'd beaten cancer before. Our daughter Emily had been only a little over two years old when the cancer first showed up in 1997. She was now twenty-one. She had never known her mom without cancer, but she'd also seen her beat it twice. Why not a third time?

Although we didn't know it when she was diagnosed, her prognosis was not good. Most people with her kind of advanced liver cancer are given five months to live after diagnosis. On we went, though, and she lived into 2017. We went on trips and had fun together like we always had as Betsy, a beautiful singer, made each day a song. The prognosis, it seemed, was wrong, and she was so healthy throughout 2017 that I sometimes forgot she had cancer. I would have forgotten entirely if I weren't driving her to her weekly chemo sessions.

Throughout early 2018, her health remained steady until the morning of May 5th when she woke up with such severe abdominal pain that she couldn't move. I took her to the emergency room where they gave her pain medication, but they couldn't do any more than that. The tumors were larger, and her liver was swollen and pressing against her other internal organs.

Now that chemo had failed, there was only one procedure left that could save her — the Y90, where they inject the liver with radioactive isotopes to kill the cancer. When we arrived for the procedure, her bilirubin was too high and calcium levels off, so they couldn't do it. There was no hope left. Soon after, the people from hospice arrived.

Betsy could no longer climb stairs and was sleeping in the living room on one couch while I had the other couch. Some nights, I would wake up to hear her whispering, and I'd ask, "Are you all right? Do you need something?"

She would answer, "I'm not talking to you. I'm talking to the angels."

In the morning, I'd ask her about it, and she'd say, "I don't know if they're angels, but they feel like angels. They feel like the same angels of light I saw in that vision at the hospital."

That vision had come to her when they were putting her under for a paracentesis. She saw bright spirits coming down from a temple and laying hands on her. She wasn't sure if they were healing her body or letting her know it was all right to leave it behind, but she wanted to go with them. In the recovery room that day, when she told me about it, she said, "I want to go where I can sing again, where I won't hurt anymore, and there aren't any more procedures or needles and no more pain."

Throughout the night of August second into the morning of the third, she talked to her angels in the darkness of the living room, and I listened to her. I couldn't make out the words — she was speaking in whispers — but I could sense the urgency in her voice and how much she wanted to leave her body behind. At 2:38 a.m., her voice rose suddenly. I said, "Are you all right? Are you talking to me?"

She whispered, "Yes," and then said, "I had an interesting

dream — wasn't a dream — was a real place — many rooms — so pretty — nice guy — like a guided tour — like when you go on a tour of a mansion — many rooms — so pretty — and I wanna go and I don't know why it's taking so long 'cause it's so pretty there, and he's such a nice guy showing me around like 'See? Nothing to fear, right? Only friends and love here' and I wanna go and I don't know why it's taking so long. She [the doctor] said I'd just fall asleep and go, and I keep falling asleep, but I don't go and I wanna go."

I wrote the vision down on a little pad I kept for notes on changes in her condition or funny things she'd say, and then I returned to the couch and tried to sleep. Sleep was impossible, though, and I lay there stroking the head of our little, brown Beagle and staring up at the ceiling.

Around 7:00 a.m., Betsy asked, "Are you awake? I had this crazy dream, but it wasn't a dream. It was real. And I was there. Did I tell you?" I said she had, and she asked if I'd written it down. I told her I had, and she said she knew that I would. Then she said, "I'm sorry. I gotta go. But I'll see you and my sweet little kid again on the other side. I love you both." She lingered throughout that day and into the next, but with all the pain medication she was on, she wasn't conscious for much of it. She died at 4:54 p.m. on August 4th. She was smiling.

Now she was free, but I was trapped in a dark nightmare. Her death was everything I'd ever feared. I felt the floor beneath me roll and surge like a little boat on high seas, and I knew I would be on that boat alone now, staggering back and forth for the rest of my life.

The next night, though, she showed up and played me her four favorite Bruce Springsteen songs. I was listening to a mixed CD we'd made years before — which had none of those songs on it — when they suddenly started playing in exactly the order she used to play them. Since then she has let Emily and me know when she's around plenty of times, often through songs — which is hardly surprising since singing was her great passion. And she still drops in from time to time, brightly smiling, in my dreams.

I don't know exactly where she is when she's not visiting us, but I think of her vision and her angels often. I know that, wherever she is, there's no more pain — and she's singing. And I can only be grateful for all our time together, for holding her in my arms, and for being able to let her go when it was right. Knowing this has stopped my little boat from being rocked so hard because, when we love someone, we only want what is best for them. If there's one thing I'm sure of, it's that she's happy now in the mansion of many rooms, so pretty, with her angels of light.

—Joshua J. Mark—

Buggy Ride

It's time to say goodbye, but I think goodbyes
are sad, and I'd much rather say hello.
Hello to a new adventure.
~Ernie Harwell

Lera, my one-hundred-year-old grandmother, was absolutely convinced that she had met a man who would be returning to take her on a trip. Apparently, he promised that he would come back and they would go by horse and buggy to a place where she could visit some of her old friends. This was a paradox because most of her old friends were deceased.

It all sounded like a scam to me. You know, one of those people who befriend old folks and convince them that they've won a trip or, better yet, someone proclaiming to be a long lost love interest who has returned to resume a previous relationship that never existed to begin with. I'd seen the tabloid talk shows where sobbing seniors woefully described identical situations. If I'd actually believed that my grandmother had met someone new, I would have been concerned.

Everyone listened and smiled respectfully as Lera told her story, but I concluded secretly that Grandma had either lost her marbles or had had a dream that seemed very real to her. However, I was sure of one thing: She hadn't met anyone new. She lived in an apartment, and my mother lived directly across the hall from her. Mom was her caregiver and rarely left her side. The man whom my grandmother described was a mystery.

As time passed, Lera told everyone about her upcoming trip. She still couldn't pinpoint when it would take place, but she talked about it often.

It was obvious that Lera was excited about this new adventure, but after several months of anticipation, the trip story began to wane. "Well, I guess he's forgotten about me," she told my mother. "I don't think he's coming back like he promised, or he would have been here by now."

In an attempt to comfort her, my mom assured Lera that the mystery man hadn't forgotten her, and that all things happen in due time.

By the beginning of February, winter was in full swing, and it enveloped the city with colder-than-usual temperatures. I had just given birth to my first child, and life was busy.

Lera was excited to be a great-grandma once again, and her new great-grandchild was a welcome topic of conversation. The mystery man had finally trailed off into the sunset, and everyone seemed to be focused on more enjoyable things like baby clothes and cute baby playthings.

On a Tuesday afternoon, Lera's good friend Carl stopped by for a visit. Carl was a nice, young man. He'd met Lera through a mutual friend several years before, and they had developed a rich and lasting friendship. He dropped by every Tuesday, and they chatted for an hour or so. When it was time to go, Carl always reassured Lera that he'd be back the following Tuesday for another visit.

This particular visit, however, ended differently. When it was time for Carl to be on his way, he gave his customary farewell and told Lera that he would stop by again the following Tuesday. In response, Lera exclaimed quickly, "Oh, I won't be here."

"You won't?" Carl questioned.

"No," Lera answered. "I'm going on a trip."

There it was: the trip story. Once again, she reiterated the story of the man who promised to return and take her on a trip. Everyone was familiar with the story. We'd heard it at least a dozen times. We knew about the man and the buggy ride. We knew that Lera was expecting to see her old friends, but we had heard the story so many times that we'd become complacent. We didn't pay attention to her newest proclamation that she wouldn't be there the following Tuesday.

Five days later, Lera complained of severe abdominal pain. The degree of pain was out of the ordinary, and it was obvious that she needed medical attention. Immediately, my mother called 911.

Lera was transported to the hospital where she had emergency exploratory surgery. Family gathered and waited anxiously for news from the operating room. Finally, it came. An obstruction was found, and it had cut off circulation to a vital organ. The organ could not be saved, and there was nothing more the doctors could do other than to try and keep her comfortable.

When I heard the news of Lera's prognosis, the buggy-ride story came to mind immediately. It became clear to me that Lera's experience, whether a dream or an actual event, had taken place for a reason. The man who had appeared to Lera had gained her trust, and he'd made a promise to return. He had encouraged her and prepared her for a very special trip. She was excited to go, and her excitement now became the primary source of our comfort.

The click-clacking of hooves and creaking of wagon wheels could not be heard by those who were with her that night. The vapor from the horses' breath and the welcoming smile from the angel driving them could not be seen by those whose time had not yet come. Lera, however, had been waiting expectantly. And in the quiet of that early Monday morning, she passed away peacefully and began her journey by horse and buggy, off to visit her old friends.

— Melinda Pritzel —

Meet Our Contributors

Jayne M. Adams has been writing all her life in various careers. She now gets to spend her time telling stories inspired by her experiences. Her story "The Token Collector" will appear in *Short Story America: Vol. VII* in February 2020. She and her husband live in the South Carolina low country.

Kristi Allen, known in many online fan communities as the Kritter Lady, is an avid crocheter, and has spent over three decades perfecting her craft. Using her own visions as her inspiration, she designs and creates her own unique stuffed animals, called Kritters.

Jean S. Anker has a B.A. in English Literature and has been a teacher and a stay-at-home mom for her three sons. Jean and her husband recently celebrated their fortieth wedding anniversary with a trip to New Zealand. She enjoys travel, tennis, and yoga. She is writing a book about Greek immigrants, drawn from her family heritage.

David-Matthew Barnes is an author, playwright, poet, and screenwriter. He loves tacos, white carnations, love stories, old movies, koalas, Nancy Drew books, everything written by Judy Blume, and all things Snoopy, Tiki, and Disney. Learn more at davidmatthewbarnes.com.

Laurie Batzel lives in Northeastern Pennsylvania with her husband, four children, and a Corgi named Stuart. She is an author of contemporary and historical women's fiction books. Her debut novel, *With My Soul*, will be released by Anaiah Press in September. She loves reading, baking, and watching British period dramas on TV.

Barbara Bennett used her natural humor and acquired wit to survive twenty-six moves in seventeen years to five foreign countries, which she shares in *Anchored Nowhere: A Navy Wife's Story*. Her first mystery is currently a work in progress and this is her third story published in the *Chicken Soup for the Soul* series. E-mail her at barbny2nc@gmail.com.

Francine L. Billingslea is originally from New Jersey and now resides in the Atlanta, GA area. She feels proud and blessed to be the author of over sixty-five published works and a frequent contributor to the *Chicken Soup for the Soul* series. She loves writing, traveling, and spending quality time with her loved ones.

Maureen Boyd Biro is an author, dream consultant, and speaker. Writing and dream work are her twin passions, and she enjoys leading creative retreats, teaching workshops, and presenting at conferences and events. She resides in California with her artist husband and rescue tabby Sophia. Learn more at lyricaldreaming.com.

S.L. Blake is an avid reader and lover of the written word. She has written for local and national publications and is currently finding the courage to self-publish her debut novel, *The Deepest Scars*, although she has already written several books. She lives where the Army sends her husband, along with their two children and two dogs.

Jackie Carman Blankenship is a self-published author of four novels. She was the editor and a contributing writer for her college newspaper and has had several articles published in online magazines. She works for an international Christian ministry, enjoys spending time with her daughters, granddaughter, friends, and being outdoors.

Theresa Brandt is a writer who lives with her three boys and lots of furry friends. She loves spending time with family and friends as well as reading, gardening, traveling, and crafts. E-mail her at tbbrandt1972@yahoo.com.

Christine Brown was born and raised in Zion, IL. She earned both a Bachelor's and Master's in Creative Writing, and loves to travel, see the world, and experience new things.

Marlene Bryenton received the Order of Prince Edward Island and an Honourary Doctorate of Laws degree from UPEI Charlottetown. She had a long career with Federal Government of Canada and developed the Joseph A. Ghiz Memorial Park. Marlene has two grown children and four grandchildren.

C. R. Chan is a stay-at-home wife and mother to three wonderful children. This foodie is a former nurse and figure skater who enjoys working out, gardening, cooking, camping, and traveling. She has been writing stories since the age of eight and this is her first published story. She resides in Calgary, AB with her husband Jon.

Ginny Huff Conahan taught for fourteen years in Los Angeles, CA schools and sixteen years in Fort Collins, CO to kindergarten through college-level students. She has a Doctorate in Education from the University of Southern California. She enjoys reading, crafting, and volunteering. E-mail her at gcona@comcast.net.

Gwen Cooper received her B.A. in English and Secondary Education in 2007 and completed the Publishing Institute at Denver University in 2009. In her free time she enjoys Krav Maga, traveling, and backpacking with her husband and Bloodhound rescue in the beautiful Rocky Mountains. Follow her on Twitter @Gwen_Cooper10.

D'ette Corona is the VP/Associate Publisher for Chicken Soup for the Soul. She doesn't find time to write often but is proud to be able to share this story.

Elizabeth C. Crognale has been married for fifty-two years and has three children and four grandchildren. She's enjoyed years of involvement with women's ministries and teaching adults and children at church. Diagnosed with breast cancer in 1993, it surprised her again in 2015. Beth thanks Kelly J. Stigliano for helping compose her story.

Born in Michigan, **Dorothy Dale** was raised on a farm with no electricity or running water where she learned many survival skills and crafts. Her knitting, crocheting, and other hand-made items have won prizes at local fairs. She writes of her experiences, observations, and dealing with the ups and downs of life.

Lynn Darmon is a Medium living in Michigan with an international clientele. She has been featured on ABC's *20/20* and *The Dr. Oz Show* along with other appearances in television and radio. When not working, Lynn enjoys traveling to spend time with her two grown children, a son in Los Angeles and a daughter in New York City.

Dr. David Davis has been a chiropractor since 1982. He currently writes and speaks on caregiving for loved ones with Alzheimer's. The message he wants to share is that caregiving is an opportunity for growth and healing. When he is not traveling, he makes his home in upstate New York.

Sergio Del Bianco has a background in fine arts and psychology. He is an artist and writer, interested in the intersection of art, psychology, and the humanities. He resides in Europe with his spouse and growing family of rescue animals. E-mail him at sergiodelbianco@yahoo.com or through Twitter @DelBianco97.

Ruth Douglas is a graduate of New Hope Christian College. She enjoyed being a pastor's wife for over fifty years. Her interests included reading, travel, entertaining, and teaching children. Ruth lives in Colorado Springs, CO where she enjoys spending time with her children, grandchildren, and great-grandchildren.

For over forty years, **Dr. Mary Edwards** has been an author, book coach, and life and legacy coach. Her acronym for LEGACY is Leaving Every Generation a Chronicle of You. In 1990, she received the 107th Point of Light Award for her community service. Mary is a widow and lives in Detroit, MI. E-mail her at leavesofgold.11c@gmail.com.

Jackie Eller has been writing since she was a child. Her deep faith in God has always helped her in her life. She attended the University of Kansas and left just three credits short of a degree, but the experience left her a better writer. She is married and lives on a farm with her husband Kenny, three cats, and four chickens.

Elizabeth Rose Reardon Farella received her Bachelor of Arts in Elementary Education from Molloy College and her Master's of Science in Literacy from Adelphi University. She is a first-grade teacher at St. Edward the Confessor School in Syosset, NY. She enjoys traveling with her husband and her three beautiful daughters.

Karleen Forwell is a diaper-changing, chaos-fixer, stay-at-home mom of two little boys. She survives by her photography, her garden and her family (and homemade wine).

Ryan Freeman received his Bachelor of Arts in Elementary Education from Clemson University. He lives in Colorado with his three daughters and teaches school and tennis. Ryan enjoys the outdoors and spending time with his family. He plans to continue to grow his nonprofit program and work with children.

Gail Gabrielle continues to passionately pursue her writing career in various venues. This is her second contribution to the *Chicken Soup for the Soul* series. Her adult children, Danielle, Alexandra, and Zachary serve as daily inspirations in supporting her as she uses the power of the written word to help others.

M. Elizabeth Gage is a Yankee currently residing in northern Mississippi.

She earned her B.S. in Biology, *cum laude*, from Lafayette College in Easton, PA, but it was the summer of 1983 at the Oregon Institute of Marine Biology that stole away part of her heart. The rest belongs to her husband of many years and their children.

Julia Gousseva was born and raised in Russia but now lives in Arizona with her husband and her son. She writes fiction and nonfiction stories set mostly in Russia.

Jeffrey Guard is a writer and media producer who lives in the greater New York City area. He is a member of the Hudson Valley Writers Center and is working on his first novel. Jeffrey has a Bachelor of Arts in Psychology from Texas A&M University.

Joanne Guidoccio retired from a thirty-one year teaching career and launched a second act as a writer. Her articles and book reviews have appeared in newspapers, magazines, and online. The author of five novels, Joanne writes cozy mysteries, paranormal romances, and inspirational literature. Learn more at joanneguidoccio.com.

Yvonne Hall is a mother of four, stepmother of three and grandmother to fourteen children ranging in age from four to thirty-one years old! She is also the adoptive mom to two very happy felines. Yvonne enjoys walking, researching health and wellness, and meeting with her small, fun-loving, and very committed writing group.

Dr. Tory Wegner Hendrix earned her Doctorate in Acupuncture and Chinese Medicine from Pacific College of Oriental Medicine in San Diego, CA. She owns a successful holistic clinic in North Carolina and enjoys life with her husband, two little girls, and a big black Lab. Learn more at acupuncturewellnessconnection.com.

Sandra Hesler is mom to two teenagers whom she homeschooled for a total of ten years. She contributes monthly to the "SDA Homeschool Families" homeschool blog and is currently working on building a freelance writing business. She enjoys writing, collecting old books, hiking, camping, canoeing, and being with her son and daughter.

Jeff Hill lives in Minnesota… even in the winter. He enjoys, biking, fishing, and spending time with family and friends. He has retired from a thirty-four year teaching career.

Renee C. Houghton attended college at the University of California, Davis. Her career included sixteen years as a banking executive. Renee has two young girls and enjoys reading, traveling, and volunteering with her pet therapy dog. She plans to continue writing to help and inspire transplant recipients and their families.

Sheryl Hutchinson is a writer and artist living in Iowa. She enjoys writing, painting, sewing, and photography. Sheryl writes adult novels and children's books.

Jennie Ivey lives and writes in Tennessee. She is the author of numerous works of fiction and nonfiction, including many stories in the *Chicken Soup for the Soul* series. Learn more at jennieivey.com.

Sergio Jauregui is a big family man. He has four daughters and a loving wife. His daughter Mayra wrote this story for him. He currently resides in Texas.

Carolyn Jaynes, M.A. is a Minnesota empath who escaped to San Diego, CA and now Hawaii. She trained in Counseling Psychology and teaches spirituality. She loves roller-skating and sings professionally. Her inspirational book, *Sprinkles from Heaven: Stories of Serendipity*, is available online. E-mail her at SprinklesfromHeaven@gmail.com.

An entrepreneur, wife, mother, and novelist, **S.R. Karfelt** enjoys spending time with her family, and summers spent writing on the tiny island of Alonissos, Greece. When not traveling she resides in Horseheads, NY.

Donna Keenan is a grandmother of four and spends her spare time crocheting, metal detecting and enjoying life to the fullest!

Kathleen Kohler is a writer and speaker from the Pacific Northwest. Her articles appear in numerous magazines and anthologies. She and her husband have three children and seven grandchildren. Kathleen enjoys gardening, and painting, and is amazed at how God intervenes in our lives. Learn more at kathleenkohler.com.

Deborah J. Konrad has a B.A. from Mount Holyoke College and an M.A. from Purdue University Global. At fifteen, she was faced with assisting her parents with the care of her paralyzed sister, Sandra. This experience, and the events that led up to it, served as the backdrop to her first book, *The Blessing of Movement*.

Sid Korpi is a former English teacher, journalist, animal chaplain, and award-winning author of *Good Grief: Finding Peace After Pet Loss*. A Renaissance woman, she is also an award-winning actress, dancer, and artist. She currently teaches private painting parties through her business "Just Arting Around."

Since before she could walk, **Stephanie Kovala** has been going on outdoor adventures with her family around her home in Northern Ontario. Her dad in particular loved being outside and always encouraged her to make the most of each day.

Tree Langdon is a Canadian writer who is inspired by her dreams for the future and by her passion for shining light in the darkness. Her work has been published in the anthology *Breathing Words* and *Chicken Soup for the Soul: The Miracle of Love*. Learn more at enticethewrite.com.

Lisa Leshaw recently retired from the mental health profession. She's spending her days building new bridges, freelance writing, and conducting empowerment workshops for women of every age.

Carrie K. Linde lives in a historic 1909 home near the Black Hills of South Dakota with her husband, two girls and a few quirky animals. This is her first published piece. Inspired by unique stories begging to be told, Carrie is writing her first novel. Look for her supernatural thriller, *Water Like Glass*, online soon.

Joshua J. Mark is an editor/director and writer for the online history site "Ancient History Encyclopedia." His nonfiction stories have also appeared in *Timeless Travels* and *History Ireland* magazines. His soul mate, Betsy Mark, passed over to the other side on 4 August 2018 but lives on with him and their daughter Emily.

Jeri McBryde loves sharing her life experiences in the *Chicken Soup for the Soul* series with the hope of helping others. Jeri lives in a small southern delta town. Retired, she spends her days reading and writing. A doting grandmother, her world revolves around her faith, family, friends, and chocolate.

Lisa McCaskill has been an educator for over twenty years. She has a great love for books, writing, and learning. The three of these, she says, are inextricably linked.

Caroline S. McKinney has retired from the School of Education at the University of Colorado where she taught children's literature, writing, and literacy courses for many years. She was also a literacy teacher and staff developer for Boulder Valley schools. She loves family, pets, her flute, and being in Assisi, Italy.

Suzanne Miley's first career was in information technology, her second accounting, and her current third act is assisting people in recognizing and accepting their innate gifts and talents via writing, coaching, and retreats. She has three grown children and two delightful grandchildren. Suzanne lives in Santa Fe, NM.

G. E. Mimms received her B.A. from the University of South Carolina in 1973. She currently resides in Indio, CA and enjoys golf, swimming and biking. She also teaches Performance Writing at the CVRep Theatre School for Performing Arts.

Marya Morin is a freelance writer. Her stories and poems have appeared in publications such as *Woman's World* and Hallmark. Marya also penned a weekly humorous column for an online newsletter, and writes custom poetry on request. She lives in the country with her husband. E-mail her at Akushla514@hotmail.com.

Evangeline Neve is a writer and editor who has lived in Nepal since 1996. Her published work includes articles on travel, food, family and cats. Evangeline also helps provide educational opportunities and a safe living space for at-risk girls. Her passions include food, travel, beer, books and more. Learn more at evangelineneve.com.

Randi O'Keefe lives in Utah with her husband Tim. Her articles have appeared in print and digital publications. She has been published in the anthologies *Dolls Remembered*, *Chicken Soup for the Soul: Touched by an Angel*, and *Serendipity*. Far too many nights she can be found reading when she should be sleeping.

Teresa Otto is a freelance writer, photographer, and retired pediatric anesthesiologist. She enjoys Taoist Tai Chi and loves her four-legged children. While Montana will always be home, she is passionate about travel, especially to off-the-beaten-path places. You can keep up with her adventures at thenomadsdaughter.com.

Tammy Parker is an analyst covering the telecommunications industry. Over the years, she has also worked as a journalist and freelance writer. She lives in her native Colorado with a longhaired tuxedo cat and a frenetic American Eskimo dog. Learn more at tammyparker.com.

Amy Rovtar Payne lives on a hobby farm with her husband and an assortment of animals. She holds a degree in education and is a certified horseback riding instructor. Amy enjoys competing in agility with her rescue dogs, working with her American mustang horses, and showing Rhinelander rabbits.

Darlene Grace Peterson, a certified court reporter in Canada's Supreme Court of British Columbia, left after many years to pursue a writing career. Published in various areas, she loves to write fiction and nonfiction about succeeding against all odds. Darlene's other loves are animal welfare, gardening, and cycling.

Retired and living in O'Fallon, MO, **Lenore Petruso** was a writer for a St. Louis-based financial services firm. Lenore enjoys early morning walks, container gardening, tea parties with her grandnieces, Mia and Rosalia, and writing personal essays. Her essays have appeared in *Reminisce*, *Good Old Days* and *AFA Care Quarterly*.

Lori Phillips enjoys writing about life experiences, spirituality, and dreams. Currently, she is working on a dream symbol dictionary series and children's fiction stories. She received her Bachelor of Arts in communications/journalism and Master of Education. She lives in Southern California with her family.

Changing seasons, unexpected blessings, love that lasts forever... these are a few of **M. Jean Pike's** favorite things. With a writing career spanning two decades, she has eight romance novels and over two hundred essays and short stories in print. Visit Jean's blog at mjeanpike. wordpress.com.

Hayley Pisciotti received her Bachelor of Arts from Lycoming College and was awarded the President's Prize in Prose. Her other works have appeared in *The Tributary*, Odyssey online, and FrayedPassport.com. Her most recent work can be viewed on her blog at hayleypisciotti. wordpress.com.

Wendy Portfors writes from her heart. She published a book that documented her journey from caregiver to ultimately being widowed. Wendy is currently working on a series of children's picture books. Wendy loves to golf and explore new countries. Recently remarried, she and her husband Dave live in Alberta, Canada.

Melinda Pritzel describes herself as a jack-of-all-trades and a master of few. She received a B.A. in business/legal assistance from Avila University in Kansas City, MO. Melinda enjoys photography and uses that and her writing skills to create greeting cards which she sells online at greetingcarduniverse.com/yowzers.

Kathryn Radeff is a health and travel writer by profession. She spends much of her time in Western New York and South Florida. She is also a Certified Pilates Instructor. She loves the freedom of the freelance life and spending time with animals. E-mail her at kradeff1@msn.com.

Mandi Raybuck is a stay-at-home mother of three spirited children, and four cats that help run the household. She's an aspiring writer, a lover of indie folk and alternative music, and a passionate perennial gardener.

Janet Rich (a.k.a. JR) worked as a publicist for Blue Note/Capitol Records for twenty-six years. She left the music business in 2015 to pursue her life-long passion for writing and storytelling. Janet is working on a memoir and posts soulful chit chats with folks fifty and (b)older on Instagram @eattheicecreambeforeitmelts.

Melody R. Ringo is an author, blogger, entrepreneur, wife, mother, and grandmother. She recently retired from the space industry. A former family caregiver, she's writing a book entitled, *The Beauty of Imperfection: Kintsugi for Caregivers*. Melody resides in Texas with her husband and one cat. Learn more at www.melodyringo.com.

Lisa Romeo is the author of the memoir *Starting With Goodbye*. Her nonfiction is listed in Best American Essays and appears frequently in literary journals. Lisa is an MFA writing instructor, freelance writer, and manuscript editor. She lives in northern New Jersey with her husband and sons and enjoys cooking and British TV.

Carrie Roope is a writer and editor based in the UK where she lives with her husband Colin and two boys Alfie and Ollie. She is passionate about history and heritage, which fortunately the UK has in abundance, and enjoys taking her boys on historical adventures that she one day hopes to turn into a fiction book for children.

Tyann Sheldon Rouw lives in Iowa with her husband and three sons. She writes poignant and funny stories about her family's adventures with autism. Visit her blog, "Turn Up the V," at tyannsheldonrouw. weebly.com or follow her on Twitter @TyannRouw.

Kathleen Ruth received her B.A. from St. Catherine University in St. Paul, MN and her M.A. in TESOL from the University of Central Florida. She taught in Minnesota and Florida, Bangkok, Thailand and Beirut, Lebanon. She loves reading, traveling, and embracing multiple cultures. Kathleen has five children and ten grandchildren.

Karen Ross Samford is a freelance journalist who has been writing for newspapers since she was in high school. She's lived in Texas for most of her life, though every summer she wonders why. When she is not writing, she is usually bird watching or gardening.

Sara Schafer attended an extension of Indiana University and Old Dominion University. She is now retired and enjoying crocheting, gardening, writing, and spending time with family. E-mail her at sara757s@aol.com.

Gwyn Schneck is currently a writer and speaker after retiring from thirty years of teaching and counseling high school students. She continues to walk through each day watching for angels. She loves to bring life lessons and humor to audiences. E-mail her at gwynschneck@gmail.com.

Judith Burnett Schneider, a research organic chemist turned writer, is the mother of three. Her work has appeared in books and magazines, on websites, and in standardized tests in the U.S. and Japan. She enjoys teaching students how to improve their writing by adding crafts and activities to make the writing process fun!

Steve Schultz is a two-time Teacher of the Year Award winner at Fountain Valley High School where he teaches English Language Arts. Steve has written a monthly column on love, leadership, and elevation for the past decade for *Fountain Valley Living* magazine and has been published in five other *Chicken Soup for the Soul* books. E-mail him at personalbest22@gmail.com.

M.J. Shea is tickled that her second story published in the *Chicken Soup for the Soul* series is about angels. She recently wrote and illustrated a children's book inspired by her favorite angel: her brother Neal. She lives on the Connecticut shoreline with her husband Brad and dogs Georgie Girl and Mac.

Dayle Allen Shockley is an award-winning writer, the author of three books, and a contributor to many other works, including over a dozen *Chicken Soup for the Soul* books. She and her husband are retired and are enjoying being grandparents.

Fran Signorino received her Bachelor of Science, with honors, from Caldwell University, New Jersey, in 1993 and Paralegal Certification in 1991. She has two children and two grandchildren. Fran and her husband enjoy being retired at the beach, traveling, and working in church ministries.

Billie Holladay Skelley received her bachelor's and master's degrees from the University of Wisconsin-Madison. A retired clinical nurse specialist, she is the mother of four and grandmother of two. Billie enjoys writing and her work crosses several genres. She spends her non-writing time reading, gardening, and traveling.

Donna Adams Stare retired after teaching the deaf and hard of hearing for thirty-four years. She lives with her husband of thirty-two years, has one daughter and recently became a grandmother to a beautiful baby girl. She loves her family, the outdoors, dogs, crafting/card-making, and writing about her childhood and family. E-mail her at mommystare@ mchsi.com.

Dana D. Sterner has worked in the healthcare industry for more than thirty years. She has written over seventy articles related to nursing and fitness, which have appeared in regional and national magazines. She's an avid hiker and has explored most of America's National Parks.

Anita Stone is a retired science and English teacher who has a passion for teaching, gardening, and freelancing. She teaches landscaping at the local community college and is a Master Gardener. Anita has recently written articles for newspapers and magazines, and is concerned about sustainability and the environment.

Delores E. Topliff divides her year between Twin Cities, MN and Corinth, MI. With degrees in education, she teaches at a Christian university. Her sons are physicians and she brags endlessly about her grandchildren. Delores also loves worldwide travel and mission projects. Learn more at delorestopliff.com.

Renée Vajko-Srch grew up in France where she obtained her French Baccalaureate. She attended IBME in Switzerland, graduating with a degree in theology. She currently lives in the Ozarks with her husband and three sons. Her first novel will be coming out later this year. She blogs at MotherhoodAutismAndGod.blogspot.com.

Gail Walkowich is a freelance writer who lives in the foothills of the Colorado Rocky Mountains. Gail and her family have traveled extensively throughout the United States. They have visited some of the Caribbean Islands, Mexico and Canada. Her passions include genealogy, swimming, and exploring.

Dorann Weber is a freelance writer living in the Pine Barrens of Southern New Jersey. She's a contributor for Getty Images and her photos and verses have appeared on Hallmark cards and magazines. Writing her first story for the *Chicken Soup for the Soul* series ignited her passion for writing. Dorann enjoys hiking with her family and dogs.

Kathy Whirity is a syndicated newspaper columnist who shares her sentimental musings on family life. When Kathy is not writing or crocheting, you will find her with her husband Bill enjoying time with the grandkids.

Soneakqua J. White is the owner of At the Table Counseling. She has been licensed to practice counseling in the state of Texas for fourteen years. Her favorite clients to work with are creatives and clergy. She encourages writing as a form of therapy and as a way of life!

Glenice Wilson enjoys nature, walking, skiing, gardening, humour, writing, visual art, and music — along with the people and surprises they all offer. She grew up on a farm on the Manitoba prairie but ventured off to live in Edmonton and Jasper. She now lives again in prairie country, but in Barrhead, Alberta.

Mary Jo Marcellus Wyse has an MFA from Vermont College of Fine Arts and an MA from Kansas State University. She enjoys running, reading, traveling, and spending time with her family. She lives in beautiful Grosse Pointe, MI.

Debra Zemke is a songwriter and music publisher in Nashville, TN. Songwriting since 1992, with over three dozen published and recorded songs, her hope is to move people emotionally and inspire them to never stop dreaming. She believes it is our relationships that make the magic in our lives.

Meet Amy Newmark

Amy Newmark is the bestselling author, editor-in-chief, and publisher of the *Chicken Soup for the Soul* book series. Since 2008, she has published 160 new books, most of them national bestsellers in the U.S. and Canada, more than doubling the number of Chicken Soup for the Soul titles in print today. She is also the author of *Simply Happy*, a crash course in Chicken Soup for the Soul advice and wisdom that is filled with easy-to-implement, practical tips for enjoying a better life.

Amy is credited with revitalizing the Chicken Soup for the Soul brand, which has been a publishing industry phenomenon since the first book came out in 1993. By compiling inspirational and aspirational true stories curated from ordinary people who have had extraordinary experiences, Amy has kept the twenty-six-year-old Chicken Soup for the Soul brand fresh and relevant.

Amy graduated *magna cum laude* from Harvard University where she majored in Portuguese and minored in French. She then embarked on a three-decade career as a Wall Street analyst, a hedge fund manager, and a corporate executive in the technology field. She is a Chartered Financial Analyst.

Her return to literary pursuits was inevitable, as her honors thesis in college involved traveling throughout Brazil's impoverished northeast region, collecting stories from regular people. She is delighted to have come full circle in her writing career — from collecting stories "from the people" in Brazil as a twenty-year-old to, three decades later, collecting stories "from the people" for Chicken Soup for the Soul.

When Amy and her husband Bill, the CEO of Chicken Soup for the Soul, are not working, they are visiting their four grown children and their grandchildren.

Follow Amy on Twitter @amynewmark. Listen to her free podcast — "Chicken Soup for the Soul with Amy Newmark" — on Apple Podcasts, Google Play, the Podcasts app on iPhone, or by using your favorite podcast app on other devices.

Thank You

We owe huge thanks to all of our contributors and fans. We were overwhelmed with thousands of submissions on this very popular topic, and we had a large team of editors that spent months reading them. Laura Dean, Crescent LoMonaco, Jamie Cahill, Susan Heim, Mary Fisher, Barbara LoMonaco, and D'ette Corona read all of them, and then D'ette and Amy Newmark narrowed down the semifinalists to make the final selections.

Susan Heim did the first round of editing, D'ette chose the perfect quotations to put at the beginning of each story, and Amy edited the stories and shaped the final manuscript.

As we finished our work, Associate Publisher D'ette Corona continued to be Amy's right-hand woman in creating the final manuscript and working with all our wonderful writers. Barbara LoMonaco and Kristiana Pastir, along with Elaine Kimbler, jumped in at the end to proof, proof, proof. And yes, there will always be typos anyway, so feel free to let us know about them at webmaster@chickensoupforthesoul. com and we will correct them in future printings.

The whole publishing team deserves a hand, including our Senior Director of Marketing Maureen Peltier, our Vice President, Production and Project Management Victor Cataldo, and our graphic designer Daniel Zaccari, who turned our manuscript into this beautiful book.

Changing your life one story at a time®
www.chickensoup.com